Africa and the International Monetary Fund

Africa and the International Monetary Fund

Edited by Gerald K. Helleiner

Papers presented at a symposium held in Nairobi, Kenya, May 13-15, 1985

International Monetary Fund • 1986

Library of Congress Cataloging-in-Publication Data

Africa and the International Monetary Fund.

Bibliography; p.
1. International Monetary Fund—Africa.
I. Helleiner, Gerald K. II. International Monetary Fund.
HG3881.5.I58A34 1986 332.1'52 86-10415
ISBN 0-939934-61-2

Price: US$10.00

Foreword

At their Eighth Regular General Assembly held in August 1983 at Arusha, Tanzania, the Governors of the Association of African Central Banks proposed the organization of a joint symposium with the Fund on the subject of Africa and the International Monetary Fund. The Governors felt that such a symposium would lead to a better mutual understanding of the approach to the design and implementation of adjustment programs. For its part, the Fund was glad to have the opportunity to discuss its policies with the monetary authorities of its member countries in a framework that was free of the pressures of time and circumstance that inevitably surround negotiations of programs.

This volume contains the proceedings of the resulting symposium held in Nairobi on May 13–15, 1985, under the joint sponsorship of the Association of African Central Banks and the Fund. Professor G.K. Helleiner of the University of Toronto acted as Chairman of the symposium and also edited the material in this book.

The lively and candid exchange of views that took place during the symposium did much to improve the understanding by participants of the realities facing Africa today and of the policies that would most appropriately respond to those realities. I hope that the publication of these proceedings will continue the dialogue in a wider public forum in furtherance of the mutual interests that the Fund and all its member countries share in the success of the adjustment and growth processes in Africa.

J. DE LAROSIÈRE
Managing Director
International Monetary Fund

June 1986

Acknowledgment

On behalf of all who participated in the symposium, I should like to express deepest thanks to our hosts in the Central Bank of Kenya and the Government of Kenya, and particularly to Governor Philip Ndegwa, who also managed to make major contributions to our deliberations despite his extraordinarily busy schedule. We were received warmly and well; the efficiency of the symposium's support system made the participants' stay in Kenya pleasant as well as productive. We were particularly honored by the unexpected opportunity of meeting His Excellency, the President of the Republic of Kenya.

Let me express my own thanks to the Association of African Central Banks (AACB) and the International Monetary Fund for affording me the privilege of serving as moderator in the Nairobi meetings and as editor of this volume. I have thoroughly enjoyed both tasks.

Above all, I should like to express my congratulations to the organizers for having conceived the idea for the symposium and for having implemented it with imagination and efficiency. The AACB deserves the credit for initiating the request for such a meeting and the Fund deserves no less praise for its enthusiastic response. I should like to express particular thanks to Azizali Mohammed and Ahmed Abushadi of the External Relations Department of the International Monetary Fund who have planned, organized, and supported the entire enterprise from the beginning.

I believe that the symposium was successful. Frank communication took place; both sides listened and learned. I hope that it may have ushered in a period of greater mutual understanding and partnership between African Governors and Fund staff. Both Governors and staff change, however, and so do the issues. I hope, therefore, that this symposium was only the first in a continuing series of similar exchanges with the Governors. I hope too that publication of the proceedings may extend the learning processes on these occasions much more widely both in Africa and in the international community.

Finally, let me express my thanks to Jennifer Johnson for her assistance in the preparation of the manuscript for publication in Toronto and to David D. Driscoll of the Editorial Division of the Fund's External Relations Department for putting it into its final published form.

G.K. Helleiner
Toronto, October 1985

Contents

Part 3

Adjustment in Africa—What Can Be Done?

Appendix

Introduction

G.K. Helleiner

The world is faced with a crisis in Africa. The word "crisis" is undoubtedly overused in today's complex and unstable world, but the current situation in Africa richly deserves its use. On top of fundamental problems of longer-run development—rapid population growth, slow economic growth, and susceptibility to drought and desertification—that had already attracted widespread concern, recent years have seen savage blows from a malfunctioning world economy dealt on Africa. The collapse in African countries' international terms of trade consequent to oil price increases and severe global recession has done the greatest damage, but high international interest rates and protectionism have also hurt. Sadly, recovery from the most recent world recession has failed to restore previous levels of primary commodity prices upon which the economic health of most African countries depends. The prospect for improvement in African terms of trade over the medium-term future remains bleak. At the same time, despite the obvious increase in African needs, net capital flows to Africa are dwindling and are projected to shrink further in the next few years. Many countries in Africa are on a downward spiral. The progress achieved since independence 25 years ago is in serious jeopardy.

"Adjustment" to external shocks as has occurred in Africa in recent years has taken the form primarily of slashing imports, investment, and already minimal levels of consumption, with the severe consequences for child nutrition now being documented by the United Nations Children's Fund (UNICEF). The price for these quasi-adjustment measures will be paid for years to come. Average per capita incomes and investment rates in Africa have fallen for four years in a row. Projections of growth, trade, per capita income, and such physical indicators of human welfare as infant mortality, which many of us consider most important of all, are all simply *unacceptable* and dangerous. Moreover, the debt servicing obligations of many African countries appear to exceed prospective servicing capacity. In the best of circumstances it will take time and many more tough policy decisions before Africa can expect to return to a stable, sustained, and acceptable development path. There is risk that low-income African nations will be unable to extricate themselves from their financial bind, at least within the "medium-term framework" employed by the Fund for its programs, and possibly longer. Hence the word "crisis" could not be more appropriate. To some degree, in consequence of the Ethiopian tragedy and the severe drought elsewhere on the continent, the world has already focused its attention on Africa. But the magnitude of the current African crisis is not yet fully appreciated in the international community: for most African countries it is a long-run disaster, centering on a shortage of foreign exchange.

The International Monetary Fund responded to the external blows rained upon Africa in recent years with unprecedented levels of lending. Although its activities in Africa had previously been modest, since 1979 the Fund has played a prominent intermediary role between African countries and the international financial community. By the early 1980s net Fund credits to Africa exceeded net flows from the World Bank group, traditionally the major multilateral actor on the continent. But the bulk of Fund credit has been offered on highly conditional terms—in keeping with the Fund's requirement for revolving its resources and its objective of restoring balance to its members' external payments position as quickly as possible. The Fund's view of its role in Africa is succinctly summarized in the papers by Richard Erb and Alassane Ouattara. African members of the Fund have not always been content with the terms of its lending, and their grievances are eloquently expressed in many papers in this volume. Indeed, the motivation of the Association of African Central Banks (AACB) in suggesting the symposium at which these papers were presented was a feeling that such an exchange would lead to a better understanding on the part of African countries of the approach of the Fund to the design and implementation of adjustment programs and a better appreciation on the part of the Fund of the special difficulties, problems, and perspectives of the African countries. At the same time, the relatively short-term character of Fund lending (three to five years) has meant that the resources lent in the recent burst of Fund activity in Africa are now coming due for repayment. Unless there is a renewed surge of lending there will be a net flow of resources from Africa back to the Fund over the next few years, well before Africa has adjusted to the shocks that gave rise to the need for credits in the first place. Nor is African discontent and frustration confined to the activities of the Fund. The international financial community as a whole, including the World Bank group and bilateral aid donors, comes in for a share of the blame for Africa's predicament and bleak prospects, since it too is reducing its commitment in Africa.

There is by now substantial agreement on how to move Africa on to self-sustaining growth and roughly on what it would cost. Despite extraordinarily little room for error, the task is not unmanageable. What is required is sustained, joint effort on the part of both African governments and the international community, including the Fund, to achieve a transition to more stable and acceptable development. Africa represents a test of the international community's capacity to respond effectively to crisis. Appropriate response will challenge the community for the next decade and perhaps longer.

One question kept recurring, sometimes explicitly, virtually always implicitly, in the symposium. To whom should policy recommendations and appeals for reform be addressed? To whom, ultimately, were the Governors of the African Central Banks and other participants talking? The world? The major powers in the Executive Board and the Board of Governors of the Fund? The management and staff of the Fund? Or, on the other side, to African politicians and governments? African civil servants? African publics?

For analytical purposes, I shall distinguish three addressees for policy recommendations: the world community, the Fund's Executive Board and Board of Governors, and the Fund management and staff. The response of the world, and particularly of industrial nations, to Africa's crisis was addressed repeatedly and variously in the symposium. There were calls from virtually all quarters for increased resource flows to Africa through official bilateral development assistance, the International Development Association (IDA), the special World Bank facility for Africa, and other devices. J.O. Sanusi of Nigeria even suggested a Marshall Plan for Africa. This analogy may be a little misleading, in that, apart from other obvious points of dissimilarity, the sums suggested for helping to meet African needs would be modest compared with those directed in an earlier day toward rebuilding Europe. Governor Moyana of Zimbabwe also drew useful parallels between the reconstruction of war-devastated Europe and current needs in Africa.

In the trade realm, there were calls both from African Governors, particularly Governor Fadiga and Mr. Sanusi, and from others for higher and more stable primary commodity prices. Appeals were unanimous for reduced protectionism against African and other low-income countries' products. African support for the initiation of new General Agreement on Tariffs and Trade (GATT) negotiations that would take adequate account of the needs of developing countries in crisis was specifically recommended by John Williamson.

Debt relief of various kinds for African and other low-income countries was repeatedly recommended. (I have not attempted to achieve consistency among the debt estimates employed by various authors; data on African debt are obviously in need of improvement.) Among the possible modes of relief that were canvassed are conversion of debt to grants, multi-year rescheduling, and the revision of various Paris Club procedures (including provision for effective follow-up on the rapid translation of multilateral commitments into bilateral action). Eduard Brau's paper was cautious about the prospect, however, and emphasized improved domestic debt-management systems.

More broadly, some invited governments to embark upon wide-ranging international monetary reform to improve the prospect for a stable and predictable international economic environment and (a particularly sore and frequently mentioned point) more symmetric sharing of adjustment burdens. In this context, Governor Gebre-Kidan of Ethiopia invited consideration of a new development-related role for the Fund; but this suggestion did not meet with full agreement.

The staff of the Fund and the World Bank can, of course, attempt to exercise some influence on world opinion and the policies of the major powers. The staff of the Bank, in their successive reports on sub-Saharan Africa, *have* tried to do so and have called repeatedly for increased official development assistance to Africa and reduced protectionism. There seemed to be general agreement that net external resource flows (and net transfers, allowing for interest payments) to Africa should not be permitted to decline, as is now projected for the medium term. Indeed, it was agreed that the "crisis" would be better met by increased net flows and transfers. Experts can and should shout loudly and univocally on these matters and publicize the relevant statistics. Realistically, however, the prospect that discussions of Fund and World Bank programs, domestic policy reform, and international debt relief will lead to greater flows of resources does seem at present rather bleak. The struggle for further resources must nevertheless continue and the Fund and World Bank management and staff can be expected to participate actively in this struggle.

What about issues within the province of the Executive Board and the Board of Governors of the Fund (or their equivalents in the World Bank)? Obviously, many issues addressed under this heading may also be considered matters within the province of the Fund's management and staff. There is some inevitable blurring and overlap in the categories I am employing, as will become apparent. Nevertheless, other suggestions made in the symposium's papers fall strictly within the jurisdiction of the Executive Board and the Board of Governors. These Boards can act, of course, only within the constraints of the existing Articles of Agreement, the conventions of relevant institutions, and, to some degree, the established positions of the major powers within these bodies.

The most direct and obvious issue of this sort relates to the amount of the Fund's own limited resources. J.O. Sanusi argued for substantial quota increases and the advance of the Fund's ninth quota review. Many also called for resumption of the issue of SDRs. Despite already considerable international support, and not merely in the developing countries, for these suggestions, progress has proven politically difficult. Particular attention was called to the potential use of returning Trust Fund resources (roughly SDR 2.7 billion between 1985 and 1991) in a manner appropriate to the needs of African and other low-income countries, perhaps in an expanded interest subsidy scheme.

The terms of access to the Fund's resources were also criticized. Low-income members' access rights were actually reduced in absolute terms in the latest quota revision and this seems an obvious matter for review. Many participants in the symposium also recommended improvement of the functioning of the compensatory financing facility so as to relate drawing rights more effectively to needs and, in particular, to return compensatory financing facility drawings to the low-conditionality status they enjoyed prior to September 1983. Expanded use of the extended fund facility in Africa also carried widespread support. Reconsideration of the rate of interest paid on Fund credit of various kinds was also urged. Former Executive Director Narasimham of India suggested exploration of the possible use of the clause concerning "exceptional circumstances" justifying special arrangements in respect of the currency of Fund repurchases for African and other low-income countries in the near future.

Fund conditionality was addressed in the papers by Samba Mawakani, Alassane Ouattara, and John Loxley, and was the subject of a great deal of discussion and debate. A review at the level of the Executive Board of the guidelines relating to conditionality, performance requirements, and waiver procedures was suggested to ensure an appropriate degree of Fund flexibility. Mr. Narasimham also suggested exploration of the possibility of prorating drawing rights according to the degree of shortfall in respect of performance.

Luis de Azcarate's reflective paper on the role of the World Bank in Africa stimulated discussion of the interaction between the Fund and the Bank in providing appropriate finance in the current circumstances of crisis. Governor Ndegwa of Kenya called for joint Fund-Bank programs coordinating the

Extended Fund Facility and structural adjustment loans; others noted the dangers of "ganging up" on borrowers and "cross-conditionality." There seemed to be general agreement that there would be much to be gained from improved cooperation between the World Bank and the Fund, and from a review of their respective roles in bridging the gap in providing adequate medium-term balance of payments finance for African and other low-income countries. A review of the appropriate degree of World Bank reliance upon structural adjustment loans, sectoral adjustment loans, and other kinds of policy-based lending in these countries, and modalities for their use, was also widely seen as timely.

Lastly, some suggested that an overall review of the future role and nature of the Fund, particularly as it relates to the needs of its lowest-income members, might well be launched by the Executive Board or the Board of Governors. Carlos Massad also suggested that the Boards might launch task-force reviews of general policies, resource use, and the relationships between members and the Fund, with a view to ensuring the Fund's own stated objectives of pragmatism and flexibility.

African Governors repeatedly called for innovation, pressure, and leadership on these issues from Fund management and staff. While there were some substantive disagreements (for example, on whether Fund and World Bank programs should be jointly formulated, or whether there is merit in encouraging each institution to play a separate role), there seemed to be less disagreement between Fund staff and Governors on what changes were desirable than there was on the likelihood of their being achieved. One must presume that the likelihood increases if the management and staff press for these changes, and the meeting gave out strong signals on the appropriate directions in which to press.

The African Governors also saw the need to deepen their own independent research on these matters so as to strengthen the hands of their hard-pressed and inadequately backed Executive Directors. Some mechanisms for backing their efforts already exist, of course, but the discussions suggested to many that they might not be enough.

By far the sharpest divergences surfacing during the symposium and contained in the papers that follow were on matters that, on the face of it, are to a degree—exactly how much is still not entirely agreed—within the discretion of the Fund management and staff. On the one hand, African Governors are frustrated and hard pressed. On the other hand, many individuals in the Fund's management and staff clearly see themselves misunderstood as international civil servants and not in a position to discuss in public weaknesses in the implementation of country programs by members. Among the matters at issue at the level of individual countries' relations with the Fund management and staff are:

- the detailed interpretation of the guidelines on conditionality and the details of performance targeting;
- the term of agreements and particularly the degree of use of the Extended Fund Facility;
- the degree of cooperation between the Fund and the World Bank and the extent to which these institutions' programs are truly complementary rather than generative of cross-conditionality;
- the details of disbursement schedules;
- the details of waiver arrangements and contingency clauses in performance criteria.

Some of these issues involve considerations extending beyond the details of individual country programs. The intercountry disposition of lending—which countries are to receive how large a percentage of quota—depends upon a specific interpretation of uniformity of treatment as it applies to African and other low-income countries. John Williamson pointed out that there may be room for some reinterpretation of the concept of revolving funds. Funds may revolve in different ways, and in some circumstances prolonged use of Fund resources may be entirely consistent with the necessary revolving character of these resources.

Roger Lawrence of the United Nations Conference on Trade and Development (UNCTAD) recommended joint frameworks at the country level for planning external-resource requirements, and extending the use of donor consultative groups to many more African countries. The specific modalities for doing this equitably probably require the establishment of general principles and approaches.

The volume of the financial flows from the Fund to its African members was not generally a major area of dispute. These flows are typically too small by themselves to be effective and under the terms under which they are released may also be inappropriate for many. Rather, the Fund's role as catalyst, or more accurately "gatekeeper," for larger and more appropriately termed financial flows from the World Bank/IDA, bilateral donors, and other sources was at the heart of the debate. The Fund's vision of what constitutes an acceptable program is what really matters. What is principally at issue therefore is program design.

The need for major structural adjustment and policy reform, usually involving exchange-rate modification and austerity, was not questioned by the

African Governors. It should therefore be possible now to put to rest the unrealistic image of uncomprehending and perverse African macroeconomic managers who simply do not understand the gravity of their own problems. Plenty of self-criticism and plenty of tough action have already been taken (though, sadly, more is needed in many places) in macroeconomic management circles in Africa. Policy is not now likely to be improved through more vigorous preaching by outsiders.

There was a remarkable degree of agreement among Governors that Fund staff, missions, and management have not always responded to their problems with the understanding that they believe they have a right to expect. Many, including some with reasonably successful Fund programs, suggested that the Fund staff is inadequately informed or insensitive with respect to local conditions and objectives, patronizing in their relationships with local professionals, and rigid or powerless or both in their negotiations with African governments. Whether or not these perceptions are accurate, their persistence must be a matter for profound regret. It does little good for the Fund staff to restate their good intentions, to proclaim their pragmatism and flexibility in principle, or to defend themselves on the ground that shortage of resources ties their hands, if these perceptions are widespread. Needless to say, the Governors are not radicals bereft of detailed knowledge or experience. Increased Fund awareness of these perceptions and the range of countries in which they are held was an important outcome of the symposium. Mr. Ouattara, in his statement in the concluding panel, assured Governors again of the Fund staff's openness, pragmatism, and flexibility. Ultimately, of course, in these matters the Fund will be assessed by the Governors in the same way it assesses its member governments—according to performance.

There appear to be plenty of plausible empirical and analytical grounds for the Governors' expressed dissatisfaction and disaffection with Fund advice and approaches. In the papers and in the discussion much was made of program failures in Africa (as well as some trumpeted successes, notably that of Ghana), as well as about structural rigidities, wider definitions of success, including concern with vulnerable groups, aspirations for food security and economic integration, the need for institutional development, and the need for longer time horizons (for import liberalization aspirations, among other matters). John Loxley's paper on alternative stabilization programs elicited by far the most vigorous responses, both positive and negative, of all the contributions at the symposium. A major issue raised by his paper and the subsequent discussion was whether better programs required more resources for their success. Of course, easier programs would be made possible by more resources, and sometimes the absence of more resources was what Governors were implicitly criticizing. They clearly want the Fund staff to press harder on their behalf for more resources, and the Fund does have some room for manoeuvre in this respect, both at the level of individual countries and in the aggregate. But it would, I believe, be quite wrong to interpret all this dissatisfaction in these terms. African central bankers and their staffs also have professional credentials. The issues are complex, and key questions of timing, phasing, and packaging are typically matters of judgment rather than of technical sophistication. They cannot be dismissed by technicians as mere politics. At a minimum, African governments should be able to expect Fund missions seriously to consider the merits of alternative programs. Fund staff might themselves construct alternative packages for members with limited capacity to develop their own.

It would also be productive for the Fund (and for other independent investigators) to generate or encourage careful analytical and empirical studies of the peculiar adjustment problems of low-income countries. Some such studies are already being done within the Fund, according to Mr. Ouattara, who also expressed the sensible view that their results should be made public. A little more open public discussion and a lot more publicly visible research effort may vastly improve the Fund's standing in Africa. Many questions raised in the following papers require investigation. For example:

- Is it true that the lags are longer for many supply responses in low-income countries? If so, why? In which sectors? What can be done about it?
- Is it true that nominal devaluations of equal size generate more or faster inflation in low-income countries? If so, why? Are such effects related to the degree of front-ending of real resource flows?
- What are the implications for policy of the possible negative price effects of collective expansion of particular primary exports?
- Is it true that interest rate reforms have more limited effects on savings and the efficiency of resource allocation in low-income countries? Is monetary policy in general less effective in such countries?
- What have been the implications for income distribution and poverty of specific adjustment programs?

There is a rich research agenda here, an agenda for expanded effort within the Fund and in member countries on the part of all who are concerned with Africa's future.

Research may show that in order for any adjustment programs to work in low-income countries, more resources will be required. If so, tough international decisions may have to be made (some are, in fact, already being taken in the face of limited resources) involving the conscious selection of fewer countries for assistance. More rationing of international support and more dispute about the appropriate meaning of the revolving nature of Fund credit could lie ahead of us. The papers and discussion in this volume have certainly not dealt with all the harsh implications of the difficulties ahead of Africa in its current crisis.

Whatever the research results, African governments must ultimately formulate their own programs. Their professional analyses and assessments must be of a quality that will earn Fund, World Bank, and international respect. Moreover, management of their programs—both of demand and of supply—must be continuously effective. Programs that work are good not only for Africa but also for the Fund and for the world, regardless of who may have designed them.

Of fundamental importance for member countries dissatisfied with the Fund's program design is the development and continual maintenance of a defensible stabilization and adjustment program of their own. Developing country governments, particularly the weaker and less experienced ones in Africa, have frequently found themselves in a basically reactive mode, objecting to various specifics of mission-suggested packages, yet without coherent and viable alternative packages of their own to propose.

The Fund management and staff steadfastly maintain that they do not impose programs on anyone and that they are open and flexible in considering alternatives. Certainly the 1979 guidelines on conditionality seem to leave plenty of room to do so. Whether one thinks that they typically have done so or not, the Fund should be interested solely in whether programs work. The likely elements in Fund-suggested programs and the possible preconceptions of its staff missions are by now well known. Member governments uncomfortable with these typical approaches must develop plausible and professionally defensible alternative packages of their own, complete with the detailed factual content and targeting required by Fund missions. No doubt they should be especially well prepared to argue their case for those policies in which Fund doubts can be anticipated. Clearly, local authorities have a comparative advantage over outsiders in their knowledge of the details of the local economy and policy. Provided that the sums are correct, the facts well documented, and the arguments professionally presented, their programs should expect to receive respectful and sympathetic Fund consideration.

*****

Part 1 of this volume contains introductory overviews of the Fund and Africa, presented in opening speeches by Governor Nyirabu of Tanzania and Finance and Planning Minister Saitoti of Kenya and in the keynote address by Richard Erb, Deputy Managing Director of the Fund. These addresses, in which the different approaches of the Fund and the African governments are fully in evidence, ably set the stage for the more detailed presentations that follow.

Part 2 contains the six papers, commissioned jointly by the Association of African Central Banks and the International Monetary Fund, and discussants' comments on them, as well as a paper prepared by Governor Ndegwa of Kenya on the economic crisis in Africa. Of the six commissioned papers, three were prepared by the staffs of the Washington-based international financial institutions (two from the Fund and one from the World Bank) and three were prepared for the AACB (two by African central bankers and one by an academic). Alassane Ouattara's paper addresses the design, implementation, and adequacy of Fund programs in Africa from the Fund's point of view. J.O. Sanusi of Nigeria considers the performance of the international monetary system and Fund, and Samba Mawakani of Zaïre considers conditionality in the context of Africa's current social and economic conditions and disequilibria. John Loxley's paper addresses possible alternative approaches to stabilization in Africa. Luis de Azcarate presents an overview of the World Bank's evolving role in adjustment and growth in Africa. Eduard Brau of the Fund analyzes the problems of external debt management in the African context.

Part 2 also contains the comments of the formal discussants of each of the papers. In some cases, comments of other participants are also presented, notably some of the comments on the Ouattara and Loxley papers, which generated particularly active debate. The concluding comments made by Luis de Azcarate, Alassane Ouattara, and John Loxley in reply to floor discussion of their papers are also presented.

Part 3 contains the presentations made by seven panelists in a concluding session entitled "Adjustment in Africa: What Can Be Done?" The panelists included two non-African former Executive Directors of the Fund (M. Narasimham from India and Carlos Massad from Chile), two current African Governors (Abdoulaye Fadiga of the Central Bank of West African States (BCEAO) and A. Tadesse Gebre-Kidan of Ethiopia), the Director of UNCTAD's Money, Finance, and Development Division (Roger Lawrence), John Williamson of Washington's independent Institute for International Economics, and Alassane Ouattara, Director of the African Department of the International Monetary Fund.

PART 1

Africa and the International Monetary Fund

A View from the Fund

Richard D. Erb

The International Monetary Fund has been playing and will continue to play a major role in supporting African members undertaking adjustment in a difficult external environment. While much attention is usually accorded to its provision of financial assistance, the Fund is, in a larger sense, a collaborative institution that provides all members with opportunities to interact within itself in a number of important ways. Through their full participation in discussions in the Executive Board, the Interim and Development Committees, and the Joint Annual Meetings of the Fund and the Bank, the representatives of African states are able to contribute to the formulation of policies of the Fund in such areas as Fund surveillance, the conditionality associated with the use of Fund resources, and international liquidity, as well as broader questions on the working of the international monetary system. The African countries are also major participants in the Fund's technical assistance programs, both at headquarters and in the field. If the greater part of my remarks today addresses the Fund's financial activities in Africa, this is simply a recognition of the extraordinary balance of payments problems that so many African states are encountering and which the Fund is seeking to help alleviate within the framework of its monetary role in the international monetary system. I shall revert to the broader issues of relations between the Fund and its members in the concluding part of my statement.

The Fund will maintain its financial assistance to its African members, and do so in cooperation with the World Bank, as long as these countries pursue their adjustment to the severe internal and external imbalances that have characterized so many of these countries since the start of the decade, if not earlier. Although the external environment has and will continue to have an important impact on the growth prospects in Africa, continued domestic policy reforms will be necessary to improve the domestic environment for economic growth and stronger external payments positions. There is no single economic formula for restoring growth and for strengthening the ability of countries to attract non-debt-creating capital flows and to mobilize domestic savings to finance expansion, but experience has pointed to the important roles that fiscal, monetary, exchange rate, and pricing policies play in providing conditions conducive to economic growth. These are the major themes of my remarks to you today and of the remarks that my colleagues will be making in the next few days. I hope these remarks will set the scene for a successful and stimulating symposium.

External Environment

The global economic environment of the late 1970s and early 1980s had a major impact on the economies of African countries. The rise in the price of oil, accompanied by a marked decline in the export prices of products typically exported by the African countries, led to a deterioration in the terms of trade for most of these countries. In addition, a slowdown in industrial country growth led to a decline in demand for exports from Africa, and a sharp rise in international interest rates increased the cost of commercial capital to those countries that were borrowing in private markets. Even countries for whom the bulk of capital flows was from official sources saw a leveling off in these flows as the economic situation of official lenders worsened with the global recession.

As to the future, the external environment for achieving orderly adjustment and restoring conditions for growth in Africa is likely to be somewhat better. In the short term, according to our latest staff assessment, gross domestic product (GDP) for all of Africa is expected to increase by 3.5 percent in 1985 and about the same level, or by 3.7 percent, in 1986. Growth in sub-Saharan Africa is projected to reach 2.9 percent per year in 1985 and 3.5 percent in 1986. Despite these improved prospects, however, the aggregate current account deficit for Africa will remain difficult to finance, narrowing to a projected $10.2 billion in 1985 and $9.3 billion in 1986. For sub-Saharan Africa this deficit is projected to be $8.3 billion in 1985 and $7.8 billion in 1986.

Projections beyond the near term are more difficult to make and subject to even greater uncertainties. The Fund's *World Economic Outlook* provides a medium-term baseline scenario for the 1987–1990 period, based on assumptions regarding the policies ''most likely'' to be pursued by both developing and industrial countries. This baseline scenario anticipates an average rate of growth of slightly over 3 percent for the industrial countries over the period to 1990. For all indebted developing countries, gross national product

(GNP) growth consistent with the underlying policy assumptions would average about 4.8 percent. For sub-Saharan Africa, the baseline scenario anticipates an average growth rate of 4.2 percent. Interest rates are expected to be somewhat lower in real terms than in early 1985. And non-oil commodity prices are expected to rise broadly in line with prices of manufactured goods exported by industrial countries.

The policies pursued by industrial countries will be especially important because their economic performance will determine the external environment within which developing countries' efforts to resume sustainable growth will take place. The industrial countries will be seeking to consolidate the recovery and to ensure that its benefits are more broadly shared. This effort will involve a range of domestic policies, including a firm rejection of protectionism. Industrial countries—especially those in Europe—will have to work to reduce structural rigidities that have led to inefficiencies and reduced employment opportunities which, in turn, have nurtured protectionism. A tightening of trade restrictions could choke off the ability of indebted countries to earn the foreign exchange necessary to meet their external debt payments.

In addition, industrial countries should be prepared to support the adjustment efforts of debtor countries by providing adequate flows of capital on realistic terms and by a readiness to consider restructuring of existing debt. The Interim Committee has urged industrial countries to consider resuming export credit cover for debtor nations making satisfactory progress with adjustment policies. Industrial countries are urged to continue to provide concessional resources, either directly or through the multilateral development banks. While commercial capital, including debt rescheduling, is important, increased official development assistance will have to play the major role in the economic recovery and growth of many low-income African countries.

Domestic Policy Requirements

Although the adverse external environment has contributed to the difficulties of many African countries, these adversities have also served to highlight certain internal rigidities and structural imbalances that have been allowed to grow for too many years. While not gainsaying the importance of the external environment, it also has to be recognized that the growth and balance of payments prospects of African countries depend fundamentally on the domestic policy course in each country. In working with African countries in the context of Article IV consultations, in the context of requests for the use of Fund resources, and the furnishing of technical assistance, the Fund has gained considerable experience of the types of policies conducive to economic growth and external payments viability.

The key requirements for achieving enduring growth are domestic financial and price stability and the allocation of resources in an efficient and effective manner. Particularly where inflation has been endemic, action to reduce fiscal deficits and to control monetary expansion is essential. Special attention has to be accorded to keeping tight control over current public expenditures so that more resources can be directed to investment. A reduction in the claims of the general budget on the banking system releases resources for use by more productive sectors of the economy.

As for improving resource allocation, pricing policies are crucial. Many countries in Africa maintain extensive systems of price controls and subsidies that might temporarily mask inflationary pressures but that lead to misallocations of resources. Low agricultural producer prices, for example, result in declining domestic availability of food grains and to a growing dependency on imports.

In the external sector, the price of foreign exchange is another key element in the adjustment process. An inappropriate exchange rate generates cost and price distortions that encourage consumption and uneconomic investment and reduce the profitability of export and import competing sectors. If exchange rates and interest rates are not allowed to respond to market conditions, domestic savings tend to flow abroad and savings by nationals working in other countries tend to be retained abroad rather than repatriated. Similarly, restrictions on trade and competition create inefficiency and tax the community for the benefit of favored groups.

Economic growth depends critically on the level of domestic capital formation, provided, of course, that investment is allocated efficiently. Member countries can call on the expertise of the World Bank to help design measures to strengthen and enhance their development prospects. This is just one way in which the Fund and the World Bank reinforce one another in best serving their members. The Fund's role is primarily to promote macroeconomic and broad pricing policies conducive to both growth and balance of payments viability. The Bank's role is primarily to promote investment policies conducive to growth and to encourage better project design, evaluation, and implementation. Our experience has convinced us that a country's productive resources cannot be properly developed if payments difficulties are overriding and if incentives—such as an appropriate exchange rate—are inadequate. At the same time, achievement of a sustainable balance of payments position depends, among other things, on the efficient deployment of resources over time.

These then are the policies that the Fund espouses, whether in the course of Article IV consultations or in the context of the use of its resources. Not only are these policies designed to mobilize larger savings in the domestic sector but they are also essential for attracting larger flows of resources from abroad on appropriate terms. Of course, these general policies must be carefully adapted to the situation of each country.

In advising countries on designing programs that can be supported by the Fund, the first step is to reach an understanding with country officials on the problems causing the balance of payments difficulties, the measures needed to correct them, and the total amount of financing that may be available from donors and creditors. There is no "optimal" adjustment path that is the same for every country seeking to restore conditions for growth. Within the constraints of available financing each country must answer for itself the critical question regarding the optimal speed and the pace of adjustment. Some countries may need, and in some cases may choose, to undertake very rapid and sharp adjustment, in which a number of corrective measures are implemented simultaneously. Others may be able to phase in their measures more gradually, assuming that such an approach does not make a call on larger external resources that are larger than can be mobilized, or even worse, discourage foreign sources of credit and development assistance from providing the required resources.

In addition, a more gradual approach to policy adjustment may, in some circumstances, directly result in a lower domestic growth rate. For example, if price incentives are inadequate, production may be discouraged. If inefficient enterprises are not strengthened or liquidated, resources will be diverted from more productive investments. Thus, it is not always appropriate to assume that more gradual adjustment will result in higher growth rates.

A number of countries of Africa have been successfully pursuing the types of policies that I have described. I would like to highlight some of the more noteworthy cases. For example, the Central Bank of Kenya, through a series of increases in domestic interest rates, has restored real interest rates to positive levels for the first time in recent years. Domestic saving as a percentage of GDP has exceeded the Government's target for every year since 1980. In addition, a series of devaluations of the Kenyan shilling and a managed float of the currency since 1983 has helped increase Kenya's exports as a percentage of GDP from 13.7 percent in 1983 to 17.9 percent in 1984. Other examples include the Côte d'Ivoire, where authorities have adopted an interest rate policy aimed at making domestic financial investments more competitive with similar investment abroad. And Mali, through adoption of important fiscal policy reforms, such as containment of public sector personnel expenditures through a wage freeze and increases in public enterprise prices and tariffs, succeeded in eliminating the deficit of the consolidated Government operations. Needless to say, while the Fund has supported these types of measures, it is the officials of the countries who chose and implemented them. Any improvements in economic conditions that resulted must be credited to the perseverance and tenacity of these officials.

The Fund's Financial Activities in Africa

The Fund has played an active role in supporting the adjustment efforts of its African members in recent years. At the end of 1984, total obligations of African countries to the Fund subject to repurchase, including repayments to the Trust Fund, amounted to SDR 7.2 billion. Of this amount, SDR 1.5 billion was provided under the Fund's compensatory financing facility in response to shortfalls in African countries' export proceeds and also, in some cases, to increases in cereal import costs. At the end of April of this year, the Fund had 14 stand-by arrangements and one extended arrangement with its African members and two more stand-by arrangements pending—for Côte d'Ivoire and Togo.

In addition to providing its own financial resources, the Fund has been a catalyst for mobilizing support from other external sources such as Paris Club official debt reschedulings and provision of new external finance. In 1984 seven African countries negotiated debt reschedulings under the Paris Club for an estimated $1.9 billion in debt relief. In that year the Fund also attended consultative groups and donor conferences involving 12 African countries, where pledges were made for significant amounts of commodity and project assistance.

The Fund's resources are a revolving pool that can be made available temporarily to members experiencing balance of payments difficulties. This assistance is designed to enable countries to restore a viable external payments position in the medium term, that is, an external current account deficit that can be covered by normal capital inflows consistent with the debt-servicing capacity of the economy. The resources of the Fund thus serve as a "second line" of reserve for its members, providing quick-disbursing financing, untied to projects or designated imports. Members draw on these second-line reserves to meet immediate financing needs while they implement corrective adjustment measures and work to attract other funds of a longer-term maturity designed to address their developmental needs. As these adjustment measures take effect, the need for exceptional financing from the Fund should recede and countries can start to rebuild their reserves as insurance against future, unforeseen crises. Part of this reserve rebuilding includes restoration of their second line of reserves through repayment to the Fund. Any failure to do so undermines the institution's unique monetary role and makes it that much harder to obtain resources for the Fund itself. As central bankers you are well aware that claims on the Fund are treated as liquid reserves by creditors.

The role of the Fund in providing short-term, quick-disbursing financing can be seen by looking at the levels of Fund assistance during the difficult 1980–84 period, compared, for example, with multilateral development bank assistance, which is longer term, more project oriented, and thus not as quickly mobilized. Purchases from the Fund by African countries in 1981 and 1982—a period in which the external environment was particularly harsh because of high interest rates and a world recession—totaled SDR 1.9 billion and SDR 1.7 billion, respectively. This compares, for example, with World Bank disbursements of $1.0 billion in 1981 and $1.3 billion in 1982. By 1984, however, World Bank disbursements to Africa totaled $1.8 billion, while Fund purchases had declined to SDR 1.2 billion. This shift in the composition of flows to Africa reflects a transformation from immediate balance of payments requirements to longer-term, structural-adjustment and development financing.

In 1984 the Fund provided $13.4 million in technical assistance to Africa, a 44 percent increase over the $9.3 million provided in 1980. The Fund provided 62 man-years of expert assistance in 1984, compared with 47 man-years of assistance in 1980.

Policy Issues

Because its assistance is provided on a short-term basis, the Fund has been perceived as expecting its members to adjust overnight. Although Fund assistance is disbursed against short-term targets, these targets are established within a medium-term framework of policy commitments. The Fund does not expect that a balance of payments turnaround will occur in one year. That many stand-by programs have a one-year duration simply reflects the reality that it is not feasible in many cases to devise policy commitments beyond one year. Additionally, the longer the time over which adjustment is spread, the larger must be the commitment of resources from abroad. The Fund and the member country can make meaningful projections only for a certain period ahead. Few authorities are willing or able to make policy commitments beyond one year ahead for many reasons, given political calendars, that is, elections, the annual budget cycles of both the country and its donors, and the normal span of official debt reschedulings.

Some members are concerned that the policy conditions imposed by the Fund are unduly harsh and have the effect of undermining their growth. I would suggest that conditionality is no more severe than it has to be to meet the essential medium-term objective of restoring growth and a viable external payments position, given the external resources that members can obtain from the Fund and from other donors and creditors. In cases where a country has postponed adjustment too long, the adjustment measures may be implemented in circumstances that are socially and politically hard to bear, and may be disruptive to the economy. But the alternatives, in terms of further deterioration of economic conditions, are even more disruptive. For most countries implementing Fund-supported programs, the decline in growth rates occurred before they embarked on the program. The provision of financing by the Fund, both directly and indirectly through its catalytic effect, helps these countries to sustain much higher levels of imports and of activity than would be possible without the Fund's support.

The Fund is prepared to use its best efforts to adapt to country preferences as long as it can carry conviction with other suppliers of finance, and is itself convinced, that a comprehensive program is being embarked upon to rectify the underlying imbalances in the economy. In every case, considerable attention will continue to be paid to supply-oriented policies consistent with the development aspirations of African countries. Any adjustment that requires a compression of net domestic absorption will appear restrictive in the short term but can enhance growth prospects in the medium run. Decontrol of interest rates may result in an increase in domestic interest rates that, in the short term, leads to liquidity pressures and problems and even bankruptcy for some domestic companies. But in the medium term these interest rates will attract higher levels of domestic savings and support increased domestic investment. In addition, these interest rates will provide better signals for a more efficient allocation of investment and, together with higher levels of domestic capital formation, contribute to increased domestic output.

Policies of the character supported by the Fund are not temporary measures to be abandoned once financial adjustment is achieved. Nor are they to be contrasted with policies aimed at development. On the contrary, they must be maintained and adapted to ever-changing conditions in the domestic and international environment if the momentum of growth is to be sustained.

Prospects

The Fund hopes to continue to assist its members through its various facilities, provided that appropriate adjustment policies are followed, and to serve the catalytic function of inducing additional finance from official and also private lenders. The Fund cannot project future use of its resources based on a specified country-by-country lending program in the same way a development financing institution can because it has no project pipeline and its funds disburse rapidly rather than being spread out over a project cycle.

The decision to approach the Fund for help is a sovereign decision of the member and cannot be taken for granted. The Fund might itself be precluded from providing additional finance by the emergence of arrears on payment of charges or on the discharge of repurchases on past transactions. However, on the basis of existing programs, and of those that are under active negotiation, it appears likely that net use of Fund credit by African countries—under the credit tranche facilities—will continue to expand in 1985, although the use of Fund financial assistance by the African countries might be expected to stabilize somewhat in the years ahead. African countries will be making repurchases under the Fund's special facilities in the next few years, but the net outcome will depend on whether conditions develop that warrant fresh purchases under these facilities.

For the Fund to remain strong, credible, and able to help its African members, it must be assured of the adequacy of its resources. The Fund's liquidity position was substantially strengthened in 1984 when quotas were increased to SDR 89.2 billion from SDR 61.1 billion and its permanent lines of credit were enlarged following the revision of the General Arrangements to Borrow. In addition, special borrowing arrangements with some Fund members have increased the Fund's access to credit by SDR 7.5 billion. But the Fund's resources are limited and, in order to be able to stand ready to meet the requirements of all its members, it must be assured of repurchases by member countries within the prescribed amount of time.

Collaboration with the Fund

There are a number of ways, in addition to the financial assistance that the Fund can provide, that the interests of African countries are served by their membership in the International Monetary Fund. One of these is consultation regarding economic and financial policies that every country undertakes in accordance with Article IV of the Fund's Articles of Agreement. These regular consultations are central to the Fund's surveillance and provide an opportunity for African members, in particular those members not currently drawing on Fund resources, to analyze and discuss their domestic policies and to benefit from the assessment of the international community on their consistency with the objectives of growth and external stability. Moreover, through the participation of their representatives in the Executive Board discussions, African members can express their views on the policies and actions of other Fund members, especially those that are important markets for African exports and suppliers of capital.

Through their participation in Board discussions, the African members also contribute to the evolution of Fund policies. Two issues keenly debated in the Board recently—Fund surveillance and the allocation of SDRs—exemplify the importance of these discussions. African members, in conjunction with a number of others from the developing world, have argued that there is a global need for liquidity that justifies an SDR allocation without delay. Other members have been unable to agree with this conclusion in part because they have difficulty in formulating the place of the SDR in a rapidly evolving structure of international liquidity. The debate therefore is broadening to take account of these more fundamental questions.

Fund surveillance has been subjected to similar reflection. African members have joined others in stressing the need for the Fund to carry out its responsibilities in an even-handed way. Given that developments in the largest industrial countries have a heavy impact on the rest of the world, they have argued the special importance of ensuring that surveillance be effective over those countries. In considering the modalities for making this process more effective, African states must be prepared to reflect on their own attitudes toward the views expressed by the Fund when they are not under the pressure of need to use Fund financial resources.

In recent years, emphasis has been given to the role that economic policies in member countries can play in improving the working of the monetary system. For example, efforts to encourage greater convergence of underlying economic and financial conditions and policies are being intensified by looking at ways to promote more effective surveillance. Increasing attention is being given to the structural characteristics of the financial and exchange markets to see if improvements in markets could result in smoother adjustments of exchange rates so as to contribute to maximizing trade and long-term investment opportunities. Improvements in the international monetary system are currently under study. The African countries, with their special concerns for the stabilization of markets, will undoubtedly have an important contribution to make to the intellectual process that will strengthen the Fund and enable it to function in the best interest of all its members.

A View from Africa: 1

G. Saitoti

It is a time of great hardship for much of the population of our continent, but also, in my view, a time of substantial promise. The problems of Africa in 1985 hardly need elaboration. The view that this is a time of substantial promise for Africa may require some explanation, since so many observers offer little else but gloomy forecasts. My guarded optimism is based on two observations. First, the natural resources of Africa and the potential of its 400 million people, which so excited the world as the continent gained independence in the 1960s, are still there in 1985. Second, everyone concerned with Africa—its people, its governments, its friends among the international agencies and bilateral donors—recognizes that Africa is facing vast problems of development. There is broad consensus on the reasons for our current problems. If recognition of a problem is a first step toward its solution, we are certainly ready for the second step.

This symposium may itself be part of that next step toward Africa's renewed development. The International Monetary Fund has, to its credit, been playing a far greater role in Africa in recent years than was true in the early post-independence period. Although the Fund's mode of operation remains close to its traditional role, I sense a growing awareness by Fund officials that the Fund may have to find innovative forms of assistance to contribute to African growth. Fund officials are showing increasing concern about African issues.

What is so special about Africa's situation in 1985 that we should hold a special symposium on its relations with the Fund? Participants will have many different answers to this question. My answer lies in the vast disparity between Africa's large economic potential and its current parlous state of economic development. This is a continent of 400 million people, only a tiny fraction of whom are producing up to their potential. Africa's agriculture can grow a wide variety of tropical and even temperate crops, often at very high yields, and the possibilities for research leading to improved productivity have hardly been touched. Africa's land is rich in mineral wealth, much of it unexplored, and its rivers contain unexploited potential for power and irrigation. With good economic management, good world market conditions, and more patience than we can perhaps afford, African economies should be capable of producing far more output than at present and of noticeably improving the well-being of their people.

Yet the stark reality of 1985 is so very far from this potential. Our population is growing much too fast, over 3 percent a year, while gross domestic product barely keeps up, having grown at 3.3 percent a year in the 1970s and growing more slowly in the mid-1980s. Moreover, Africa may be going through that part of the demographic transition in which population growth necessarily accelerates before it begins slowing down. In fact, one of Africa's greatest successes—a marked improvement in the health standards since 1960—only intensifies the population dilemma. The almost chronic drought in the Sahelian region may be causing desertification, a situation made worse by population pressure that leads to overgrazing and deforestation. Agricultural growth for the continent has slowed to 1.4 percent a year, making Africa the only part of the world suffering a decline in per capita food consumption. A continent that should feed itself and even export food finds itself instead increasing food imports by 9 percent a year for the past two decades. Export volumes actually fell during the 1970s, and exports remain heavily concentrated in primary materials. These deep structural weaknesses in our economies manifest themselves in statistics familiar to all participants in Fund discussions: continentwide reserves not far above a month's imports, high debt service ratios, high government deficits, and savings rates that, at 16 percent, are low by international standards.

No one questions that Africa's economic ills have structural causes, nor that the cures must also be structural. How, then, can the Fund, which operates primarily on short-term macroeconomic variables, help us toward solutions for structural ills? That, I think, is the core question before us.

The Fund, in its stand-by and extended arrangements, concentrates on a set of short-term macroeconomic policy variables that also have long-run impacts. These variables include the exchange rate, interest rates, external borrowing, domestic credit and the money supply, and government deficits. Sometimes food prices become an issue, as does trade liberalization. Targets based on these policy variables are packaged into what have come to be called "stabilization programs." Economic stabilization is frequently an essential first step toward long-term structural adjustment, and, as such, contributes to ultimate solutions for deep-seated economic problems. Some of the chosen Fund variables—the exchange rate, interest rates, and food prices, for example—have key roles to play in long-term structural change. So the underlying issue is not the chosen variables or the stabilization package. Rather, the basic problems with the Fund's assistance are questions of quantity, timing, and conditionality. The Fund lends too little in the light of the required adjustments and expects results too soon.

One-year or even three-year stabilization packages can have remarkable effects in developed or industrial economies. When a country enjoys an array of industries that are competitive or nearly competitive in world markets, a change in the exchange rate can quickly develop new exports and make profitable new ways of replacing imports. When foreign capital flows readily into and out of a country's financial markets, stabilization is often rewarded with substantial private capital inflows that ease adjustment. When capital markets are well developed, higher interest rates can curb excess demand for loans and even induce new domestic saving, while monetary instruments can work rapidly to influence rates and control the expansion of domestic credit. When rural credit and goods markets work efficiently, high farm prices can quickly stimulate more market grains, and markets will distribute them widely.

By and large, African economies do not meet these conditions. Some of our economies certainly have some elements amenable to rapid response, and in this respect African countries differ from one another. But probably no African country encompasses all, or even most, of the market conditions that would make a one-year stand-by program effective. Our exports are concentrated in a few products, often minerals or tree crops, that need years to yield increased output. The export of these commodities suffers from large swings in prices, too large to permit complete dependence on liberalized markets. Many farmers are not well integrated within the national market and either miss chances to exploit higher prices for cash crops or are unable to procure credit and material inputs needed to increase production. Many of our industries emerged behind high protective barriers and cannot be made competitive with an exchange rate adjustment, however politically or even economically advisable. Capital markets are fragmented and hardly touch some sectors, while credit instruments are poorly developed, leaving central bankers impotent to affect credit conditions in important parts of our economies.

There are solutions to these structural deficiencies, and indeed the typical stabilization package includes some of the solutions. But the solutions involve basic development measures that require years to become effective.

What is needed is the amalgamation of segmented markets or even the creation of new markets where highly imperfect ones now exist. This involves action on several fronts: macroeconomic policy adjustments certainly, but also institutional development and change, focused political commitment, and a radical reorientation of administrative practices and attitudes.

Let me illustrate my point with an example from only one of the typical policy changes embodied in Fund stand-by arrangements. Import liberalization and exchange rate management are areas that both the Fund and the World Bank have concentrated upon in recent years. The Fund's prescription generally involves an initial devaluation, followed by a flexibly managed exchange rate that maintains real incentives to export and to reduce or replace imports. This prescription is accompanied by a relaxation of quantitative controls over imports and thus a greater dependence upon exchange rate management, tariffs, and fiscal and monetary policy to control the demand for imports. This is a sensible path to take over a long period of time, not least because it contains elements that will themselves help break up the structural rigidities of African economies. But in the short term, structural rigidities prevail and counteract the intended effects of policy changes.

I have already mentioned that export response is likely to be long delayed. Aside from Africa's staple export commodities, which can be expanded only to a limited extent in the short run, we have few alternative export commodities and little existing capacity for manufacturing exports. What is needed is a long period—perhaps three to five years—of enhanced and steadily maintained export incentives to convince farmers and manufacturers that there are profits in producing for export. Only then will they invest in the needed capacity for export. Now what happens if we go too far toward liberalization and exchange rate flexibility? In the face of continuing fluctuations in prices of our primary exports, there will have to be large compensating swings in the exchange rate, as well as changes in fiscal balances and in rates of credit expansion. This would create an environment of changing price incentives that works directly against the steady price signals required by potential investors in new export goods or import substitutes. What we require instead is a gradual shift toward the new regime, backed by substantial balance of payments support to insulate the economy from short, sharp changes in earnings from our traditional exports. This example could be extended to other policies that are part of Fund packages. The Fund ought to help us through this kind of transition, and I believe it wishes to do so. Its style of lending needs to evolve towards larger amounts, committed over longer periods and with more emphasis on longer-term structural changes.

Aside from structural rigidities that prevent rapid responses to Fund policies, African economies face another kind of problem that limits their ability to try stabilization cures. In the long run, I am convinced stabilization and liberalization prescriptions will lead to renewed economic growth. Under these conditions, in most African economies depending foremost on the output of small farms for general prosperity, renewed growth will spread its benefits widely among the population, benefiting small farmers, rural workers, small traders, and those currently unemployed. But we have to deal first with the short run to preserve both basic standards of living and political stability. In some instances, Fund programs jeopardize the well-being of the poorest members of society. In Africa, where poverty is at bare subsistence level for many people, governments have to be careful about prescriptions for long-run recovery that raise prices of commodities essential to the very poor. In redesigning Fund programs to suit the long-run needs of our countries, we have to find innovative mechanisms that accommodate the very poor, especially in the short term.

My description of African economic problems suggests several general lines along which changes in Fund procedures and conditions would be welcome. First and most obviously, we need loans that are larger and cover longer periods for both disbursement and repayment. Second, African countries would be helped by a more flexible approach to the conditions of Fund assistance. In some cases, for example, adverse changes in circumstances may require larger disbursements to support certain policy initiatives, and in such instances it should be possible either to increase the funds available or to scale down our policy ambitions without forfeiting the next tranche of a stand-by. Third, the Fund should become more directly involved in the difficult institutional changes needed to make markets work more effectively and, if necessary, be prepared to lend funds in support of such changes. Finally, the Fund should become more directly concerned about the distributional aspects of their conditions and assistance to ameliorate their effects on the poorest in our societies.

With regard to the international setting in which stabilization and structural adjustment take place, I said earlier that African governments and their people recognize the vast problems facing the continent. Further, we recognize the heavy burden that rests upon our own governments to take the difficult measures necessary to renew economic growth. But we cannot succeed, no matter how bold and effective we may be, unless the international economy supports our efforts. African economies need buoyant, open, and stable world markets in which to sell their exports and purchase their imports, and they need access to capital markets at low cost. Instead, what do we see in the world economy today? We see growing tariff barriers, quotas, and other protective devices imposed precisely by those countries best able to afford the costs of adjustment. African countries have learned the textbook lessons of comparative advantage and want to sell the products of their land and labor to the industrial world. But it often seems that the industrial countries do not truly understand the basis of free trade and prefer to produce themselves many things that we and other developing countries could sell to them at lower cost. This evidence of an inhospitable international environment is discouraging to African governments, especially when those most responsible for it are often those pushing us forcefully toward stabilization and structural adjustment. The Fund itself is not responsible for these hostile policies, but by virtue of its operations it is seen as among those supporting developing countries' stabilization and adjustment. Therefore, it bears some responsibility to convince the industrial countries to do their own adjusting. Unless the Fund turns its considerable powers of persuasion on the North as well as on the South, it will in effect be asking those with the least economic resources to do most of the adjusting. This is inequitable as well as impractical.

A View from Africa: 2

C.M. Nyirabu

No one would be happier than I if I am proved wrong on this point, but I believe that the excellent relationship between the Fund and its African members in the early years of their membership in that organization unfortunately no longer exists. There is a feeling that neither side understands the difficulties of the other. There is no meeting of minds either on the diagnosis of the present ills of Africa or on the remedies prescribed for their cure. Such a state of affairs should not be allowed to persist, for it is certainly neither in the interest of Africa nor in the interest of the Fund. This situation makes it difficult both for African countries to make progress and for the Fund to achieve its fundamental objectives of contributing to the promotion and maintenance of high levels of employment and real income. It is crucially important to clear up this situation so that the earlier harmonious relationship between the Fund and its African members will be restored, and both sides will be able to make progress in a spirit of mutual understanding and cooperation.

Many excellent, detailed studies diagnosing our present ills have been made by international, regional, and national organizations, and by individual scholars. I think there is a unanimity of opinion that these ills are the combined result of severe exogenous shocks, such as the steep oil-price escalations in the last decade, persistent drought, prolonged recession in industrial countries and their resort to increased protectionism, continued policies of strict monetarism, and reduction in real terms of external assistance. Our own mistakes in investment allocation—in many cases aided and abetted by aid donors—or in management of the economy, coupled with certain long-term trends, such as rapidly increasing population, declining demand for our exports, principally of primary goods, and increasing competition from synthetic substitutes developed by the industrial countries, have contributed to these ills.

I specified persistent and recurrent drought among the exogenous factors that have strained many African economies. Let me elaborate on this. Half of Africa's nations lie partly or completely in arid or semi-arid zones. Drought occurs somewhere in Africa every year; two or more droughts affecting large areas of the continent occur every decade; and extremely protracted and widespread droughts occur about once every 30 years. Since 1965 average annual rainfall in Africa has been significantly lower than over the previous 20 years. The net result of successive recent calamities is that Africa has moved from an earlier self-sufficiency in food and agricultural products to present deficits, which are on the increase. While the rate of growth of food production has been on the decline, the growth rate of population has not abated. In fact, estimates of population growth rates of the low-income developing countries point to a disturbing upward trend. The cumulative impact of both these factors is seen in the widening gap between the availability of food and the demand for it. The continent thus has to live with the frightening prospect of dependence on other countries for feeding its millions. It is a paradox that a continent with relatively high per capita availability of land has to import food from countries with less land. We have to improve the productivity of land use. This is a herculean task, but, given the will and international cooperation, it is not impossible. We have seen that other countries that were once importers of food grains have not only turned the trade corner, but are in a position to create adequate reserve stocks of food for effective management of domestic supply.

With only very few exceptions, the developing countries in Africa are industrially undeveloped, with the result that they have to import many manufactured consumer items from the industrial world. The prices of these manufactured items rise with every bout of inflation in the producing countries. The export receipts of the African countries, on the other hand, do not show corresponding growth because our exports consist of primary products, many of them agricultural. Exportable surpluses are dwindling because of erratic production trends and uncertainties of climatic conditions, and demand for them is limited by the user countries' increasing resort to synthetic substitutes. We therefore have to export much larger volumes than we did a few years back to import a given quantity of our consumer basket.

The long-term solution to our present day maladies lies in improving the productivity of land and in rapidly industrializing the continent. We need external resources for this restructuring of our economies. Unfortunately, the outlook in this regard is dismal. The African countries are already indebted to the extent of over $100 billion. In addition, many countries have substantial short-term debt comprised of trade and services credits and arrears on payments. Delays and defaults in payment of trade bills have choked off imports and thereby strangled vital sectors of many national economies. Many export-oriented units with large import content in their products have to work at suboptimal levels, causing further reduction in export receipts. The vicious circle revolves, pushing these countries deeper into debt. The level of debt of African countries is estimated to be around 40 percent of gross domestic product and equal to some 20 months of their export earnings. The yearly flow of resources from Africa to lender countries by way of debt service is of the order of $17 billion. Apart from these frightening statistics, what is even more disturbing from the point of view of future prospects is the hardening—in all respects—of the terms of new loans. Interest rates are rising, the maturity and grace periods are shortening, and the grant element is being reduced. We are guilty of passing a heavy backlog of debt to the next generation. We could feel less remorse if, along with the debt, we also bequeath them a larger production base and a sound infrastructure. To accomplish this, however, we need to tighten our belts further and reduce consumption so that the resources thus saved can be employed in capital formation.

Domestic savings mobilization is low in African countries relative to other regions. What is more serious, the savings ratio has been declining in recent times. In turn, the domestic resource gap is widening. All are aware of the high dependence of the level of savings on the level of income and on the structure of national economies. Income levels in African countries are generally low and economic bases fragile. Added to these disadvantages, the trend in international economics in recent years has been unfavorable, particularly to African countries, and again this is partly because of the economic structure we have inherited. Appropriate institutions and mechanisms for the mobilization of savings are lacking in African countries. Our institutions need to be restructured and our policies reexamined. There is perhaps little we can do as individual countries about the deteriorating international economic situation, but there is certainly something we can do—and we are doing—about our own institutions and the organization of our own savings and capital formation. In fact, we are quite aware that unless we take measures to raise the levels of domestic savings in our African countries, our economic position and our already low standard of living will deteriorate further.

The damage which these current ills and misfortunes have done to the young developing economies of Africa is deep and extensive, and right now all of us in Africa are still bewildered about what shocks are in store for us and about how to cope with the day-to-day business of managing our economies. Even if there are no more shocks, it will take considerable time before this damage is repaired and we are able to resume the normal path of economic development. The problem of structural readjustment is truly formidable. Even in the better-off countries in our part of the world, the level of domestic resources has fallen so much that very little is available for investment. In the low-income countries even current consumption, at the already low standards of the 1970s, cannot in most cases be maintained. The need for external resources for many of us is not so much for project investment as for sheer maintenance of the economy.

In most of our economies we cannot operate our present capital stock at anything like optimum capacity, primarily because we can no longer afford imported inputs. This is independent of whether these inputs are a high or low percentage of final output; so long as domestic substitutes are not available, cuts in operating imports mean cuts in capacity utilization and domestic value added. Equally, we cannot afford foreign exchange for spares and replacements to maintain our existing capital stock. In these circumstances project aid that neither leads to net export increases nor substitutes for existing import needs is not helpful. It merely adds to the overall level of unusable, unmaintainable capital stock. A far higher share of foreign exchange devoted to operating, maintaining, and rehabilitating inputs and to efficient export development and import substitution would, economically speaking, be much more efficient.

The economic conditions under which we made use of the Fund's resources in the 1960s and the middle 1970s are far different from the conditions under which we need them now. The disequilibrium we are faced with did not arise primarily from demand distortions, let alone from the increasing use of real resources, but from the recent damage done to domestic supply mechanisms. This damage has been compounded by several international factors that have reduced the availability of external resources just when the need for them is most pressing. Domestically, we are in a critical supply situation; externally, the crisis is one of liquidity. Both crises are likely to persist for a long time.

This brings me to our expectations of the role the Fund should play and our actual experiences with, and current perceptions of, the performance of the Fund. We all know that the Fund is the institution par excellence for providing relief to members in an external liquidity crisis. We also know that the Fund's resources for doing so are not unlimited and accept that, in making them available, the Fund has to design conditions to ensure that the resources will have maximum effectiveness in mitigating the crisis, not only in the immediate context but also over a medium term, and that the use of these resources by a member will have to be temporary so as to preserve their revolving character. After all, as central bankers we adopt similar attitudes toward our own borrowers. So far so good. But when these general principles get translated into specific programs for action, there seems to be a wide gulf between the Fund's and the Africans' diagnosis of the true cause of the malaise, the prescriptions of remedies, the perceptions of how the remedies will work in practice, and the periods within which a more healthy and normal condition will return.

Thus there is a general feeling among us that the Fund gives excessive importance to achieving internal monetary balance and exchange rate adjustment, irrespective of the causes of the present disequilibria in payments. It is unclear whether this is due to the particular set of assumptions the Fund has made about the way in which the disequilibria are produced—what in technical jargon is called "the model"—or whether it is due to the Fund's feeling that it can usefully work only in these areas.

One problem I would wish the Fund to consider is that monetary policy is rather less effective in African countries than it may be in relatively developed countries. (Even there its role is in dispute.) First, there is greater liquidity outside the banking system in African countries. Further, monetary policy is bound to be less successful in a developing African economy with its narrow and ill-connected money markets, structural rigidities, and nonmonetary obstacles to growth. In this context, the limitations on influencing macroeconomic activity, let alone fostering development, merely by acting on the money supply are particularly great and cannot be ignored. Another constraint for the central bankers of Africa is the problem of monetary data. "Errors and omissions" attain large dimensions in the measurement of monetary aggregates in the absence in most commercial banks of statistical and research cells and in the lack of mechanized collection and compilation of essential data. Sophisticated monetary policies cannot be evolved and implemented under such circumstances. In short, central banks in African countries are highly exposed to uncertain influences and forces emanating from the undeveloped economic environment.

Central banking in less developed economies, as in Africa, is further conditioned by the need on the part of the banks to assume a more positive role in development. Although the precise nature of this role varies from country to country, in addition to their usual responsibilities central banks are often charged with operational responsibilities in regard to programs of economic development. (In developed economies this work is left either to private sector or to special public-sector institutions operating in the capital market.) This development-banking role of central banks in our economies implies some restrictions on the free use of monetary-policy instruments, such as the allocation of credit and setting of interest rates. A great deal more can be said to elaborate and illustrate this proposition, but I think the point is obvious. In the special conditions obtaining in African countries, for the reasons explained, the sharp edges of the instruments of monetary policy get blunted.

In pointing out the especially restrictive conditions in which African central bankers must work, I certainly do not intend to undermine the role of central banks. Nor is it my intention to suggest that the external balance and the level of the exchange rate are unimportant. No responsible central banker would do that. But, and this is the crux of the matter, there seems to be a wide divergence of view between the Fund and ourselves as to the appropriate exchange rate and other levels, how to reach them, and their likely effects. The matter is complicated by differing perceptions of how particular economies are actually structured, how they will react to particular measures, how long the interval will be between taking a particular step and its becoming fully effective (the speed of adjustment), and how changes build up self-reversing factors (e.g., inflation) before they can increase real exports, savings, and recurrent revenues. Our economies are mostly fragmented, the poorer ones being more highly fragmented than the rest. Income and asset distributions are skewed, and the speed of adjustment is quite slow. We are therefore understandably hesitant about the efficacy of the Fund's prescriptions, especially when there are quite legitimate and serious doubts, even at technical and factual levels, about the benefits which much better articulated and richer economies than ours have derived from the kind of policies we are often called upon to implement. We feel that much more thought than ever before needs to be given at technical levels in the Fund to these questions.

The correct assessment of the prevailing situation and understanding of how a particular economy works in practice have assumed much greater importance than was the case, say, 10 to 15 years ago. Not only are the present balance of payments problems of African countries of wider dimensions and more intractable than before, but the Fund's viewpoint on the creditworthiness of a country or soundness of its policies has acquired much greater importance than in the past. Whether it is a question of rescheduling commercial-bank debt or official loans or of granting further bank loans or more official assistance, concerned authorities place great reliance on the Fund's conclusions. That the Fund's own resources are not adequate to the magnitude of the problem places great responsibility on the Fund. If its judgment is inaccurate, the recipient country or the donor organization will suffer. All the more reason therefore that the Fund should take every care to arrive at a judgment well substantiated by a thorough study of the facts and, in particular, of the path and speed of adjustment to the suggested policy measures. I am sure all of us will be happy to assist the Fund in such endeavors.

In the present difficult circumstances, our African economies are in most cases too import intensive and insufficiently export intensive. Therefore efficient import substitution and efficient export promotion are not alternatives, but necessary complements, if we are ever to regain external balance. This is particularly true of industry that must play an important part in restructuring Africa.

About 60–70 percent of our agricultural exports are of products for which—given their price elasticities, rates of demand growth, and Africa's share of world trade—rapid growth in export volume would reduce export earnings throughout Africa. At the same time, the demand for minerals is problematic at best and even the prospect for petroleum is none too bright to the end of the decade.

Three ways to enhance export earnings, however, lie in industrialization. The first is processing existing primary exports. Not all are suitable for processing, but many are. India, for example, no longer exports raw hides and foresees the day when it will no longer export leather, but only leather products. Tanning and the manufacture of leather products involve high value added and are not, in world terms, very technical nor capital intensive. That is one example. Another is specialty textiles, such as African prints and garments made from them. A second way is developing new manufacturing units based on natural resources and exporting finished or semifinished manufactures, such as, for example, pulp and paper from softwoods and ammonia and urea from natural gas. A third way—which straddles the border between export promotion and import substitution—is regionally oriented manufacturing. This is by no means as cost-inefficient across the board as is sometimes assumed. Tanzania's electrical-transmission and switchgear factory has won several aid-financed orders in international tendering; so has Zimbabwe's railway-vehicles industry. Malawi, Botswana, and Zimbabwe have substantial manufactured exports that receive little protection against world sources and next to none against South African products. I am sure many of my colleagues could quote similar examples. Viewed regionally, collective import substitution is, in some cases, both more practicable and more cost efficient than purely national import substitution. Viewed nationally, it is export promotion. So long as we can buy imports from each other in return for exports to each other (in unusual cases the purchaser can readily pay in convertible currency despite highly unbalanced trade), exports to our neighbors are every bit as valuable as those to our traditional northern markets, and, for manufactures, often pose fewer taste, marketing, and transport-cost barriers.

On the domestic side, efficient import substitution in manufactures as well as food and energy is critical. We need to increase both domestic output and domestic employment, as well as to reduce the marginal import to gross domestic product ratio. Clearly not all industries are suitable. For example, unsuitable are those with high direct and indirect recurrent import content or those producing and using technology designed for much larger markets and plant sizes than we can provide (although regional exporting may help reduce this scale barrier). But the sweeping characterization of all African industry as involving high import content, low domestic value added (including domestic purchases of goods and services), and hopelessly high cost is simply not empirically correct.

On protection there is a problem. In the 1960s three countries were commonly characterized as having developed intolerably high costs and globally uncompetitive industrial sectors behind high protection barriers. Analysts confidently explained why they would forever remain sickly infants. Those three countries are South Korea, Singapore, and Brazil. Especially in South Korea and Brazil protectionism is alive and well, but after 20 to 40 years of building a strong industrial sector oriented to the home market, global market competitiveness of these countries across a wide range of manufactures has been demonstrated. One hundred years earlier, similar analyses of the U.S. and German manufacturing sectors "demonstrated" that protection would forever prevent their becoming globally competitive. There is I know, a catch. Building a home or regional market base is, historically the commonest means to building a strong industrial sector that can serve as a springboard to global market penetration. But building this market base is not a sufficient condition to becoming globally competitive—many infant industries and industrial sectors do become eternal juvenile delinquents, rather than healthy adults. Moreover, it is not the only route to competitiveness, nor for very small economies, such as Botswana and Mauritius, is it likely to be practicable.

In the perspective of medium-term structural adjustment as well as long-term development, industrialization is critical. The Lagos Plan of Action was right to pick out basic food self-sufficiency and industrialization as the focus of attention until the year 2000. The Southern African Development Coordination Conference is correct to emphasize building up, step by step (beginning with selected agricultural inputs, basic consumer goods, and construction inputs), a coordinated regional approach to industrialization.

In the short run, different but no less urgent considerations apply. Unless peasants can buy basic manufactured consumer goods and construction materials (rather grandly termed "incentive goods") no producer price increases can be real to them. Unless inputs—hoes, seeds, fertilizers, gunny bags, plows—are more readily available, they will find it well nigh impossible to achieve sustained output increases. Unless and until these conditions are met, massive increases in nominal producer prices (whether official, private, or parallel market) are not engines to increase production so much as dynamos for reving up inflation and currency overvaluation.

Today many African countries have the capacity to produce these incentive goods and inputs. In their production, the ratio of imports (of operating inputs and spares) to output often averages 20–25 percent. That is, local production is far more foreign-exchange efficient than final goods imports. Yet these industries stand 25–75 percent idle because we cannot afford that 20–25 percent import content. Frankly, I believe that one of the necessary preconditions for reversing the 1970–85 secular decline in agricultural output per capita in Africa is to revive our manufacturing, so that peasants can actually buy the inputs they need and the consumption and construction goods they want. Without that, better nominal prices, better private and public procurement policies and enterprises, more research, even improved processing and transport capacity will not result in the sustained 4 percent or better annual agricultural growth trend we need. I will go further. Without it, many African nations will never get back to past peak agricultural output levels and will continue on a downward trend punctuated by short-lived, partial recoveries, when—as this year in most of East and Southern Africa (but not in the Horn, or Sudan, or the Sahel)—the weather is kind to us. It is, I believe, no accident that the bulk of the World Bank's first program loan to Mozambique is allocated to inputs and spares for basic consumer goods and for industries producing agricultural inputs. I salute that judgment by Mozambique and the Bank not because it downgrades Mozambique's agricultural crisis, but, on the contrary, because it is a critical step toward making possible the recovery of Mozambique's agricultural production and rural economy.

I should like at this point to make a couple of observations on the low-income countries that form the majority on our continent. Their plight is particularly difficult because, apart from the severity of external shocks and the rigidity of their export sectors, many are very much restricted to the Fund as the only source for balance of payments assistance—a lender of first, last, and only resort. Nevertheless, there seems little recognition of this reality in Fund policies relating to the amount and duration of its assistance. The innovations the Fund resorted to in the 1970s to meet the problems created by external shocks, such as the oil facilities, the Trust Fund, and the interest subsidy, are seen no more. This is ironic since the ability of low-income countries to service high-interest, short-term drawings is now lower than it was then. Moreover, the 1973–74 economic shocks were certainly not comparable in duration and cumulative impact to those beginning in 1979. Even the question of further SDR allocations has been hanging fire for several years. Many of these countries are forced to do without Fund assistance because they are already in the "high conditionality" status, and, for one reason or another, are unable to satisfy the conditions. Satisfying these conditions would only move them to still higher conditionality status without any assurance that the Fund, by itself or in consort with others, would provide adequate resources to enable them to achieve a satisfactory external position within a reasonable period.

For major debtors using basically commercial bank funding, the Fund has not merely encouraged parallel negotiations between commercial banks and these countries, leading to rescheduling and new money, but has insisted on such negotiations and on lenders releasing enough funds to ensure the success of stabilization programs. Those nations whose chief sources of external finance are governments (including their export credit windows) and international development agencies wonder why the Fund has not made equally forceful efforts on their behalf to mobilize from these sources the complementary finance needed, in parallel with Fund drawings, for any Fund stabilization program in Africa to succeed or even to endure beyond the first few quarterly checks.

Mr. Ruding, the current Chairman of the Interim Committee, recently warned that insufficient financing leads to too large a depreciation of exchange rates, too tight restrictions on imports and other payments, and ultimately to defaults. He also indicated that some African stabilization programs are so austere as to give little incentive or room for increased investment, economic growth, or employment. Those two comments relate directly to the context in which we are forced to operate.

We are passing through a critical phase in the history of our relations with the Fund. Our balance of payments situation will take time to set itself right. In the meantime, if the present policies of the Fund continue, most of us will be forced to repay large amounts of previously contracted Fund debt, as indeed some of us are already doing. In other words, instead of being of assistance in an already grave situation, it is likely that the Fund will become an instrument of its aggravation! I am sure no one, including the management and staff at the Fund, wants that to happen. It is therefore of the greatest importance that the Fund and African central bankers sit together to discuss all aspects of our relations, practical as well as theoretical, in an atmosphere free from the tensions of negotiations that generally obtain during our bilateral discussions with the Fund, so as to arrive at a better understanding of mutual problems and to help in the evolution of ways and means of responding to Africa's external liquidity crisis.

PART 2

Africa and the Bretton Woods Institutions

The Economic Crisis in Africa

Philip Ndegwa

Africa is currently in a dangerous economic crisis, whose real severity, dimensions, and social and political consequences are not fully appreciated even in Africa itself. The causes of this worsening crisis include a wide range of internal weaknesses, a hostile external economic environment, and, in recent years, climatic factors. The African crisis is also unique in that many of its elements are uncharacteristic of other developing regions.

It is essential that the nature of this crisis be clearly understood by African governments, the multilateral organizations, and donor countries. Without that understanding, communication is impossible, nor is it possible to design economic measures and assistance programs to attack the crisis effectively and consistently.

Indeed, valuable time may continue to be lost in trying to sort out misunderstandings. Africa's economic situation, already serious, is deteriorating. In fact unless effective measures are taken now, the already fragile fabric of the economic, social, and political systems in many parts of Africa will break down. The starting point for discussions between the International Monetary Fund and the World Bank, on the one hand, and African central banks, on the other, should be a fresh examination of this crisis. The African situation should first be looked at objectively, and then strategies appropriate for dealing with it should be considered. This sounds simple, but it will require determination by all parties to consider new approaches to the problems. In this connection, there appears happily to be no disagreement about the overall objective. Every African country is seeking balanced and sustainable economic growth, the same objective which the Fund and the World Bank wish

---

Author's Note: The author would like to thank A.K. Mullei and A.C. Fenwick for their assistance in preparing the final draft of this paper. The views expressed in this paper do not necessarily reflect those of the Central Bank of Kenya or the Government of the Republic of Kenya.

to support. Disagreements continue to take place over strategies, such as policies needed, appropriate economic measures, and their timing. To overcome misunderstanding, the crisis facing Africa and its principal causes must first be understood. After that, since there is no disagreement about the basic objective, it is easier to discuss strategies appropriate for dealing with the crisis. In short, the first task is diagnosis, and only then should medicine be prescribed. To deal with the situation the other way around is to invite even more misunderstanding and disagreement.

The African Situation

The World Bank and other organizations have published materials on some aspects of the crisis and the complex range of issues resulting from it: mass poverty, unsustainable population growth rates, havoc wreaked by drought, the rapidly decreasing ability of the continent to feed itself, unemployment, shortage of domestic savings, accelerating desertification, and shortcomings in domestic policies. Two observations are in order. First, for many African countries poverty and other hardships are more severe now than 20 years ago. In other words, in certain respects, such as per capita incomes and employment, the two United Nations Development Decades have seen virtually no development in many parts of Africa. Second, the interaction between rapidly increasing populations, shortage of resources and skills, and weak or ineffective administrative machineries will in many cases lead to greater human misery and to total collapse of many African countries unless appropriate measures are taken immediately. While appropriate internal measures by Africans themselves are necessary, many of these countries' economies are often substantially influenced by forces beyond their control. Climatic conditions are one such factor, but external trade (e.g., commodity prices) and other factors are of equal importance and capable of management, given willingness at the international level. Ten primary products account for 75 percent of Africa's export earnings, making Africa's export earnings extremely vulnerable to changes in demand.

Africa's access to alternative sources of foreign exchange, especially the private loan markets, is circumscribed by its special circumstances. Africa gets only 10 percent of total foreign private investment flowing to developing countries, compared with 60 percent to Latin America and 30 percent to Asia.

The steep rises in oil prices in the last 12 years and the recent global recession have considerably inhibited African countries to handle their economic problems. For example, between 1979 and 1984, growth in output of African countries averaged only 2 percent a year.[1] That was much slower than population growth, which averaged nearly 3 percent and reached a high of 4 percent in several countries. The growth of export volumes has averaged 2.8 percent for Africa, compared with 6.5 percent for all non-oil developing countries as a group. Import volumes have fallen on average by 1.1 percent, compared with growth of 2.9 percent for all non-oil developing countries. At the same time, food production per capita has fallen by about 20 percent during the last two decades. Imports of grain on commercial terms have grown by about 9 percent a year on average over that period.

The terms of trade of African countries have been weak, suffering an average decline of 2 percent in the last six years. The current account deficits of African countries have been little reduced over the last few years (to a total of $10 billion in 1984, compared with a peak of $14 billion in 1981), but the improvement is largely attributable to the curtailment of imports essential for development. The smaller deficit is not therefore something to be applauded. External indebtedness (excluding outstanding Fund purchases) has risen to over 60 percent of gross domestic product, compared with around 35 percent in the late 1970s, while debt service ratios have risen to around 25 percent.

The outlook for Africa is likewise unfavorable. The Fund's most recent set of scenarios, based on assumptions which I consider optimistic, indicate that many aspects of economic performance of 43 low income countries (26 of which are African) are unlikely to improve, and some aspects will worsen. The picture, of course, becomes worse on less optimistic assumptions.

In summary, the causes of the economic crisis in Africa reflect a difficult combination of internal weakness, unfavorable external economic conditions, and noneconomic factors, such as adverse weather. The crisis calls for a coordinated approach, focused broadly on development rather than on economic stabilization. African governments, the donor countries, and the multilateral institutions must now embark on a dialogue on development possibilities to be tackled not tomorrow, but now. Time is running out. If insufficient effort is made in the 1980s, it may be beyond joint abilities of the Africans and their well-wishers to handle the problems in the 1990s.

---

[1]Many of the figures in this and the following paragraphs are taken from *World Economic Outlook* (Washington: International Monetary Fund, 1984).

Solutions

As stressed above, the task of dealing with the African crisis is too large and urgent for anything less than a sustained effort by all parties on all fronts. The solutions must focus on internal measures in individual countries, regional cooperation, and bilateral and multilateral assistance. Progress will be insufficient unless material steps are taken in each of these areas.

A considerable amount of literature, prepared by such bodies as the World Bank, already exists on how African countries can themselves improve their economic performance. There can be little disagreement on the value of the intellectual and practical contributions made by that literature on agricultural policy, population planning, improvements in administration, and abandonment of practices that inhibit personal productive effort. African countries must take the necessary measures in these areas. In particular, there must be a determination to implement those macroeconomic policies (e.g., monetary and exchange-rate policies) demanded by changing circumstances, so that economic imbalances, endemic in many African countries, can be arrested before they reach proportions at which surgical operations are unavoidable. It is equally important to deal urgently with those internal bottlenecks that threaten to hinder production, such as inappropriate pricing systems, administrative and regulatory constraints that thwart the efficient operation of markets, inadequate support of popular efforts, overreliance on government investments, and inappropriate import and tariff policies.

Economic cooperation needs the urgent attention of African countries. This cooperation is absolutely essential in food production and industrialization. Cooperation should not be regarded, as hitherto, as something to be mentioned in meetings in order to appear neighborly.[2] Economic cooperation is necessary for the development and survival of each and every African country. In the past the highest barrier to economic cooperation has been political resistance because of ideological differences, disputes about sharing the expected benefits from cooperation, narrow and short-run political ambitions. African political leaders must recognize that there will be no rapid and sustainable development in their countries without cooperation. In this they must demonstrate their complete commitment if only because without that

[2] I have discussed this matter in some depth in *Africa's Development Crisis* (Nairobi: Heinemann, 1985) and in greater detail in "Cooperation Among Sub-Saharan African Countries: An Engine of Growth?" *Journal of Development Planning* (New York), No. 15 (1985), pp. 137–61.

commitment other benefits, especially those expected from donors, will not materialize.

The African crisis needs, in addition to more practical and committed action by the African countries themselves, appropriate external support if the strong forces now leading to greater poverty are to be overcome before it is too late. In that connection, bilateral and multilateral donors must recognize that the unique economic crisis confronting Africa requires alternative development strategies which, in turn, require alternative external-support programs.

Proposals for an enlargement of the resources available to (and from) the Fund and the World Bank, for a new SDR allocation, and for ways to reduce indebtedness by cancellation or conversion to grants have much logic and necessity to support them. Other useful proposals include bringing about a substantial reduction in protectionism in the industrialized countries and applying Fund surveillance with equal force to creditor countries in a position to increase incomes in their own and in other countries by increasing imports.

There is, of course, nothing new about these proposals, important though they are, and most of them have a somewhat dated air, with the result that they are now often dismissed out of hand. Yet the need to implement them is overwhelming. The recent and present inaction contrasts starkly with the spirit of innovation and international cooperation of the early 1970s, when several steps were taken, within the Fund's framework in particular, to deal with the needs of that time. The oil facilities were created then, interest subsidy accounts were set up, the Trust Fund was established, the compensatory financing facility was extended, and the extended Fund facility instituted. Many of these, however, were temporary steps.

A renewal of this spirit is now required to deal with the crisis of the 1980s. As far as Africa is concerned, efforts such as the World Bank's special action program for Africa are clearly along the right lines, and there is no doubt that emergency programs to deal with certain aspects of the African crisis, especially famine, are necessary. In that connection perhaps a portion of the Fund's gold holdings could be used to fight famine, as indeed some of those assets were used in the 1970s. But these emergency efforts must not obscure the urgent and imperative need for long-term measures. Those measures are not necessary only for Africa: they are needed for all developing regions and the international community as a whole. A new approach to the management of international interdependence, based on equity and realization that prosperity everywhere is augmented and sustained by fighting poverty wherever it might be found, is now imperative.

Seen in this context and in that of the preceding discussion about the African economic crisis, African countries often find some aspects of Fund conditionality difficult to accept. Short-term "adjustment" programs in countries that already have very low and declining per capita income and in which unemployment is high and basic daily food requirements expensive in relation to incomes can have economic and political implications that are difficult to foresee and certainly not easy to handle. Steps to reduce economic activity already at minimum levels are not the answer in these cases, over and above the intellectual difficulty of justifying such measures. Unsustainable balance of payments deficits and other economic imbalances must, of course, be corrected but this should only be contemplated in a realistic framework of growth. The longer-term Fund and World Bank facilities (the extended Fund facility and structural adjustment loans) are in principle the kinds of efforts appropriate in this regard. A greater proportion of the lending activities of these bodies should be effected through these kinds of programs.

The Fund and the World Bank have crucial roles to play in the development of Africa through such measures. It should also be emphasized that this is not just a question of the amount of funding available. It is equally important that these organizations participate fully and appropriately with developing countries at the earliest stages in formulating development plans and strategies. As already mentioned, the job at hand requires open minds and alternative strategies. Working closely together in formulating such strategies should also help improve mutual understanding of the various perspectives on development that exist on each side of the Atlantic. The extended Fund facility and structural adjustment loans are essentially learning processes and not mechanisms to force standard prescriptions. In any case, it should not be the attitude that "produce a good program and you will get a loan from the Fund or Bank." These institutions should be prepared to participate actively in the formulation of the program, especially when the country concerned may be unable to produce a working document on its own.

Conclusion

The African situation calls for a definite, objective, and large commitment. But this commitment will not occur unless there is a more open and constructive dialogue between Africa and the international community. To be constructive, that dialogue must recognize the problem in its most basic human terms.

Finally, I would like to invite consideration of ways to facilitate communication. A new office in Africa, perhaps sponsored by the Fund and the World Bank and responsible for ensuring that perspectives on each side are adequately represented, might help in this regard. I know that there are such organizations as the Economic Commission for Africa and offices of a number of specialized agencies and the World Bank in Africa, but in my view more than that is needed. Hence my suggestion for a special Fund/World Bank office in Africa.

African Economic Disequilibria and the International Monetary System

J.O. Sanusi

Developing African countries are currently in the grip of an economic and social crisis of an unprecedented scale and severity that threatens the existence of many of these countries. To be sure, the crisis did not suddenly emerge. It is the cumulation of adverse developments whose smoldering embers are traceable back to the 1970s. Its tempo has recently so accelerated that unless urgent measures are taken, the situation spells disaster. Several interrelated factors have combined to create the economic crisis. In addition to structural rigidities, developing African countries are also the victims of unfavorable exogenous shocks that have kept them in a perpetual state of disequilibrium.

This paper will not rehash the economic malaise affecting the developing African countries. Documents on the subject are abundant. Rather, it will analyze the nature and causes of disequilibria in Africa and how the international monetary system has responded to the crisis. The leitmotiv of the paper is that, in relation to the magnitude and severity of the economic crisis, the response of the various international financial institutions, as well as private capital markets (which constitute the international monetary and financial system), has been inadequate.

For the purpose of this paper, the concept of "disequilibrium" is loosely employed. The concept is akin to, but in a singular way departs from, its now familiar neoclassical meaning because this paper is essentially an exercise in political economy. The concept here simply refers to the constellation of destabilizing forces that have operated on one another so as to keep the African economies in a state of external and internal imbalance (crisis).

The first section of this paper analyzes the nature and causes of the economic disequilibria in Africa. The second section examines the response of the international monetary and financial system to the crisis, particularly how the modus operandi of the international monetary system affects the access of the developing African countries to financial resources and why the African countries have benefited so marginally from the system. Finally, the third section draws together some of the major measures, short, medium, and long term, needed to stem the crisis, allow for adjustment consistent with the capability of the countries, and set the African economies on a self-sustained and dynamic growth path.

Nature and Causes of the Disequilibria

Internal structural rigidity and acts of nature have been aggravated by deterioration in the international economic environment. These factors have been responsible for generating the constellation of problems that constitute the present economic and social crisis in Africa.

Of the countries classified by the United Nations as "the least developed," two thirds are in Africa. As compared with other developing countries, social and economic indicators of development, such as output growth, health, and literacy, have shown persistently weak performance in Africa. Economic growth rates in Africa in the 1970s averaged only 4–5 percent as compared with the 6–7 percent recorded by Latin America. Average per capita GNP in 1981 was $770, as compared with $973 for Asia, and $2044 for Latin America. Food production in Africa between 1970 and 1980 was much lower than in the other regions and rose by an average of only 1.7 percent as compared with 2.3 percent for Asia, and 3.5 percent for Latin America.

The rate of growth of population in Africa is among the highest in the world. This trend has put pressure on land where average per hectare production has been lagging behind other developing regions. Furthermore, population growth increases the need for additional social services and puts further pressure on government expenditure. In terms of the physical quality of life, Africa has the lowest index of all developing country groups, as well as the highest infant mortality rate and the lowest average literacy rate (36 percent). The vast majority of the people in Africa are living in abject poverty and social deprivation.

The economic structure in Africa is usually dualistic with a large subsistence sector (accounting in some cases for over 70 percent of the gross domestic product) and a relatively small monetized modern sector frequently dominated by mining and other extractive industries operated by multinational corporations. The production structure in the monetized sector is typically export oriented and consists of a narrow range of primary products—mainly from agriculture and mining.

The development of African economies has been constrained by their primary export-oriented economic structure that has been historically determined and that, after more than two decades of independence, remains virtually unchanged. In addition, as open economies, African countries are more prone to the vagaries of international economic events.

Since the early 1970s, the terms of trade of the region have deteriorated sharply because of asymmetrical movements in the prices of imports and exports. While the African countries have been beset with enormous increases in the prices of their imports (e.g., oil, intermediate and capital goods, and food), the prices of their exports (especially coffee, cocoa, and tea) have declined significantly.

With deficits in current accounts and the worsening terms of trade, developing African countries have become mired in the debt trap. Total external debts of the region account for only about 18.7 percent of total developing countries' debt. This figure, however, conceals the fact that as a ratio of their GNP, total external debts are higher than in any other region of the world. Developing African countries' outstanding external debt, both disbursed and undisbursed, was put at about $150 billion at the end of 1983, as compared with $143 billion at the end of 1982. As a proportion of the value of their annual exports, the external debt of the region rose from 138 percent in 1981 to 161 percent in 1982 and is estimated to be about 180 percent in 1983.

A number of African countries are by nature disadvantaged since they are landlocked or located in an arid zone that imposes physical constraints on development efforts. In addition to physical structural limitations, many of these countries are also prone to drought, earthquakes, floods, desertification, deforestation, and crop and animal diseases. The severity and scale of these devastating natural factors in Africa are greater than in the other regions of the world.

By far the single most devastating plague on African countries is the drought, which has been persistent and severe and is rapidly spreading to hitherto unaffected areas. In addition, desertification is said to be spreading at a pace that spells disaster for the continent if it is not checked. It is estimated that 44 percent of the land in Africa has been affected by drought and desertification, which together have reduced agricultural production by more than one half. The United Nations Disaster Relief Coordinator's Office reported that between 1970 and 1981, because of natural disasters, over

1 million people in Africa lost their lives, while material damages were put conservatively at $46 million. In addition to the loss of human life, outbreaks of disease and pest infestation also took their tolls on crops and livestock on a large scale in various parts of the continent.

Moreover, rapid population growth rates have put pressure on arable land, thus forcing marginal lands to be brought into cultivation, which in turn has drastically reduced agricultural output, incomes, and employment and has accentuated domestic inflation. To these problems are added the prevalence of subsistence production, which renders Africa's food supply prone to adverse weather conditions, disease, and pests. The situation has been further exacerbated by the "international demonstration effect" that shifts tastes away from traditional African staples in favor of imported foods. (This is especially true for manufactured food products.) These influences have led to a sharp rise in the total food import bill for the region and a worsening of the external payments position. A growing dependence on imported foods has reduced the possibility of using trade, specifically imports, for economic growth and development.

These factors, along with internal structural rigidity, have militated against economic progress in the developing African countries. Inappropriate and imprudent economic policies have also accentuated the economic difficulties facing some of these countries. In particular, many countries have adopted domestic and external policies, as well as institutional arrangements, such as unprofitable parastatals and costly commodity marketing boards, that have compounded the problems of adjustment. Official policies have in some cases failed to accord priority to food production by providing advantageous pricing, incentives, and investment.

The external causes of the disequilibria in Africa can be attributed to the deterioration in terms of trade, exchange rate volatility, external indebtedness, high interest rates, and protectionism.

On a general plane, and in varying degrees, all developing countries have suffered from adverse external developments in the late 1970s and early 1980s. Nevertheless, the impact of external shocks on the developing African countries has been more severe because of the weak base of their economies, the greater weight of primary products in their exports, and a series of natural disasters.

External economic disequilibria are a manifestation of the dependence of developing countries on industrial countries and their susceptibility to external shocks. African exports depend on the production of primary products (from agriculture and mining). The supply of these products is inelastic in the short run and prone to a capricious international economy. African countries are price-takers rather than price-makers with respect to their exports. Moreover, imports into African developing countries consist largely of intermediate and capital goods, whose prices these countries are unable to influence. As African terms of trade declined by 3 percent in 1970–75 and fell by a further 5 percent in 1976–81, current account deficits rose dramatically from $437 million in 1970 to over $20 billion in 1982.

In the efficient and effective functioning of the international monetary system, both surpluses and deficits can be equally destabilizing. Adjustment, to be equitable, must therefore be symmetrical between deficit and surplus countries. The present asymmetry in the international adjustment process, however, implies that the burden of adjustment in terms of forgone output, unemployment, and inflation, tends to be borne largely by deficit countries. In the developing countries, this situation has severely constrained their growth. In some cases, the adjustment in African countries has taken the form of large cutbacks in imports of capital goods, spare parts, and raw materials, reduction in social services, and massive retrenchment of workers, particularly in countries with limited opportunities for alternative employment. The social and economic costs of these measures could be politically destabilizing.

With economic activity slackening largely because of deflationary measures in the industrial countries, the prices for developing African countries' exports have fallen sharply in real terms. Furthermore, volatility and misalignment in the exchange rates of the major currencies, particularly the appreciation of the dollar, have destabilized the trade position of the African countries and deepened their external payments problems. The attempt to ride out unexpected massive external deficits by maintaining a critical minimum level of imports has compelled African countries to run down their external reserves to precarious levels and to have recourse to external borrowing. Only four African countries had sufficient reserves to finance three months' imports in 1982. Between 1971 and 1983, the external debt of Africa is estimated to have increased from $11 billion to $150 billion (disbursed and undisbursed).

Economic policies in the industrial countries have also resulted in higher nominal and real interest rates. Record interest rates have in turn increased the cost of servicing external debts for the African countries. Total debt service payments by developing African countries rose steeply from $1.4 billion in 1972 to $15.3 billion in 1982. The high rate of increase in debt-service payments accounts for the sharp decline in net resource inflows, which reached a peak of $10.1 billion in 1978 and thereafter fell every year, turning to a net outflow of resources totalling $0.3 billion in 1982.

Furthermore, a surge in protectionism in the developed countries, manifested in a marked increase in tariff and nontariff barriers, has resulted in a substantial reduction in the exports of the developing countries to the industrial countries.

In sum, this constellation of mutually reinforcing problems has resulted in deterioration in African countries' terms of trade and external payments position and has increased debt-service commitments, causing in turn a vicious circle of low income, savings, investment, and output.

Response of the International Monetary System

The preceding section focused attention on the nature, causes, and consequences of the crisis. Although some of the economic problems facing developing African countries are internal, demanding internal solutions, it is clear that these problems are for the most part exogenously determined and that the overall solutions are therefore beyond the capability of these countries alone. Surely the African countries are aware of the magnitude of the problems facing them and have accordingly undertaken bold and often painful adjustment measures to address the situation. These measures include policies aimed at pruning non-core programs, holding down already low wages, improving revenue positions, and compressing imports (including essential capital goods, as well as food). All these measures put enormous strain on social and political stability.

Moreover, at the regional level the African countries recognize intraregional economic cooperation, as envisaged in the Lagos Plan of Action and the Monrovia Strategy, as a means of promoting collective economic self-reliance. Noticeable progress has been made in the Economic Community of West African States, for example, but efforts in this direction are being seriously constrained by the economic crisis facing all African nations.

What has been the response of the international monetary system to the crisis? How much financial assistance have the developing African countries received from the system?

For the purpose of this essay, the international monetary system refers to the international monetary and financial institutions, overseas development assistance (bilateral and multilateral), and private capital markets. In this context, it encompasses the Bretton Woods system, other multilateral institutions such as the Organization for Economic Cooperation and Development (OECD) and the Organization of Petroleum Exporting Countries (OPEC), the Euromarkets, and private foreign investment.

The deterioration in the economic conditions in Africa during the late 1970s was met with an increase in the International Monetary Fund's activities in the region. Like other developing regions in the world, Africa made significant use of Fund resources including its compensatory financing facility and extended Fund facility. But, as in other regions, these resources fell far short of African needs.

From 1979 to 1983, purchases by developing African countries from the Fund amounted to SDR 5,152 million, or 22 percent of total Fund lending, as compared with SDR 8,096 million, or 35 percent, for Asia and SDR 9,805 million, or 43 percent, for Latin America.

As of June 30, 1984, the cumulative flow of resources to Africa under the compensatory financing facility totaled SDR 2,121 million, representing about 28 percent of cumulative flows to the developing countries, as compared with SDR 3,005 million, or over 40 percent, that went to Latin America. African countries made only negligible use of the buffer stock financing facility—a mere SDR 8.6 million, as compared with SDR 281 million for Asia and SDR 139 million for Latin America.

As of May 1984, the cumulative flow of Fund resources under the extended Fund facility to all developing countries amounted to SDR 5,906 million, of which Asia received SDR 2,946 million, or nearly 50 percent, closely followed by Latin America with SDR 2,296 million, or about 39 percent. Developing African countries received SDR 613 million, or about 10 percent. On a cumulative basis, as of May 1984, Fund assistance to African countries under the supplementary financing facility totaled SDR 586 million, representing 21 percent of aggregate supplementary financing resources, while SDR 1,847 million, or 69.5 percent of total assistance, went to Asia.

By the time the oil facilities were wound up in March 1976, of the 53 countries which benefited from the scheme, six industrial countries accounted for about 51 percent of total drawings, as compared with 7 percent for Africa.

The record of the World Bank's distribution of resources clearly shows that despite the unprecedented economic crisis that has ravaged the continent recently, Africa has up until now received an inadequate flow of funds from the Bank. The cumulative flow of World Bank resources to African countries amounted to $10 billion in 1982, representing 18.6 percent of Bank aggregate resource transfers. (Asia received $20 billion, or 36 percent, and Latin America over $17 billion, or 32 percent.)

Cumulative IDA credits totaled about $20 billion in 1982. Of this, Africa's share amounted to $5.9 billion, or 29.5 percent, compared with $13.6 billion, or 68 percent, for Asia.

Until the late 1970s, for most countries of Africa, overseas development assistance loomed large in the total package of external resource flows, accounting on the average, for about 50 percent of their external resource flows in the 1960s. The magnitude and composition of aid flows changed markedly, however, in the late 1970s, a period that witnessed increased privatization. From 1980 onward, such assistance to Africa actually fell in nominal terms from 53 percent in 1971–73 to 38 percent in 1979–81, while private flows rose from 10.9 percent in 1971–73 to 59.4 percent in 1979–81.

With the relative decline in overseas development assistance, the developing countries were compelled to turn to the international money and capital markets for funds. This development had the effect of putting pressure on the markets as competition for syndicated Euroloans increased. Terms hardened, and for the African countries with their special circumstances, borrowing from the markets became extremely difficult. Africa's resort to Euroloans rose from $1 billion in 1974 to $5 billion in 1978, but declined thereafter to $3 billion in 1981, compared with $3 billion, $12 billion, and $13 billion for Asia in the same period. For Latin America, the respective figures were $5 billion, $20 billion, and $27 billion.

OPEC has played an increasingly significant role in the provision of aid to developing countries since the mid-1970s.

In absolute terms, OPEC lags behind the traditional aid donors, notably the Development Assistance Committee (DAC) members. Nevertheless, in relative terms, OPEC aid compares favorably with that of DAC countries. As a ratio of GNP, the average OPEC figure of 1.87 percent from 1975 through 1982 is five times as high as the DAC average of 0.36 percent, which is far below the internationally recommended target of 0.70 percent.

As of December 31, 1983, OPEC's cumulative aid to the developing countries totaled $1.8 billion. Of this, Africa's share amounted to $810 million, or 45 percent, compared with $803 million, or 44 percent for Asia, and $198 million, or 11 percent for Latin America. Clearly, OPEC has played an important role in filling the resource gaps in developing countries.

Why have the developing African countries not benefited more from the international monetary system? The paucity of the flow of resources from the system to the developing African countries, as highlighted in the preceding subsection, may be ascribed to the operational philosophy of the financial institutions in the system and to the historical and geopolitical setting of the African continent.

The major financial institutions in the present system, the Bretton Woods twins of the International Monetary Fund and the International Bank for Reconstruction and Development, were created when the developing countries in general and the African countries in particular were colonies, with little or no say in the establishment of these arrangements. Despite changes in the international economic structure, particularly since the 1970s, neither the structure nor the operational philosophy of the Bretton Woods system has shown a significant shift to reflect contemporary realities of the situation in the developing countries, in particular with regard to their adjustment and development requirements.

The determinant of the power structure and access to the resources of the Fund is the quota system. The formula on which quotas are based takes little explicit recognition of export instability, structural imbalance, or dependence on imported inputs and therefore tends to underestimate the financial requirements of the African countries for balance of payments assistance. But more important, voting power is weighted by quota, and the amount of resources a member can draw from the Fund is predicated on the size of the member's quota. Since the African countries as a whole have a relatively small share of total quotas in the Fund, they have been mere onlookers in the system with little or no leverage. These factors partly explain the relatively paltry flow of resources to the region from the Fund.

A serious defect in the flow of resources to the African countries the Fund's standard conditionality that still puts rigid emphasis on demand contraction and exchange rate devaluation. Lately, there has been a hardening of the Fund's conditionality, including a proliferation of cross-conditionality with other sources of finance, and a growing practice of tying drawings under the compensatory financing facility to other conditional arrangements. The Fund's compensatory facility, in any case, supplied only about 4 percent of the finance that would have been required to offset the worsening of developing African countries' terms of trade in 1980–82.[1] Many arrangements have been canceled, a significant number of them in developing Africa, on the grounds that members had failed to meet the Fund's rigid performance criteria.

The Fund's conditionality is regarded in Africa as onerous in relation to the magnitude of the loans and, for this reason, members have shied away

---

[1]G.K. Helleiner, *The IMF and Africa in the 1980s*, Essays in International Finance, No. 152 (Princeton, New Jersey: Princeton University, 1983), p. 51.

from using the Fund's resources, except in dire cases. It is, therefore, not entirely correct to say that countries failed to approach the Fund early; in fact, they have been discouraged by the conditionality that they perceived to be stringent.

But more serious is the fact that the adjustment problems in the developing countries have been aggravated by the policies of the Fund. The thrust of the Fund's adjustment programs has been to focus more sharply on reducing demand than on stimulating supply. The Fund has treated the balance of payments objective as overriding and has not been sufficiently accommodating to other government objectives in designing stabilization programs. Given the peculiar case of the African countries, restoration of a healthy payments position requires long-term changes in the structure of production and demand. Although the Fund offers some financial support, there is still scope for substantial improvement to reflect the influences of deteriorating terms of trade and other exogenous factors that have worsened the balance of payments situation in most developing countries. Admittedly, over the years, there has been some liberalization of the Fund's conditionality, including the introduction of the new lending facilities mentioned earlier. Nevertheless, the Fund's current approach offers only a high-cost solution, as the conventional stand-by arrangements of one-to-three years' duration are ill suited to address the problem of structural adjustment in developing countries.

The Fund's Articles of Agreement refer to the maintenance of high levels of employment, income, and economic development as "the primary objectives of economic policy," objectives that the Fund can assist through balance of payments support. In practice, the Fund would appear to have treated these objectives as secondary to the restoration of payments equilibrium and has tended to neglect the potentially negative impact of its programs on the "primary objective" set out in the Articles of Agreement.

As with the Fund, access to the resources of the World Bank is largely conditioned by its operational philosophy. The Bank has traditionally perceived its main function as that of providing finance for projects and not for correcting external payments imbalances. This perception has, to a considerable extent, hindered the effectiveness of the Bank's response to the resource requirements of the developing African countries. It is, of course, acknowledged that the Bank has recently introduced programs aimed at expanding imports, and, while it is too early to assess their effectiveness, these programs are nevertheless a step in the right direction.

The undue emphasis which the Bank places on per capita income, reserve position, savings rates, and terms of trade in evaluating creditworthiness generally counts heavily against African countries because, given the nature of their economic problems, they score low marks on these criteria. There has never been a dearth of projects in Africa to justify the region's small share of total Bank lending. Real problems exist in the articulation and preparation of projects and sometimes in the inability of local institutions to provide local counterpart financing. In this regard, the Bank can assist positively in assessing viable projects and in the handling of local costs. Some circles, notably potential foreign direct investors, perceive that Africa is a high-risk zone, ignoring the fact that a lot of investment in Africa earns adequate return.

To some extent, the Bank has acknowledged the structural adjustment problems facing the developing African countries and has responded with its structural adjustment loan program.[2] The distribution of IDA credits is generally skewed by concentration in a few developing countries, notably India, Pakistan, and Bangladesh. Together, these three countries account for well over 50 percent of IDA credits. Although there has been some noticeable increase in IDA credits to the African countries, the increase has not kept pace with their growing needs. A major constraint on the African countries' access to this highly concessional assistance has been the inadequacy of IDA's resources, which have been crippled by the failure of some major donors to fulfill their financial obligations to that institution. Efforts to augment IDA resources under the seventh replenishment have met with serious difficulties owing largely to the opposition of the United States of America. The U.S. action limits IDA's seventh replenishment to $9 billion instead of the $12 billion that is required for the 1984–86 period.

As mentioned earlier, overseas development assistance flows are conditioned largely by the strategic interests of the donor countries. Historically, Africa has never been regarded of strategic importance in the global balance of power and hence has been unable to attract enough such assistance, as compared with other areas perceived as more strategic. One consequence of this pattern of flows has been a broadening of the development gulf between the African countries and other developing areas.

Lately, developing countries have been required to obtain a clean bill of financial health from the Fund as a sine qua non for further access to loans or even for renegotiation of their existing debts. This has been a source of seri-

---

[2]The case for substantial transfer of real resources to Africa has been reinforced in the World Bank's study, *Toward Sustained Development in Sub-Saharan Africa: A Joint Program of Action* (Washington: World Bank, 1984).

ous friction between some African borrowers and the lending syndicates. The Fund's seal of approval is contingent upon a prior undertaking to accept the standard stabilization program and to meet the acid test of performance criteria. In effect, the outcome of all manner of loan negotiations, debt reschedulings, or refinancings has come to depend crucially on the role of the Fund.

Finally, the present economic crisis in developing African countries calls for urgent and concerted action at the international level to ameliorate the deteriorating situation. Attention has earlier been drawn to the determined efforts being made at both national and regional levels to deal with the crisis. There is no denying that during the last few years the terrifying scale of the crisis has elicited positive response from the international community. In relation to the magnitude of the problem, however, the response of the multilateral financial institutions, especially the Fund, the World Bank, bilateral and multilateral overseas development assistance, and the private international financial markets has been totally indequate.

Measures to Be Taken

A consensus has emerged recently on the nature and causes of the present disequilibria in Africa and the policy tools to be used in addressing the crisis. What has been lacking is the political will to translate the consensus into concrete action both at the national and international levels.

Certain obvious measures can only be taken at the national level. African countries have taken, and are taking, painful adjustment measures which in some cases over time are neither socially nor politically sustainable. These countries have no choice in putting their own economies in balance but to continue to take these actions, including efficient use of the external resources which come their way. There is undoubtedly need for the African countries to be more prudent than in the past in the use of fiscal and monetary policies. And there is need to encourage agriculture in Africa.

The proposals I suggest are intended as sui generis treatment of the African countries in their relation with the international monetary system. The measures proposed could be adopted within the existing system without awaiting long-term structural reforms. They constitute not an alternative to such reform, but rather interim action urgently needed to avert catastrophic collapse and global instability, pending sustained world economic recovery and the negotiation of longer-term structural reforms.

To begin with, in order to attenuate economic disequilibria in Africa and set the stage for self-sustained economic growth and development, fundamental changes are needed in the mode and operational philosophy of the international monetary and financial system. The present crisis calls for purposive and concerted action by the international community through the transfer of adequate real resources to the African countries to complement their adjustment efforts.

With greater resources, multilateral institutions would be able to offer support to needy countries and accordingly set the stage for a movement back toward the international financial institutions, as opposed to private markets, as the main conduit for channeling international finance to developing countries, particularly the African countries.

That the Fund, the pivot of the system, needs an enlargement of resources to cope with demands of member countries cannot be overstressed. The resources of the Fund should be substantially increased to enable it to meet its obligations to members in need of financial support, especially the structurally disadvantaged least-developed countries, the majority of which are in Africa. The Ninth Review of Quotas should be advanced by at least two years, and, more important, the distribution of such additonal resources should be weighted heavily in favor of the least developed countries as a way of redressing past inequities in the distribution of Fund resources.

There should be a substantial allocation of SDRs. In light of the present economic crisis, there is a compelling need to link the allocation of SDRs with the needs of development.

Augmenting the Fund's resources alone will not per se suffice to enhance the efficient working and equity of the adjustment process. Perhaps more important, the Fund's rules and mode of operation must be fundamentally changed if the institution is to play an effective catalytic role in the alleviation of the economic crisis facing the African countries. Consider, for instance, the compensatory financing facility. Although this facility has been liberalized, the liberalization has not gone far enough to address the roots of the problems of the poor countries. First, drawings from the facility should ideally be related to shortfalls in export earnings and upward movements in overall import prices (rather than cereal imports only) since one of the raisons d'être of balance of payments support is to arrest harmful cutbacks in imports. Second, the repayment period should be extended when a user is unable to reverse a shortfall in a short period. Third, compensatory drawings should be disassociated from quotas and related instead to the balance of payments needs of members. In this way, a greater number of African nations that have seen a deterioration in their terms of trade would qualify for compensation under this facility.

Although the extended Fund facility has been hailed as an attempt to address the structural and supply-side factors in the balance of payments difficulties of developing countries, it suffers from the shortcomings of traditional Fund conditionality, which attaches undue primacy to demand-side considerations. Above all, the Fund should design conditionality in a manner that takes cognizance of the peculiarities of member countries who perhaps have common problems, but by no means common adaptability.

To reverse the current downward trend in economic activity in Africa, it would be desirable to create a new Trust Fund for Africa to provide additional resources to the hardest-hit countries that face severe adjustment problems with limited access to financial markets. Drawings under the facility should be eligible for interest rate subsidy.

There is also an urgent need to work out the possible modalities for arbitration and settlement of conflict when a disagreement between the Fund and a member country has become excessively costly to the welfare and growth prospects of the borrowing country.

Similarly, the resources of the World Bank Group, particularly the IDA, should be substantially expanded to enable the institutions to meet the challenges not only of the moment, but also of the future. Because it is the least developed region within the developing world, and because of its current grave economic crisis, Africa should not only have its share of IDA resources maintained, but substantially increased. There is also a clear need for increased structural adjustment lending by the Bank beyond the present 10 percent limit, particularly in the case of the hard-pressed African countries.

To address the crisis, the Bank would need substantially to increase its program lending to the developing African countries. There is urgent need for quick-disbursing loans to finance not only imports of raw materials and spare parts, but also local costs, and to support adjustment. Furthermore, to alleviate the present crisis, it would be desirable to create a special window in the Bank, targeting exclusively developing African countries, or to earmark, say, about 50–60 percent of IDA loans for the next 10 years or so for the developing African countries.

Also important is the need to increase overseas development assistance and other forms of concessional assistance beyond their historical real levels. In this regard, donor countries whose aid has not yet reached the internationally agreed targets of 0.7 percent of their GNP to developing countries and 0.15

percent of their GNP to the least-developed countries should take urgent action to do so. Specifically, donor countries should show a willingness to transfer more aid in quick-disbursing form.

An important supplement to concessionary resource flows is the Euromarket. Nevertheless high and variable interests charged by commercial lenders have virtually eliminated balance of payments advantages expected from this borrowing by African countries. One way to minimize the overall debt-servicing cost for these countries is to charge a lower and fixed interest rate on their official loans. There is a persuasive case for conversion of official debts from loans to grants and, in the case of private debts, for longer-term maturity and grace periods. Commercial loans should be made accessible to a larger number of African countries to overcome the present concentration on a few countries considered more creditworthy.

In general, for the policies of the developing African countries to succeed, the industrial countries will not only have to generate more steady economic expansion, but will also have to make a substantial concession by offering better prices for African commodities. In addition, reasonable prospects for the resumption of growth and development in Africa, will require not only lengthening the term of its debt, but also a reduction in high interest rates. These measures are crucial to the solution of the debt problem.

In order to raise agricultural and industrial output, African countries will themselves have to pursue more realistic agricultural and industrial policies, ensuring that the new funds they borrow are for productive investment rather than for increasing consumption. Closely related is building up reserves in good years to enable these countries to withstand the inevitable fluctuations in commodity export prices.

What the African countries need now to lift their decimated economies from the abyss of retrogression is a sort of Marshall Plan for Africa similar to that designed to rehabilitate and reconstruct Western Europe at the end of World War II.

The upshot of the policy measures adumbrated above is that the African countries constitute a special case and therefore what is required is special treatment. This, in fact, is the central message in this paper. There is a compelling need for a change in attitude in the analysis and prescriptions for the African countries in the international monetary system. Hitherto, although the very serious and almost intractable economic problems of African countries have been recognized and indeed emphasized in discussions in many international fora, prescriptions for international reform have often been too general or global in approach, invariably by-passing the African countries in their implementation. Thus, even if all the current reform proposals, such as the Group of Twenty Four Program of Action and the Brandt Commission recommendations, were to be implemented, African countries would benefit only marginally.

There is therefore a plausible case to move away from the global or aggregative approach in dealing with the problems of the developing countries. In the reform of the system, special provisions or special windows must be created for the African countries, tailored to the particular and peculiar circumstances of the countries or groups of countries with similar problems.

In the final analysis, the African countries recognize that the existing structure and pattern of trade relations—a historical legacy—cannot and should not continue indefinitely. Nor can the formulation of their economic development plans be perennially contingent upon the availability of external resource inflows. For a variety of reasons, the conventional trade model that placed emphasis on foreign trade as an engine of growth is losing its power. Economic recovery, which began in 1983 in North America and Japan, has had no significant impact on the economies of the African countries. Moreover, the various prospective economic scenarios for Africa in the years ahead do not depict substantial improvement. If anything, they require further years of painful adjustment measures.

Against this background, it is imperative for the African countries to take concerted action to implement the Lagos Plan of Action which calls for economic cooperation to achieve collective self-reliance, rapid economic development, and sustained growth. The African countries have the capability and potential resources to achieve this goal. Given the present precarious economic situation in Africa, what is required is the political will to act with the understanding, cooperation, and support of the international monetary system.

In the end, it is in the mutual interests of both the industrial economies and the African countries that the international monetary system should give active support to the adjustment efforts by the African countries as a means of ensuring efficient allocation of resources and equitable distribution of the gains from economic interdependence.

Design, Implementation, and Adequacy of Fund Programs in Africa

Alassane D. Ouattara

In the second half of the 1970s and early 1980s the African countries, in common with other developing countries, were seriously affected by the adverse developments in the international economic environment, notably the oil price shocks, the economic recession in industrial countries, the steep rise in international interest rates, and the decline in prices of raw materials. The impact of these external shocks was compounded by inadequate domestic economic and financial policies pursued in many countries. The convergence of these factors thus resulted in large and growing domestic and external financial imbalances, high rates of inflation, and slackening economic growth in most African countries. Furthermore, the situation was exacerbated by structural weaknesses and the damaging impact of protracted droughts, particularly in the Sahelian region.

Faced with mounting economic and financial difficulties, a number of African countries embarked, especially since 1980, on adjustment programs supported by the International Monetary Fund. This paper examines the design, implementation, and adequacy of these programs. The discussion of these elements will be preceded by a brief overview of the causes of economic and financial difficulties in African countries and the role the Fund is playing in assisting these countries in their adjustment efforts. The paper will conclude with some remarks on the lessons that can be drawn from the recent experience with Fund-supported programs and on future prospects in Africa.

Causes and Magnitude of the Economic Problems

The economic and financial situation of most African countries deteriorated markedly in the second half of the 1970s and early 1980s.[1] The annual rate of economic growth in the non-oil African countries, which reached 6.3 percent in 1974 and 5.8 percent in 1976, fell to less than 2.5 percent in 1977–80 and to only 1.3 percent in 1981–83 (Table 1), a rate significantly lower than the 3 percent annual increase in population, resulting in a significant decline in real per capita income. Over this period, their combined external current account deficit grew sharply, rising from $4.5 billion in 1973 to $14.1 billion in 1981, or from an average of about 10 percent of exports of goods

Table 1. Africa:[1] Selected Economic Indicators, 1973–84

	1973	1975	1977	1979	1981	1983	Estimate 1984
				(percent)			
Economic growth	2.39	2.75	2.30	2.00	1.70	0.80	3.20
Inflation	9.86	15.84	24.30	22.90	28.00	26.50	17.00
Terms of trade	8.30	– 12.19	18.10	2.70	– 3.00	– 0.10	3.50
Ratio of external debt to GDP	24.90	27.50	36.00	37.90	43.40	54.60	57.70
Debt service ratio	. . .	9.50	11.90	15.50	18.70	22.60	24.90
				(billions of dollars)			
Current account	– 4.50	– 7.20	– 6.60	– 9.60	– 14.10	– 10.20	– 9.40
Net official transfers	1.10	1.70	2.30	3.00	3.40	3.30	3.40
Net capital inflows	3.80	4.90	5.00	6.40	8.40	5.40	5.10
Overall balance of payments	0.50	– 0.60	0.70	– 0.20	– 2.30	– 1.50	– 0.90
Total outstanding debt	11.60	18.40	31.00	45.10	56.30	62.20	69.30

Source: International Monetary Fund, Current Studies Division, Research Department, and *World Economic Outlook* (Occasional Paper No. 27, 1984).

[1] This follows the International Monetary Fund's *International Financial Statistics* classification of the African countries. These include all the African member countries, with exception of Algeria, Egypt, Nigeria, and Libya, which are classified under different headings. In this table, South Africa is also excluded.

---

[1]See Calamitsis (1984); Tun Wai and Acquah (1984); and Zulu and Nsouli (1985).

and services to almost 43 percent, respectively.[2] To finance these large and growing deficits, a number of countries resorted to foreign borrowing which was facilitated, in the mid-1970s, by relatively easy access to external sources of financing. However, the heavy borrowing, combined with the steep rise in interest rates at the turn of the decade, led to a debt crisis in some countries.[3] The weakening in economic growth and the large external payments imbalances were accompanied by an intensification of inflationary pressures. The average annual rate of inflation in the non-oil African countries rose almost continuously, from 10 percent in 1973 to over 20 percent during 1977–83.

This deterioration in the economic and financial situation of most African countries was due in part to adverse external factors. The sharp increase in oil prices in 1973–74 and again in 1979–80 resulted in a marked rise in the import bill of the oil-importing countries, thereby affecting significantly their external position. Although the cost of oil imports has been reduced by the recent decline in oil prices, such imports still constitute a heavy burden on the balance of payments. The African countries that are net exporters of oil of course benefited from the increases in oil prices, but have been adversely affected by the recent decline in these prices. The severe recession in industrial countries in the early 1980s affected both the oil and non-oil African countries. The recession resulted in a marked weakening in demand for exports of many countries, which was exacerbated by a sizable decline in prices of primary commodities and a significant deterioration in the terms of trade, estimated at about 15 percent over the period 1978–83. Meanwhile, the unprecedented rise in international interest rates aggravated the already heavy burden of debt servicing. High interest rates affected especially those countries with large indebtedness, but was also a factor for small borrowers. During 1974–83 the debt service payments of the non-oil African countries rose elevenfold; as the growth of their export earnings slowed, the average debt service ratio increased from 8 percent in 1974 to 23 percent in 1983 and further to 25 percent in 1984.

The adverse impact of external factors was compounded by inadequate domestic demand management and structural policies, which contributed to the worsening in the balance of payments position, the weakening of the real sector, and the rise in inflationary pressures. Many African countries continued to pursue expansionary financial policies, even though the changing

[2]See IMF, *World Economic Outlook* (1984).

[3]See Bhatia and Tahari (1984).

world economic environment increased the urgency for restraint. These policies were reflected in large and growing fiscal deficits and in rapid expansion of domestic credit and liquidity. The widening fiscal deficits were the result of increases in both current and capital expenditures which were out of line with the growth of revenue. In many cases, large spending was initially caused by ambitious development programs which had been initiated when, in the early 1970s, world prices of certain primary and mineral products were highly favorable, thereby raising export receipts and budgetary revenues (e.g., Gabon, Liberia, Madagascar, Mauritania, Morocco, and Zaïre). However, as exports weakened and revenues tapered off as a result of subsequent declines in world prices and a weakening of world demand, many countries continued with their expansionary expenditure policy, resulting in the widening of their fiscal deficits. In other cases, high expenditures reflected social and political pressures, as well as security needs. In several countries, rapidly rising wage outlays, large recruitment in the public sector, consumer subsidies, and transfers to public enterprises represented a growing budgetary burden and were frequently major causes of the widening fiscal deficits. These deficits were financed by external borrowing, large recourse to domestic credit, and, in certain cases, by an accumulation of domestic and external arrears. In a number of countries, the expansion of credit to the government was made at the expense of the nongovernment and productive sectors. This misallocation of credit was compounded by credit and interest rate controls which resulted in an inefficient sectoral allocation of resources. Negative real interest rates in many countries hampered the mobilization of savings and also contributed to the misallocation of resources.

In addition to inappropriate demand management policies, inadequate structural policies played a significant role in the deterioration of the economic and financial situation in many African countries. There was a tendency to allow exchange rates to appreciate in real terms and become increasingly overvalued, resulting in a reduction in the profitability of the export- and import-substitution sectors, an erosion of the competitiveness of domestic production, and widespread distortions in the economy. In many instances, overvalued exchange rates were accompanied by a wide range of restrictions, as well as administrative and price controls, leading to parallel markets for goods and foreign exchange. In particular, the rigidity in consumer prices led to increases in budgetary subsidies, encouraged consumption, and thereby raised imports of consumer goods. Moreover, low consumer prices were reflected in low agricultural producer prices which did not keep up with higher costs of production, thus eroding the profitability and productivity of the agricultural sector, which was also hampered by recurring droughts, especially in the Sahelian region. Frequently, controls on prices and utility tariffs added to the problems the public enterprise sector was facing as a result of poor management and overstaffing. As the development strategy in many African countries relied heavily on the public sector, the growing difficulties of public enterprises increased the magnitude of the economic and financial problems of these countries. In addition, during the last decade, there were large public investments in infrastructure and in nonviable projects, instead of quick-yielding projects; as such, these investments contributed little to export promotion or import substitution and to generating the foreign exchange needed to service the debts contracted to finance the projects.

Faced with large and mounting domestic and external imbalances, in the 1970s most countries resorted to external borrowing to finance their financial deficits while running down their foreign reserves; few countries took corrective measures to contain the deterioration of their financial situation. As financing was used as a substitute for adjustment, in many countries the debt service burden rose sharply, creditworthiness was eroded, and additional borrowing became much more costly and less available. At the turn of the decade, it became evident to these countries that financing was only a temporary solution and that there was a need for appropriate adjustment to tackle the existing problems. Since many of these problems were deep-seated and structural, however, adjustment could not be realized in a short period of time, and additional financing was needed to support an orderly adjustment process. Accordingly, a proper combination of adjustment and financing was required to achieve over the medium term a viable balance of payments position that would be consonant with sustainable economic growth and relative price stability.

The Role of the Fund in the Adjustment Process[4]

In recent years the International Monetary Fund has been playing an important role in assisting a number of African countries in the design and financing of their adjustment programs. The Fund's role in Africa, as else-

[4]Kanesa-Thasan (1981); Crockett (1982); Guitian (1982); de Larosière (1983); Calamitsis (1984); and Zulu and Nsouli (1985).

where, is governed by its Articles of Agreement, which state at the outset (Article I) that its purposes are:

> (ii) to facilitate the expansion and balanced growth of international trade, and to contribute thereby to the promotion and maintenance of high levels of employment and real income and the development of the productive resources of all members as primary objectives of economic policy; (iii) . . . to maintain orderly exchange arrangements . . .; (v) to give confidence to members by making the general resources of the Fund temporarily available to them under adequate safeguards, thus providing them with opportunity to correct maladjustments in their balance of payments without resorting to measures destructive of national or international prosperity; and (vi) . . . to shorten the duration and lessen the degree of disequilibrium in the international balance of payments of members.

In accordance with these objectives, the Fund has developed a pragmatic and flexible approach in assisting member countries in their adjustment efforts and in providing them with technical and financial assistance. In particular, the Fund has continuously adapted its policies and procedures in response to the changing international economic environment and the needs of member countries. To deal with balance of payments disturbances that are temporary and beyond the control of the authorities, the Fund introduced certain special facilities with low conditionality. These included the oil facilities, the Trust Fund, the subsidy accounts, the compensatory financing facility, and, more recently, the so-called cereal facility. The oil facilities were introduced in 1974–75 to help members cushion their economies against the adverse impact of the sharp increases in oil prices in 1973–74. The Trust Fund was created in 1976 to extend low-interest loans to low-income members out of profits derived from sales of a portion of the Fund's gold holdings. The subsidy accounts were set up in 1975 and 1980 to help the same group of members meet the higher charges on amounts lent to them from resources borrowed by the Fund at market-related interest rates. In addition, in 1979 the maximum entitlement under the compensatory financing facility, which was established in 1963 to help countries finance deficits due to temporary export shortfalls, was enlarged to 100 percent of quota. More recently, in 1981 the Fund introduced the cereal facility, as an integral part of the compensatory financing facility, to provide assistance to members experiencing temporary increases in the cost of cereal imports. Many members benefited from these special facilities. Purchases under the oil facilities by African countries amounted to SDR 465 million in 1974–76, and Trust Fund loans disbursed to them totaled SDR 962 million over the period 1977–81. The drawings under the compensatory financing facility increased from SDR 968 million during 1974–79 to SDR 1,620 million during 1980–84 (Table 2).

Table 2. Compensatory Financing Facility Purchases by African Countries, 1980–84
(millions of SDRs)

	1980		1981		1982		1983		1984	
	Export short-falls	Cereal import excesses	Export short-falls	Cereal import excesses	Export short-falls	Cereal import excesses	Export short-falls	Cereal import excesses	Export short-falls	Cereal import excesses
Central African Republic	...	...	9.0	...	...	...	...	...	...	...
Chad	...	...	7.1	...	...	...	...	...	...	...
Côte d'Ivoire	...	...	114.0	...	...	...	...	...	...	...
Egypt	...	...	...	...	...	...	...	...	...	...
Equatorial Guinea	6.4	...	4.7	...	...	...	...	...	...	...
Ethiopia	...	...	18.0	...	...	...	...	...	...	...
Gambia, The	...	...	9.0	...	...	...	...	...	...	...
Ghana	...	...	...	...	...	...	120.5	...	58.2	9.0
Guinea-Bissau	...	...	...	1.9	...	...	...	...	...	...
Kenya	...	...	...	...	28.8	31.6	...	...	...	...
Liberia	...	...	...	...	34.7	...	...	...	14.4	...
Madagascar	29.2	...	...	...	21.8	...	...	...	13.8	...

Malawi	. . .	. . .	. . .	12.0	. . .	. . .	12.2	. . .	. . .	. . .
Mali	5.1	. . .	. . .	. . .	. . .	. . .	. . .	. . .	. . .	. . .
Mauritania	10.5	. . .	. . .	. . .	. . .	. . .	. . .	. . .	. . .	. . .
Mauritius	. . .	. . .	40.5	. . .	. . .	. . .	. . .	. . .	. . .	. . .
Morocco	. . .	. . .	. . .	. . .	113.0	123.4	. . .	. . .	. . .	. . .
Niger	. . .	. . .	. . .	. . .	. . .	. . .	24.0	. . .	. . .	. . .
Senegal	. . .	. . .	42.0	. . .	. . .	. . .	. . .	. . .	. . .	. . .
Sierra Leone	. . .	. . .	. . .	. . .	. . .	. . .	20.7	. . .	. . .	. . .
Sudan	21.8	. . .	45.7	. . .	. . .	. . .	39.1	. . .	. . .	. . .
Swaziland	. . .	. . .	. . .	. . .	. . .	. . .	9.0	. . .	. . .	. . .
Tanzania	15.0	. . .	15.9	. . .	. . .	. . .	. . .	. . .	. . .	. . .
Uganda	25.0	. . .	45.0	. . .	. . .	. . .	. . .	. . .	. . .	. . .
Zaïre	. . .	. . .	. . .	. . .	106.9	. . .	114.5	. . .	. . .	. . .
Zambia	. . .	. . .	59.3	. . .	34.0	. . .	97.2	. . .	. . .	. . .
Zimbabwe	. . .	. . .	. . .	. . .	. . .	. . .	56.1	. . .	. . .	. . .
Total (both facilities)	113.0		424.1		494.2		493.3		95.4	
Total (excluding Egypt and Sudan)	91.2		378.4		494.2		454.2		95.4	

Source: International Monetary Fund, Bureau of Statistics.

While these facilities were helpful to African countries, it was evident that most countries were facing fundamental disequilibria that can only be corrected over a number of years through the adoption of appropriate corrective policies, formulated in the context of comprehensive adjustment programs. The number of African countries that implemented such adjustment programs and were supported by stand-by and extended arrangements from the Fund increased from 8 during the period 1974–79 to 27 in 1980–84. The amount of Fund assistance drawn under these arrangements rose from SDR 600 million to over SDR 5 billion, respectively. As shown in Table 3, at the end of 1980, there were 11 stand-by arrangements and 5 extended arrangements in effect; the total amount committed was SDR 2,685 million, of which SDR 685 million was drawn. By the end of 1981, the number of arrangements rose to 13 stand-by arrangements and 7 extended arrangements; consequently, the amount committed reached a record level of SDR 4,722 million, of which SDR 1,525 million was drawn. Subsequently, with the cancellations of some arrangements, the number of extended arrangements declined in 1982 to only 1 while the number of stand-by arrangements remained at 13, with a total amount of SDR 1,583 million committed and SDR 827 million drawn. By the end of 1983, the number of stand-by arrangements rose again to 16 while that of extended arrangements increased to 2; the total amount committed was SDR 2,629 million, and the amount drawn increased to SDR 1,298 million. At the end of 1984, there were 14 stand-by arrangements and 1 extended arrangement, with a total amount of SDR 1,435 million committed and SDR 719 million drawn under these arrangements.

Design of Fund-Supported Programs

The formulation of an adjustment program supported by the Fund usually involves four steps: (i) a diagnosis of the problems and the adjustment needed; (ii) a definition of the program's objectives; (iii) setting the policies and time frame required to achieve these objectives; and (iv) specifying the performance criteria to monitor the program.[5]

The first step in the design of an adjustment program is an assessment of the problems causing the balance of payments difficulties and the adjustment needed to correct them. This diagnosis, which is undertaken by the

[5]See Kanesa-Thasan (1981) and Crockett (1982).

Table 3. Stand-By Arrangements and Arrangements Under Extended Fund Facility at End of Year, 1980–84
(millions of SDRs)

	Stand-By or Extended Fund Facility	Date of Agreement	Expiration Date	Amount Agreed	Amount Purchased	Undrawn Balance
1980						
Central African Republic	SBA	Feb. 15, 1980	Feb. 14, 1981	4.00	4.00	. . .
Egypt	EFF	July 28, 1978	June 30, 1980	425.00	75.00	350.00
Equatorial Guinea	SBA	July 1, 1980	June 30, 1981	5.50	3.00	2.50
Gabon	EFF	July 27, 1980	Dec. 31, 1982	34.00	. . .	34.00
Kenya	SBA	Oct. 15, 1980	Oct. 14, 1982	241.50	60.00	181.50
Liberia	SBA	Sept. 15, 1980	Sept. 14, 1982	65.00	18.40	46.60
Madagascar	SBA	June 27, 1980	June 26, 1982	64.50	10.00	54.50
Malawi	SBA	May 9, 1980	March 31, 1982	49.90	22.00	27.90
Mauritania	SBA	July 23, 1980	March 31, 1982	29.70	8.90	20.80
Mauritius	SBA	Sept. 5, 1980	Sept. 4, 1981	35.00	15.00	20.00
Morocco	EFF	Oct. 8, 1980	Oct. 7, 1983	810.00	147.00	663.00
Senegal	EFF	Aug. 8, 1980	Aug. 7, 1983	184.80	41.10	143.70
Somalia	SBA	Feb. 27, 1980	Feb. 26, 1981	11.50	6.00	5.50
Sudan	EFF	May 4, 1979	May 3, 1982	427.00	150.00	276.00
Tanzania	SBA	Sept. 15, 1980	June 30, 1982	179.60	25.00	154.60
Zaïre	SBA	Aug. 27, 1979	Feb. 26, 1981	118.00	98.40	19.60
Total				2,685.00	684.80	2,000.00
Total (excluding Egypt and Sudan)				1,833.00	458.80	1,374.20

Table 3 (continued). Stand-By Arrangements and Arrangements Under Extended Fund Facility at End of Year, 1980–84
(millions of SDRs)

	Stand-By or Extended Fund Facility	Date of Agreement	Expiration Date	Amount Agreed	Amount Purchased	Undrawn Balance
1981						
Côte d'Ivoire	EFF	Feb. 27, 1981	Feb. 22, 1984	484.50	176.70	307.80
Ethiopia	SBA	May 8, 1981	June 30, 1982	67.50	44.00	23.50
Gabon	EFF	June 27, 1980	Dec. 31, 1982	34.00	...	34.00
Kenya	SBA	Oct. 15, 1980	Oct. 14, 1982	241.50	90.00	151.50
Liberia	SBA	Aug. 16, 1981	Sept. 15, 1982	55.00	33.00	22.00
Madagascar	SBA	April 13, 1981	June 26, 1982	109.00	39.00	70.00
Malawi	SBA	May 9, 1980	March 31, 1982	49.90	40.00	9.90
Mauritania	SBA	June 1, 1981	March 31, 1982	25.80	10.30	15.50
Mauritius	SBA	Dec. 21, 1981	Dec. 20, 1982	30.00	7.50	22.50
Morocco	EFF	March 9, 1981	Oct. 7, 1983	817.10	136.50	680.60
Senegal	SBA	Sept. 11, 1981	Sept. 10, 1982	63.00	15.70	47.30
Sierra Leone	EFF	March 30, 1981	Feb. 22, 1984	186.00	33.50	152.50
Somalia	SBA	July 15, 1981	July 14, 1982	43.10	25.90	17.20
Sudan	EFF	May 4, 1979	May 3, 1982	427.00	251.00	176.00
Tanzania	SBA	Sept. 15, 1980	June 30, 1982	179.60	25.00	154.60
Togo	SBA	Feb. 13, 1981	Feb. 12, 1983	47.50	7.25	40.25
Uganda	SBA	June 5, 1981	June 30, 1982	112.50	77.50	35.00
Zaïre	EFF	June 22, 1981	June 21, 1984	912.00	175.00	737.00
Zambia	EFF	May 8, 1981	May 7, 1984	800.00	300.00	500.00
Zimbabwe	SBA	April 8, 1981	April 7, 1982	37.50	37.50	...
Total				4,722.50	1,525.35	3,197.15
Total (excluding Sudan)				4,295.50	1,274.35	3,021.15

Table 3 (continued). Stand-By Arrangements and Arrangements Under Extended Fund Facility at End of Year, 1980–84
(millions of SDRs)

	Stand-By or Extended Fund Facility	Date of Agreement	Expiration Date	Amount Agreed	Amount Purchased	Undrawn Balance
1982						
Côte d'Ivoire	EFF	Feb. 27, 1981	Feb. 22, 1984	484.50	292.14	192.36
Gambia, The	SBA	Feb. 22, 1982	Feb. 21, 1983	16.90	16.90	. . .
Guinea	SBA	Dec. 1, 1982	Nov. 30, 1983	25.00	11.50	13.50
Kenya	SBA	Jan. 8, 1982	Jan. 7, 1983	151.50	90.00	61.50
Liberia	SBA	Sept. 29, 1982	Sept. 28, 1983	55.00	5.00	50.00
Madagascar	SBA	July 9, 1982	July 8, 1983	51.00	30.60	20.40
Malawi	SBA	Aug. 6, 1982	Aug. 5, 1983	22.00	10.00	12.00
Mali	SBA	May 21, 1982	May 20, 1983	30.40	25.40	5.00
Morocco	SBA	April 26, 1982	April 25, 1983	281.30	196.90	84.40
Senegal	SBA	Nov. 24, 1982	Nov. 23, 1983	47.30	6.00	41.30
Somalia	SBA	July 15, 1982	Jan. 14, 1984	60.00	15.00	45.00
Sudan	SBA	Feb. 22, 1982	Feb. 21, 1983	198.00	70.00	128.00
Togo	SBA	Feb. 13, 1981	Feb. 12, 1983	47.50	7.25	40.25
Uganda	SBA	Aug. 11, 1982	Aug. 10, 1983	112.50	50.00	62.50
Total				1,582.90	826.69	756.21
Total (excluding Sudan)				1,384.90	756.69	628.21

Table 3 (continued). Stand-By Arrangements and Arrangements Under Extended Fund Facility at End of Year, 1980–84
(millions of SDRs)

	Stand-By or Extended Fund Facility	Date of Agreement	Expiration Date	Amount Agreed	Amount Purchased	Undrawn Balance
1983						
Central African Republic	SBA	April 22, 1983	April 21, 1984	18.00	4.50	13.50
Côte d'Ivoire	EFF	Feb. 27, 1981	Feb. 22, 1984	484.50	446.00	38.50
Ghana	SBA	Aug. 3, 1983	Aug. 2, 1984	238.50	143.10	95.40
Kenya	SBA	March 21, 1983	Sept. 20, 1984	175.95	129.80	46.15
Liberia	SBA	Sept. 14, 1983	Sept. 13, 1984	55.00	28.00	27.00
Malawi	EFF	Sept. 19, 1983	Sept. 18, 1986	100.00	10.00	90.00
Mali	SBA	Dec. 9, 1983	May 31, 1985	40.50	10.00	30.50
Mauritius	SBA	May 18, 1983	Aug. 17, 1984	49.50	24.75	24.75
Morocco	SBA	Sept. 16, 1983	March 15, 1985	300.00	30.00	270.00
Niger	SBA	Oct. 5, 1983	Dec. 4, 1984	18.00	6.80	11.20
Senegal	SBA	Sept. 19, 1983	Sept. 18, 1984	63.00	31.50	31.50
Somalia	SBA	July 15, 1982	Jan. 14, 1984	60.00	51.25	8.75
Sudan	SBA	Feb. 23, 1983	Feb. 22, 1984	170.00	144.50	25.50
Togo	SBA	March 4, 1983	April 3, 1984	21.40	19.41	1.99
Uganda	SBA	Sept. 16, 1983	Sept. 15, 1984	95.00	44.00	51.00
Zaïre	SBA	Dec. 27, 1985	March 26, 1985	228.00	. . .	228.00
Zambia	SBA	April 18, 1983	April 17, 1984	211.50	76.50	135.00
Zimbabwe	SBA	March 23, 1983	Sept. 22, 1984	300.00	97.50	202.50
Total				2,628.85	1,297.61	1,331.24
Total (excluding Sudan)				2,458.85	1,153.11	1,305.74

Table 3 (concluded). Stand-By Arrangements and Arrangements Under Extended Fund Facility at End of Year, 1980–84
(millions of SDRs)

	Stand-By or Extended Fund Facility	Date of Agreement	Expiration Date	Amount Agreed	Amount Purchased	Undrawn Balance
1984						
Central African Republic	SBA	July 6, 1984	July 5, 1985	15.00	5.00	10.00
Côte d'Ivoire	SBA	Aug. 3, 1984	Aug. 2, 1985	82.75	41.38	41.37
Gambia, The	SBA	April 23, 1984	July 22, 1985	12.83	2.63	10.20
Ghana	SBA	Aug. 27, 1984	Dec. 31, 1985	180.00	66.00	120.00
Liberia	SBA	Dec. 7, 1984	June 6, 1986	42.78	8.50	34.28
Madagascar	SBA	April 10, 1984	March 31, 1985	33.00	27.00	6.00
Malawi	EFF	Sept. 19, 1983	Sept. 18, 1986	100.00	34.00	66.00
Mali	SBA	Dec. 9, 1983	May 31, 1985	40.50	34.00	6.50
Morocco	SBA	Sept. 16, 1983	March 15, 1985	300.00	210.00	90.00
Niger	SBA	Oct. 5, 1983	Dec. 4, 1984	18.00	35.20	12.80
Sierra Leone	SBA	Feb. 3, 1984	Feb. 2, 1985	50.20	19.00	31.20
Sudan	SBA	June 25, 1984	June 24, 1985	90.00	20.00	70.00
Togo	SBA	May 7, 1984	May 6, 1985	19.00	16.00	3.00
Zaïre	SBA	Dec. 27, 1983	March 26, 1985	228.00	158.00	70.00
Zambia	SBA	July 26, 1984	April 30, 1986	225.00	80.00	145.00
Total				1,435.06	718.71	716.35
Total (excluding Sudan)				1,345.06	698.71	646.35

Source: International Monetary Fund, Treasurer's Department.

authorities and the Fund staff, aims at identifying the causes of the disequilibrium, the adjustment needed to achieve a viable or sustainable situation, and the time span required to achieve it. A viable external position means that the external current account deficit can be covered by normal capital inflows which are consistent with the debt servicing capacity of the economy, and that such a viable situation is consonant with a sustainable economic growth and relative price stability. The estimate of normal capital inflows is an important factor in the formulation of an adjustment program and is arrived at by assessing the economic assistance that is likely to be available to the country over the medium term. Accordingly, the recently adopted adjustment programs in Africa were formulated in the context of medium-term frameworks that foresee the achievement of viable external positions and sustainable economic growth, usually over a five-year period.

Once broad agreement is reached with the authorities on the diagnosis of the problems and the adjustment period needed for achieving a viable position, specific objectives are established for the program period (usually one year). The three main objectives generally included in most programs are a reduction in the external current account deficit, the stimulation of economic growth, and the containment of inflation.

The ability to finance the overall balance of payments deficit is also a crucial element in the formulation of the program. Before a program is approved by the Executive Board, assurances are needed that the financing gaps will be covered to ensure the successful implementation of the program. In addition to purchases made available by the Fund, the Fund plays an important role in the gap-fill exercise by sensitizing creditors and donors to the importance of closing the gap through debt relief, refinancing, or additional balance of payments assistance. The Fund is invited to the rescheduling meetings of official creditors under the auspices of the Paris Club and remains in close contact with commercial banks in the rescheduling exercises of the London Club. Furthermore, in a few cases, the Fund, in close cooperation with the World Bank, has taken the lead in organizing donor country meetings for balance of payments assistance. The Bank also plays an important role in organizing consultative group meetings to ensure the availability of development financing from these countries over the medium term.

After agreeing on the specific objectives for the program period, the Fund staff works out with the authorities the measures to be implemented in order to achieve them. The measures included in recent Fund programs in Africa have involved both demand management and supply-oriented measures, taking into account the specific circumstances of each country. The package of measures adopted, as well as the emphasis on specific elements, depend on the peculiarities and options available in each case. On the demand side, the measures called for in the programs have included a reduction in the fiscal deficit, the pursuit of a cautious credit policy accompanied in certain cases by increases in interest rates and reforms of the financial sector, and prudent external debt management. On the supply side, the main measures have comprised the adoption of appropriate exchange and tariff policies, liberalization of marketing and pricing policies, including in particular adjustments in producer prices, rehabilitation of public enterprises, and appropriate public investment programs. Of course, some of these measures have an impact on both demand and supply conditions.

As discussed above, growing fiscal deficits have played an important role in the deterioration of the balance of payments position of many African countries. Accordingly, a restrained fiscal policy has been a crucial element in most adjustment programs undertaken by these countries. The reduction in the fiscal deficit was to be achieved through both expenditure-containing and revenue-raising measures. On the expenditure side, adjustment programs usually aimed at containing and in some cases reducing both current and capital outlays. The emphasis on specific measures varied from case to case. In certain cases, to limit current expenditures, the emphasis was placed on wages and recruitment policies, including at times the institution of wage and hiring freezes (e.g., Kenya, Liberia, Madagascar, Mauritania, and Morocco). In cases where budgetary subsidies and transfers to public enterprises represented a heavy burden on the budget, scaling down of these subsidies and transfers was an important element in the adjustment (e.g., Kenya, Senegal, and Morocco). In most programs, efforts were made to improve expenditure control and administrative efficiency. For those countries that have accumulated domestic arrears, their gradual elimination was also an important element in the programs. Restraining, and in certain cases reducing, capital outlays in line with resource availability and the absorptive capacity of the economy was also essential in certain cases (e.g., Liberia, Madagascar, Morocco, and Niger). On the revenue side, programs generally contained specific measures to strengthen revenue performance through the introduction of new tax measures and improvements in tax administration and collections (e.g., Gabon, Liberia, Madagascar, Malawi, Mauritania, Morocco, and Niger). In this context, the Fund has been providing technical assistance to member countries to reform their tax systems.

With regard to monetary policy, programs generally emphasized the pursuit of a cautious policy, consistent with the balance of payments and fiscal objectives, while accommodating the credit needs of the productive sectors and crop financing requirements. In addition, many programs included structural reforms of the financial sector aimed at strengthening financial intermediation and enhancing central bank management (e.g., Morocco and Somalia). Furthermore, to improve resource allocation and the mobilization of savings, many programs included upward revisions in interest rates.

Appropriate external debt management was also a crucial element in all the programs. The aim was to contain the debt to levels consistent with debt servicing capacity. The Fund also provided technical assistance to help countries improve their debt management. For those countries that accumulated external arrears, the program provided for their gradual elimination.

For the countries in which the exchange rate was overvalued or the exchange rate system was inappropriate (e.g., multiple-currency practices), exchange rate actions were a key element in the programs. The aim of adopting an appropriate exchange rate policy was to alleviate the distortions in the economy, to enhance the profitability and competitiveness of domestic products, particularly export and import substitutes, and to reduce the excess demand for imports. A wide variety of actions have been included in recent programs. In some cases, exchange rates were depreciated in order to restore and sometimes enhance the competitiveness of the domestic economy. In other instances, the depreciation of the exchange rate was accompanied by a modification of exchange arrangements, such as the move from a multiple currency peg to an SDR or a basket peg, or the change in the currencies included in a basket or their weights in line with the weights of the country's major trading partners in its trade and payments transactions. The adoption of a flexible exchange rate policy during the program period was also called for in some cases. More recently, some countries introduced a freely floating or managed floating exchange rate system (e.g., Somalia and Zaïre).

Other changes in exchange systems included, where appropriate, the elimination of dual or multiple markets (e.g., Malawi, Mauritania, and Uganda). In certain cases, this was effected gradually and the unification of rates was allowed to be completed over a period of time (e.g., Somalia and Uganda). The exchange rate actions were accompanied, in a number of cases, by an easing of import restrictions and tariff adjustments, aimed at reducing the rate of effective protection (e.g., Kenya and Morocco).

To improve resource allocation and promote domestic production, in particular in the agricultural sector, the adoption of appropriate pricing and marketing policies was a key element in a number of programs. Adjustments in prices and utility tariffs were also necessary to improve the operations of public enterprises and reduce the budgetary burden of subsidies and transfers. Accordingly, many programs called for increases in retail and producer prices, easing of price controls, and gradual liberalization of marketing.

In cases where the public enterprise sector was a major source of difficulties, the programs contained specific measures to improve the financial performance of public enterprises (e.g., Central African Republic, Malawi, Morocco, Niger, Senegal, and Togo). The measures included adjustments in prices and tariffs of the goods and services provided by these enterprises, and steps to improve their management, as well as to reduce overstaffing. Several countries also embarked on comprehensive reform programs of the public enterprise sector aimed at improving the public enterprise policy environment and institutional framework and at determining which enterprise can be privatized or liquidated. These reforms were often undertaken with technical and financial assistance from the World Bank and bilateral donor countries.

The adoption of appropriate investment programs supported by the World Bank was also a key element in recently approved programs. In many cases, this involved setting the level of public investment in line with resource availability and absorptive capacity of the country and the reallocation of investment in favor of the directly productive sectors. This reorientation often aimed at providing more resources to the agricultural and small- and medium-scale industrial enterprises, and less to infrastructure and projects with low productivity. In addition, this reorientation was accompanied, in certain cases, by the adoption of incentives to promote investment by the private sector and to attract foreign capital.

To ensure successful implementation of the programs and provide the Fund with assurances that its resources are being used to support needed adjustment, all Fund-supported programs in the upper credit tranches included "performance criteria." These criteria are relatively few in number and easily quantifiable. They typically included quarterly ceilings on total domestic bank credit and net credit to the government, as well as limitations on contracting or guaranteeing by the government of nonconcessional external loans. For countries that accumulated external or domestic arrears, their gradual elimination also constituted performance criteria. In a few cases where the monitoring of fiscal developments was crucial to the successful implementation of programs, a ceiling was placed on the fiscal deficit. In addition to the above quantitative ceilings, there were a number of qualitative performance criteria dealing with a member's intention not to introduce or intensify restrictions on payments and transfers for current international transactions, or conclude bilateral payment arrangements with other members.

During the program period, if any performance criterion was not met, the member's right to make subsequent drawings under the arrangement was interrupted. Consultation was held between the authorities and the staff to examine the reasons. In cases where the excess over the ceilings was not substantial and did not jeopardize the realization of the objectives of the program, and additional adjustment measures could be taken to ensure the attainability of subsequent ceilings, a "waiver" was recommended to the Executive Board. If approved, this restored the member's drawing rights. However, if the excess was substantial and it was determined that the program's objectives were not attainable, or that no agreement could be reached on additional measures, the program was canceled and efforts were made to formulate a new program taking into account the new circumstances.

In addition to the above mentioned performance criteria, the programs were monitored through periodic reviews to assess the progress made in the implementation of the programs, and to agree on any additional measures that may be needed to ensure the realization of the program objectives. These review clauses also constituted performance criteria.

Implementation of the Programs

Although there is a wide variety of standards that can be used to assess the performance under the programs adopted in recent years in Africa, the following two standards have been used in this paper: (i) a comparison between actual results and targets; and (ii) a comparison between actual results and previous year's performance.

The comparison against program targets shows that the performance under the programs adopted in 1980–84 was mixed. The targeted rates of economic growth were attained in only about one third of the cases. The results with regard to the external current account deficit as a proportion of GDP and to the rate of inflation were somewhat better; the external current account deficit targets were achieved in 43 percent of the cases, while the targeted rates of inflation were realized in more than half of the cases. In most of the countries involved, there was a shortfall in policy implementation as evidenced by higher fiscal deficits and larger domestic credit expansion than envisaged under the programs. The fiscal deficits in terms of GDP were exceeded in almost two thirds of the cases, reflecting higher spending than programmed, and also, in some cases, shortfalls in budgetary revenue. The higher deficits generally resulted in larger expansion of credit to the government than programmed. As credit to the private sector also exceeded the programs' targets in numerous cases, the expansion of total domestic credit exceeded the targets in as many cases and resulted in higher than targeted growth of domestic liquidity.

Compared with the results achieved in the year prior to the program's inception, the outcome was generally better, indicating that, while in a number of cases the program targets were not achieved, a larger number of countries were able to improve their situation. The growth performance during the program year compared with the previous year was better in about half of the cases. There was also a decline in the rate of inflation in almost 60 percent of the cases, and the current account deficit of the balance of payments improved in approximately two thirds of the countries. With regard to policy instruments, the fiscal position as measured by the ratio of the deficit to GDP declined in about two thirds of the cases. The rate of growth of net credit to the government and the expansion of total domestic credit, as well as the rate of growth of the money supply, were nearly equal or lower than in the previous year in a large number of countries.

There are several reasons for the problems that African countries faced in carrying out their adjustment programs in 1980–84. The main reasons are unexpected adverse developments, weaknesses in the implementation of policies, and ambitious program targets or insufficient policy measures to achieve them.

First, several countries faced unforeseen and adverse exogenous developments. These included sharp declines in world prices and weakening in world demand for main export commodities, shortfalls in capital inflows, increases in international interest rates, unfavorable weather conditions, and, in a few cases, social and political disturbances. For example, performance in Côte d'Ivoire was adversely affected by external shocks, as well as drought, which necessitated revisions in the annual targets of the 1981–83 program supported by an extended arrangement, and the authorities had to intensify their adjustment efforts to partly offset the impact of these adverse developments. Kenya, Mali, Mauritania, Niger, and several other countries were seriously affected by severe droughts that decimated livestock and necessitated large imports of cereals. In Liberia, the implementation of the program in 1982 was made more difficult by the onset of economic recession in the principal markets for Liberia's exports of iron ore. Ghana's performance in 1983–84 was adversely affected by unfavorable weather conditions and slower-than-expected disbursement of external resources. In Madagascar, the weakening in world demand and prices for coffee resulted in a shortfall in export receipts. In 1980 Mauritius was severely affected by the cyclones that led to a sharp fall in sugar output and exports. Morocco suffered during the implementation of its programs from a slackened world demand for its main export commodity, phosphates, and from drought. The program with Senegal in 1982–83 ran into difficulties partly because of the sharp downturn in world market prices for groundnut oil. Sierra Leone also suffered from a weakening of export prices and unexpectedly high levels of rice imports to compensate for domestic shortfalls in production due to drought. In Somalia, the external ban imposed on its exports of livestock placed severe pressure on the balance of payments. Zambia's performance was seriously affected by a sharp decline in copper prices.

Second, many countries encountered difficulties in implementing the intended policies. In some cases, there were problems in mobilizing sufficient political support for the implementation of the programs. In others, after some initial success, the authorities had to yield to political and social pressure and relaxed their austerity measures, particularly in the fiscal field. Limited administrative capabilities were also a factor in certain cases, and the government was not able to improve expenditure control and revenue collection, or effect requisite measures to rehabilitate public enterprises as envisaged under the programs.

A third factor related to the design of the programs. In retrospect, in some cases, the targets were too ambitious, and the package of policy instruments was not sufficient to achieve fully the desired results. Data limitations in some countries may also have affected economic forecasting and financial programming.

Adequacy of the Programs

Were the Fund-supported adjustment programs adequate for African countries? To address this important question, let me first refer to the criticisms which have been made, in both official and academic circles, regarding Fund-supported programs, particularly in the African context. The main criticisms are the following:

1. Fund-supported programs are generally "standard" and do not take into account the specific situation of African countries;

2. Fund-supported programs aim at restoring economic and financial viability in a relatively short period of time, while most African countries are faced with structural problems that can be resolved only over the long term;

3. the policies envisaged in these programs are not appropriate in the context of African countries and are harmful to economic growth; and

4. the financial support provided by the Fund is small and is subject to very harsh conditionality.

With regard to the first point, it should be noted that while technically certain macroeconomic variables, policy instruments, and performance criteria are common to most programs, the specific objectives and appropriate combination of policies, as well as the emphasis on key measures, have clearly depended on the circumstances of each country. Invariably, the different nature and severity of the problems were fully taken into account in the design of the programs. In fact, each program was formulated after detailed and lengthy discussions with the authorities on the problems each country was facing, the root causes of the problems, and the measures needed to tackle them.

Regarding the time span required to restore viable economic and financial positions, while most of the stand-by arrangements covered one to two years, the annual programs supported by these arrangements were formulated in a medium-term framework which usually foresaw that a viable situation would be achieved over three to five years, provided, in particular, that the country pursued its adjustment efforts with determination. Furthermore, in many cases, successive one-year stand-by arrangements were approved. Thus, the programs clearly recognized that a reasonable time horizon for adjustment is needed.

Turning to the appropriateness of the policy measures envisaged in the adjustment programs for African countries, as mentioned earlier, the design of the programs takes into account the specific situation of each country. As to whether particular measures such as exchange rate actions or increases in interest rates are effective instruments, experience has shown that these measures play an important role in correcting the disequilibrium. In addition, in recent programs increasing emphasis has been placed on supply-oriented measures such as appropriate pricing policies, reform of public enterprises, and adequate investment programs. The programs have not ignored economic growth; on the contrary, the policies undertaken in the context of Fund-supported programs in Africa, as elsewhere, have been designed to restore domestic and external balance in the economy and thus establish a sound basis for sustainable growth over the medium term.

With respect to the amount and conditions attached to Fund financial assistance, it should be borne in mind that the Fund is a monetary institution with limited resources. Hence, it is essential that there are adequate safeguards to ensure that Fund resources are effectively utilized in support of appropriate adjustment programs. It should also be recalled that, in view of the revolving nature of the Fund's resources, the use of Fund credit must not remain outstanding for more than a temporary period, during which the required adjustment is undertaken by a member to restore its balance of payments viability.

As indicated earlier, Fund financial assistance to African countries has been substantial, especially since 1980. In addition, by making its own resources available in accordance with its access policies, the Fund has been playing a catalytic role in helping these countries to obtain additional balance of payments assistance from other sources to support their adjustment efforts. In this way, the Fund has been instrumental in easing the hardships that are inevitably involved in the adjustment process. In the absence of such financing, African countries would evidently need to place stricter limits on domestic demand and imports to achieve internal and external balance.

The discussion on the implementation of Fund-supported adjustment programs in Africa has made it clear that performance relative to the targets has been mixed for a variety of reasons. However, there is no doubt that those countries that have undertaken such programs promptly and pursued them with determination have made significant progress, especially in relation to the conditions that prevailed in the preadjustment period. By contrast, those countries that have retarded the adoption of adjustment measures now face much more difficult circumstances. To conclude this brief section on the adequacy of Fund-supported adjustment programs in the African context, the following points should be emphasized. First, the analysis has shown that Fund-supported programs have generally succeeded in narrowing the external current account deficit, reducing inflationary pressures, and improving the growth prospects of the economy over the medium term. Second, those countries that fully implemented the requisite adjustment policies and measures registered much better results than those where policy slippages occurred, suggesting that the policy mix has been adequate in the circumstances and that policy implementation is critically important. Finally, it should be recognized that it is very difficult in a number of cases to assess the full impact of adjustment policies and measures within a short period of time. For example, the effects of a reduction in economic distortions may not be easily quantifiable and may not be felt until after a considerable gestation period. However, if the adjustment effort is pursued with determination, its full benefits become more evident over the medium term.

Concluding Remarks

The recent experience with Fund-supported adjustment programs in Africa has shown that, for a program to be successful, the design of the program has to be adequate and its policy content has to be effectively implemented. Because of the structural difficulties facing most African countries, a comprehensive policy package has to aim at addressing not only demand management issues but also the structural problems. While adverse exogenous factors may have been a major cause for unsuccessful implementation of programs, this only highlights the need for countries to continuously review, readapt, and reinforce their policies to achieve the desired objectives. Delays or interrupted adjustment efforts can only compound the problems and make the necessary adjustment more severe and more difficult.

Although in a number of cases there were slippages from program targets, a large number of African countries, in implementing Fund-supported programs, were able to make significant progress toward reducing domestic and external imbalances. However, as these imbalances remain large, African countries should persevere in their adjustment efforts. Clearly, adjustment cannot be achieved in a short period of time, and hence continuous and effective implementation of adjustment policies is necessary. Strong and sustained adjustment efforts that will contain demand pressures and promote supply are required to restore a viable financial situation and a satisfactory path of economic growth. These efforts will, undoubtedly, be helped by the current economic revival in the major industrial countries and the consequent improvement in the international economic environment. However, in the final analysis, there can be no lasting solution to the problems of African countries in the absence of appropriate domestic economic and financial policies.

The Fund stands ready to assist African countries in their adjustment efforts. As in the past, the Fund will continue to work closely with other international organizations, particularly the World Bank, and all members of the international community, in order to assure an integrated and coordinated effort to assist African countries.

References

Berg, E., "The IMF in Africa," unpublished paper prepared for Conference on Africa and the IMF, U.S. Department of State, November 1, 1984.

Bhatia, J.B. and Amor Tahari, "External Debt Management and Macroeconomic Variables: Problems of African Countries in the 1980s" (unpublished, International Monetary Fund, 1984); presented at a seminar on external debt problems of African countries organized by the African Center for Monetary Studies, Tunis, Tunisia, September 1983.

Calamitsis, Evangelos A., "Les problèmes et les programmes d'ajustement en Afrique et le rôle du Fonds Monétaire International," in *Croissance et Ajustement,* ed. by P. Guillaumont (Paris: Economica, 1985), pp. 167–94.

Crockett, Andrew D., "Issues in the Use of Fund Resources," *Finance and Development* (Washington), Vol. 19, No. 2 (June 1982), pp. 10–15.

de Larosière, J., "The IMF and the Developing Countries," *IMF Survey* (Washington), March 7, 1983, p. 73.

Guitian, Manuel, "Economic Management and International Monetary Fund Conditionality," in *Adjustment and Financing in the Developing World*, ed. by T. Killick (Washington: International Monetary Fund, 1982), pp. 16–18.

Helleiner, Gerald K., *The IMF and Africa in the 1980s*, Essays in International Finance, No. 152 (Princeton, New Jersey: Princeton University, 1983).

International Monetary Fund, *World Economic Outlook*, Occasional Paper No. 27 (Washington: International Monetary Fund, 1984).

Kanesa-Thasan, S., "The Fund and Adjustment Policies in Africa," *Finance and Development* (Washington), Vol. 18, No. 3 (September 1981), pp. 20–24.

Nowzad, Bahram, *The IMF and its Critics*, Essays in International Finance, No. 146 (Princeton, New Jersey: Princeton University, 1981).

Wai, U Tun and Paul A. Acquah, "Experience with Exchange Rate Adjustment in African Countries" (unpublished, International Monetary Fund, 1984).

Williamson, John, "The Lending Policies of the International Monetary Fund," Institute for International Economics Policy Analyses in International Economics, No. 1 (Washington: Institute for International Economics, 1982).

World Bank, *Toward Sustained Development in Sub-Saharan Africa: A Joint Program of Action* (Washington: World Bank, 1984).

Zulu, Justin and Saleh M. Nsouli, *Adjustment Programs in Africa: The Recent Experience*, Occasional Paper No. 34 (Washington: International Monetary Fund, 1985).

Comments

David Phiri

I begin by congratulating Mr. Ouattara for a comprehensive and interesting paper. The paper gives a factual account of how Fund programs in Africa are designed and implemented. One striking feature of the paper is its variety of coverage. It might have been better, however, if the author had taken a specific case and gone through the various stages of designing, implementing, and assessing the adequacy of the recovery program. In addition to this general comment, a number of observations can be made on the paper.

The author correctly points out that both external and internal factors have played their role in the current difficult external payments position of African countries. It seems to me, however, that great emphasis has been placed on the inadequacy of internal policies as the main factor for the plight of the majority of our economies. Prominence has been given to the deficiencies of both demand management and structural policies reflected in expansionary financial policies, rising wage outlays, consumer subsidies, on the one hand, and inappropriate exchange rates, supported by a wide range of restrictions and price controls, on the other. This emphasis seems misleading. The hostile world economic environment has been the dominant factor in the problems now confronting developing countries. The steep increase in oil prices in the 1970s, followed by recession, protectionism, and high interest rates in industrial countries, set in motion forces that are still straining the economies of developing countries today. The subsequent decline in prices of their export commodities and the higher import prices have led to sharp falls in the terms of trade; hence the current economic crisis. Take, for example, my own country, Zambia. The price of copper, which is the country's sole product, is probably at its lowest level in the last 15 years in real terms, and Zambia is not being adequately compensated for its copper exports. Moreover, the drought that has ravaged our economies, though out of our control, has made our position more difficult. Even the debt burden of almost all African countries rose in the first place from external developments that have led to reduced export proceeds, necessitating heavy foreign borrowings. In my view, therefore, external and exogenous factors are the root causes of the current intolerable economic conditions in African countries, and it is these factors that any recovery program must address. These factors are reflected both in balance of payments difficulties and in lower economic growth, high unemployment levels, deteriorating living standards, and indeed dire poverty in our countries.

Although, in designing stabilization programs, the Fund should take all these factors into account, the main feature of the programs in our countries has been the overriding importance given to the balance of payments. In a way, this is not surprising, given the emphasis that the Fund puts on internal developments and policies as causes of the deterioration in the external positions of our countries. To restore payments equilibrium, the goal of Fund programs, countries are urged to pursue painful demand management policies, which in many ways tend to negate the very objectives of the Fund—higher levels of employment and income, economic growth and price stability—through their deflationary impact. In any case, demand management policies, usually in the form of budgetary stringency, credit restrictions, wage restraint, interest rate reform, devaluation, all undertaken in deficit countries, fall short of the objectives of global balance of payments management.

The emphasis on the balance of payments objective also means that Fund programs are designed to achieve results in the short term, whereas the problem, being structural, requires medium-term solutions. Economic growth as an objective requires not only demand management policies, but more importantly supply-side policies. Since structural adjustment is a lengthy process, it is questionable whether conventional stand-by arrangements of one-year duration are well designed to assist with this task, even if they are set within some kind of medium-term framework. Supply-side measures have merit in our situation, particularly given the excess capacity in our economies. The strategy of adjustment with growth is therefore more beneficial to our countries. With this strategy, a viable balance of payments situation will be achieved with minimum conflict with current objectives. The supply-side measures will ensure an improvement in the balance of payments through increased volume and value of exports, while imports would be reduced through higher domestic output to meet domestic demand.

A further criticism of balance of payments equilibrium as a major objective of Fund programs is that imports may have to be suppressed in a way that denies essential intermediate and capital goods to those sectors needing to expand if the structural problem is to be overcome. The nature of the beneficiaries of Fund assistance has changed tremendously over time, and yet this change seems not to be taken into account in designing programs. The majority of stand-by credits have recently gone to the poorer developing countries, and yet in these countries the Fund's traditional policies are least suitable. Tightening conditionality in the 1980s has contracted the economies of these poor countries. The current design of Fund programs reduces the Fund's ability to achieve its objectives, especially because of the nature of the economies of the recipients of this credit.

The emphasis on internal factors as chiefly responsible for the current economic situation of developing countries seems to have resulted in making adjustment into a prescription reserved for low-income deficit countries, when in fact it should apply to all countries. It is imperative and just that surplus countries reduce their surpluses, thus helping the deficit low-income countries reduce their deficits. Unfortunately, the kind of adjustment process now pursued places the heaviest burdens upon those least able to bear them.

Some Fund programs are treated like mere intellectual exercises. The human element is not given the prominence it deserves. Political and social unrest have been constraints on the successful implementation of stabilization programs in most developing countries and, as such, cannot be overlooked in our efforts to correct imbalances of our economies. Some programs have had to be abandoned in the past because of inbuilt inflexibility on the part of the Fund regarding such unforeseen developments as deviations of official commodity prices from price assumptions. The Fund has normally been reluctant to change program targets in light of new developments, preferring to render the program inoperative. Canceling a program is costly to a country that finds itself in such a situation not of its own making.

There is no question that the Fund has been of assistance to the ailing economies in Africa. This assistance should have been even greater, however, and it could have been, if the current approach to stabilization and adjustment had been changed in light of changing circumstances. Nobody advocates that the Fund turn into a development agency, but the structural nature of the problems in developing countries in general, and African countries in particular, dictates that changes of approach take place if the Fund is to meet the primary objectives of economic policy. In this context, the question of conditionality is crucial if African countries are to benefit from the Fund. The Fund should particularly try to avoid ''overkill'' in the application of severe demand-management policies. It should use a richer mixture of policies, oriented to both demand and supply, in designing a stabilization program, taking into account the practical capabilities of each country.

I have been dealing with the Fund since 1976 (except for about two years when I was not in Zambia), and want it said that conditionality is becoming more difficult and politically more unacceptable. With population in Africa increasing annually at over 3 percent, unemployment has reached a dangerous point. We are now producing graduates who may never find employment, and yet we are given conditions by the Fund that may actually increase unemployment. The consequences are grave. There should be a human element in whatever conditionality we have to bear from the Fund. There is no point in accepting a program that, following mass demonstrations, has to be scrapped. Whatever we do, we must be sure of the support of the entire country and that people understand what conditionality implies.

Substantial public relations effort is needed to make the Fund acceptable to most countries. Some countries blame their own shortcomings and problems on the Fund. We should rather accept our responsibilities and develop and implement our own programs. Any program we enter into with the Fund must be a joint program, not one imposed by the Fund. The Fund must understand these problems better and show itself less rigid. Unfortunately, to be acceptable to the international community—the Paris Club and the London Club, for example—a country has to have a program with the Fund, whatever the consequences. Consequently, there are times when we reluctantly enter into programs with the Fund even though we know only too well that they will not work, and we do so only so that the Paris Club and the London Club can reschedule our debts. This is unhealthy, and I feel strongly that whatever program we accept must be a joint program, well understood and agreed to by both sides.

E.I.M. Mtei

To my mind, the success of a program very much depends on its design. An inappropriately designed program can hardly achieve the desired objectives no matter how determined the authorities are in its implementation. Mr. Ouattara has described the steps and the various elements involved in the formulation of a Fund-supported program. By and large, there has been a convergence of views in this symposium on the nature and severity of the problems to be addressed as well as on specific program objectives—reduction in the external current account deficit, containment of inflation, and economic growth. Whether these objectives are achievable within a timeframe ranging from one to two years, or at best three years, and with the recommended mix of policy measures is another matter. This point is crucial in the context of the structure of African economies. That structure is known to all of us, and needs no further elaboration.

The success rate of African countries in implementing Fund-supported adjustment programs is, to say the least, far from satisfactory. Mr. Ouattara has provided some insight on this in his paper, as have the tables at the end of the paper showing, on a yearly basis, the amounts drawn under Fund arrangements. The magnitude of the problem with Fund programs could, however, have been more vividly brought into focus if he had provided us with information on the number of programs agreed, the number that were effectively implemented in the sense that all the quantitative and qualitative performance criteria were met and the full amounts agreed drawn, and the number that went off the rails. Further information is also required on what happened with the set objectives of those programs in which the policies were fully implemented, in particular, whether or not they resulted in higher growth rates, a reduction in inflation, and a sustainable payments position. Did any such fully implemented programs fail to achieve their set objectives? If so, why? Unless analysis is organized along this line, it will be difficult to apportion blame between inadequate program design and the inability of countries to carry out agreed measures.

As is evident in Mr. Ouattara's paper, a Fund-designed stabilization program, whether for an African, Asian, Latin American, or European country, involves a package of measures oriented essentially toward demand management, including variations in exchange and interest rates, and reduction in both the fiscal deficit and the rate of expansion of domestic credit. Exchange-rate devaluations and interest-rate changes in the African context are more of a demand-management than a supply-oriented measure. So are the various recommended pricing measures, including the elimination of subsidies. Let me stress that no one will seriously question the use of these tools to ensure prudent fiscal and monetary policies and realistic exchange rates. One is inclined to wonder, however, whether they are adequate to meet the particular African situation. These are tools best suited to correct short-term departures from equilibrium caused by imbalances like temporary loss of budgetary control. There is no gainsaying the fact that the payments problems confronting African countries are due not only to temporary disequilibria but also to the problems rooted in the very nature of African economies. Adjustment measures that take no cognizance of these structural weaknesses stand little chance of success. Unfortunately, measures that could ease these problems, including improvements in the quality of manpower through education and of agricultural and other infrastructures, are issues which the Fund has not been able to address. In most cases, institution building is a paramount need. In the absence of a properly functioning financial system, interest rates, for example, no matter how positive in real terms, will not produce the desired results. I know of an African country where the interest rate was raised in the context of a Fund program to a level higher than that prevailing in the major financial centers. Yet, during the mid-term review, it had generated extra resources of not more than $5,000 (in six months). A poor result indeed. What is needed is institution building and, in many cases, confidence that goes beyond financial considerations.

Furthermore, Fund programs do not sufficiently reflect the extent to which African countries can adjust to a harsh external economic and financial environment. Many of these countries rely on one or two export commodities, either agricultural or mineral, whose prices have been declining. The often recommended use of exchange rate adjustment, though relevant, may not do the trick in all cases. Obviously devaluation has its limitations. First, many of these countries produce more or less the same commodities for export. With the sort of competitive devaluation which the Fund seems to encourage among them, we have witnessed continuous increases in output and export volumes, but reduced foreign exchange earnings. The net beneficiaries are the developed countries importing these commodities. The situation becomes ridiculous when the Fund tends to link the extent of exchange rate depreciation with the fall in the price of a particular export commodity, say, copper. Far from encouraging diversification, such a stance tends to impede it. Also, it is not often acknowledged that the best designed program could be rendered inoperative by other countries' policies, particularly trade and financial policies of major trading partners, and that trade liberalization measures in an increasingly protectionist world could prove self-defeating. Neither do programs anticipate natural disasters, such as the drought that has taken its toll on African economies.

The fact that growth has proved elusive in Fund programs may suggest that something is fundamentally wrong with program designs. The expectation under a Fund program is that the main elements of a policy package will be complementary. Any recessionary impact of reduced fiscal deficits should be offset by the stimulative effect of devaluation. This expectation fails to take into account the possibility that devaluation may itself have recessionary implications, thereby compounding the recessionary effects of cuts in government spending and money supply.

Of particular importance is the period during which adjustment should be effected. In this regard, the responsiveness of African economies to adjustment measures cannot be expected to be as rapid as in the economies of the advanced countries. It is unfortunate to note the small number of extended arrangements that could have taken more into account the needs of Africa. I cannot see how the formulation of one-year programs in a so-called "medium-term framework" that the Fund claims to use can surmount this problem. One should call a spade a spade, and a one-year program precisely what it is.

Finally, the crucial matter of financing deserves mention. In many programs there are financing gaps. The Fund has been extraordinarily stringent when it comes to determining access to its resources by African countries. Although the Fund has tried to bring creditors together to pledge the filling of such gaps, in some cases the pledges are either not honored or honored too late to save the program. Even though adjustment and financing go together, if success is to be assured, financing gaps to be filled by donors' pledges introduce a new element of uncertainty into programs and tend to result in traditional aid donors shifting emphasis from long-term development aid to short-term balance of payments support. Without the former, the economies of many African countries cannot take off. At best, Fund programs can provide the basis for sustained growth in African countries. Long-term development is needed to guarantee that growth.

H.B.B. Oliver

Mr. Ouattara mentioned that strong and sustained adjustment efforts are required to restore a solid financial structure and that these efforts will undoubtedly be helped by the current economic revival in the major industrial countries and the consequent improvement in the international economic environment. I am glad that members of the staff of the Fund take an optimistic view of the prices for raw materials, because if they did not, it might be difficult for them to get programs through the Executive Board. Nevertheless, I suggest that the word "undoubtedly" was put in by the author because he felt some doubts. The great triumph and the great pride of European governments lately has been that they have succeeded in stopping the inexorable rise of prices. They have succeeded in stopping the prices, that is, of those things they do not produce themselves. This is the problem that we have to face. It is the prices of primary products that must go down and, indeed, perhaps permanently. It is fortunate for a sugar producer that the Fund staff has consistently, for some time, been able to foresee increases in sugar prices. On that basis, we have been able to get the compensatory financing facility, which would not be available to us if that estimate had not been made. Now that the price for sugar is down to 3 cents a pound, a pretty useless figure in the world market, we wonder whether indeed an adjustment effort based upon the same crop is indeed the best advice that could have been given. Should we not have used the funds from this facility to develop a substitute for a product that is obviously now in world surplus and likely to so remain as long as the Europeans decide to continue to grow beet sugar and to protect their beet sugar producers. Here we have a really drastic problem. If any sugar producer defaults, it will not be, of course, because of failure to follow his own part of the agreed program, but because the price forecasts incorporating the program proved erroneous. In such circumstances, there is need—and I believe this applies to many other products besides our own—for a facility for developing substitutes for products that are no longer economical. It is hardly likely that the Fund can adapt itself within its charter to solve the sort of problem that has arisen in many cases in which countries have gone on depending upon a product that is no longer going to be the means of gaining their livelihood. Perhaps we should persuade the Bank in its structural adjustment program to include bailing out those countries that have borrowed from the Fund on a short-term basis and find it impossible to fulfill their obligations because of changes unforeseen, even by those whose job it is to foresee the future price trends.

Reply

Alassane Ouattara

As some of you know, I took on my job as Director of the African Department only last year. Before that, I was for 12 years a central banker. I know the realities and the problems of the African countries. The West African Monetary Union, with which I was associated, comprises seven countries, five of which have programs with the Fund, and these programs are all on track. This is why I said that the determination of the authorities to apply some of the policies and measures agreed to is essential. I agree with the Executive Director of the Fund, Mr. Mtei, that the design of programs is important. I did not deal in my paper with the details of how we develop our views on what type of program or policies might be appropriate for a country. Let me do so now.

As you know, the Fund holds Article IV consultations with every country once a year. This is the occasion to look at recent developments, to hear from the authorities about their policies, their intentions, their problems, the solutions, and the way in which they want to address the possibly difficult economic situation of their country. Consultation takes quite some time because, after the Fund consultative mission has returned from the country, a report is written. This report is examined by the Board. The conclusions of the Board discussions are sent to the country within about three months. Afterwards, some countries request another staff visit, and we respond. We provide technical assistance so that designing a program is not a magic process. In some countries, negotiations go on for two years and occasionally longer. Mr. Mtei asked me how many programs are on track—in effect, asking whether the way we have looked at the problem is the accurate way of doing it. Of course, one could have chosen a different approach, but, of the 15 programs in force at the end of 1984 (14 stand-bys and a single extended Fund facility program), 10 are on track. These countries have made drawings without any problem. Five have had difficulties. The Fund is not, however, inflexible. Of the countries I have mentioned, one has had no fewer than three waivers over the past 12 months because of the type of unfavorable development Governor Oliver was addressing.

A program is designed on the basis of a whole series of assumptions, both on the domestic economic situation, the policy intentions of the authorities, and the projections about the external environment. If there is a major external development, we look at it, and if this development warrants a waiver, we propose this to the Board, which, under most circumstances, grants this waiver.

Governor Phiri proposed that one should not generalize. I welcome this suggestion, and I propose that for the next seminar, we use Zambia as a case study, going through the negotiation step by step, arriving at a program, implementing the program, and analyzing the difficulties in the follow-up of the program, the use of Fund resources, and so on.

Another general topic of interest is the speed of adjustment. It was said here that maybe the Fund should have a slower adjustment process for African countries, that our countries have peculiarities, that they are special, that they have specific structural problems, drought, and other circumstances that make it difficult for these countries to adjust quickly. A stand-by for one year is therefore not a good way of dealing with problems of African countries. It is true that the framework of a stand-by is one year or 18 months, but for 12 of the 15 countries I referred to, this is the fourth consecutive year of stand-by arrangements. There are good indications that we will still be involved with these countries in the framework of stand-by arrangements for the next two to three years. So, suggesting that the turnaround of the balance of payments has to be in one year or two is not correct. It is true that the statutes of the Fund require adjustment to be made within a specified period, and this is linked to the monetary character of the Fund. It is also true that the management has to take into account the basic law that guides this institution. But in applying these guidelines, we do take into account the special circumstances of countries. If a country, after five years of stand-by arrangements, has the same imbalances that it had in the first year, however, I think most of you will agree that having a program with that country is not useful and that seeking other solutions would have been better.

With reference to the basic design of a program, a slow pace of adjustment is not necessarily the best course of action. Depending on circumstances, a country may prefer a slower pace of adjustment, but the slower it is, the larger, probably, will be the external debt. The larger the external debt, the more difficulty there will be to fill that gap, and if you cannot fill the gap, then you have slower growth. If the pace is so slow that you do not give the right signal to the countries with which you have specific relationships and whose assistance is necessary to help bridge the gap, the concessionary inflows may not be forthcoming in optimum amounts. There may be cases in which a slow pace of adjustment is required because there is fairly strong and constant external support; the adjustment measures can then be spread over a longer period. But there are cases in which the authorities may prefer to have a stronger adjustment effort to give the right signal and to get back to a faster pace of economic growth. This has happened in several cases in Africa, and it has been successful. There have been cases in which the trade balance was in deficit, with imports twice as large as exports three or four years ago, but in which the trade balance has now turned into surplus.

These cases lead to the question of exchange rate action and current account financing. We had some discussions here about whether exchange rate adjustment is good for growth and for export diversification, and whether the exchange rate impact is positive if there is a large foreign sector. Africa has a large agricultural sector, and there are countries in which these supply responses are real and significant. Like all of you here, I am from a village in Africa. I know that farmers are responsive to price increases. If you double the price, they will produce more. Of course, if it does not rain, they cannot produce. But if conditions are normal and you double prices, you have a good chance of increasing production.

It is obviously not true to say that domestic conditions are the sole factors that play a role in an adjustment process. Of course, there must also be external adjustment, but what I have tried to say is that once we have an adjustment program, it is important that the authorities implement this program with determination. The degree to which a country can influence external conditions is strictly limited. If conditions are deteriorating, if, for example, the terms of trade are getting worse, there will be additional difficulties for the country in balancing its current accounts. But domestic efforts give the international community the assurance that the country needs help and that it is worthy of help, and, therefore, there will be a greater input of capital. Consequently, I can only support the view that African countries should have remunerative prices for their basic products, though a mechanism for this purpose does not yet exist. We have a compensatory financing facility, but this is a short-term measure that does not really solve the problem of investment. There is already an improvement in the external environment, and our projections indicate that it will improve further in terms of trade, in international interest rates, and a greater stability of exchange rates. With a better international environment, and with appropriate policies in our own countries, African countries can strengthen their adjustment and therefore their economic growth.

Fund Conditionality and the Socioeconomic Situation in Africa

Samba Mawakani

Over the last few years, Fund conditionality for access to its resources has engendered abundant literature and controversial discussion. This paper serves as an introduction to an exchange of views on this widely discussed issue of great concern to Africa, with attention particularly on recent developments in Africa's relations with the Fund.

Needless to say, Africa's growing interest in Fund conditionality derives from the precarious economic and financial situation in which African countries have found themselves for several years. In response to their problems, many African countries have resorted to the Fund's financial assistance, which is extended under certain conditions. Such conditionality has had an impact on both the economic and social environment of these African countries.

Section I of this paper gives a description of the economic situation in Africa so as to clarify the environment in which the Fund has operated over the last few years. Section II outlines the main characteristics of Fund conditionality. Section III describes the impact of conditionality on Africa's economic and social position. Section IV identifies several issues to be examined by the Fund over the next few years in light of the requirements for economic adjustment in Africa.

The Economic Situation in Africa

Africa includes about 30 independent states with tremendous natural resources: 97 percent of world chromium resources, 85 percent of platinum, 64 percent of manganese, 25 percent of uranium, 13 percent of copper, 20 percent of hydroelectric potential, and vast bauxite, nickel, and lead resources. Africa also accounts for a large share of world production in other sectors: 70

percent of cocoa, 66 percent of coffee, 50 percent of palm oil, and 20 percent of petroleum traded in the world, excluding the United States and the Soviet Union.

There are certain general similarities in the economic structure of African countries: small domestic markets because of low per capita incomes and quite small populations, predominantly agricultural activities, high dependence on some basic export commodities, and concentration of foreign trade on a few partners. In addition, the education level is low, the reproduction rate is high, and the urban population is constantly increasing.

Over the last two decades, most African countries have recorded slow economic development, with annual per capita income only rising by 1.3 percent in 1969–70 and by 0.8 percent in 1970–79, while food production grew by only 1.5 percent a year during the 1970s, against 2 percent a year during the previous decade. In relation to size of population, food production fell by 0.9 percent in 1970–79, while cereal imports skyrocketed, thus increasing food dependency. Export production, which had grown by 20 percent in the 1960s, shrank by about 20 percent during the 1970s, while per capita exports declined by 3.5 percent from one decade to the next. During the present decade, production growth rates decelerated in African countries: from 3 percent in 1980 to 1.8 percent, 1.2 percent, and 0.1 percent in 1981, 1982, and 1983; while the inflation rate rose to 19.5 percent in 1983 from an average 7.5 percent in 1967–76.

The stagnation recorded in African economies since the early 1970s originated from both external and internal factors. The economic development of African countries depends on external resources in the form, of both export receipts, whose level depends on world market terms, and venture or borrowed capital. The external orientation of African economies, however, makes these countries sensitive to shocks and cycles in world markets. The crisis of the 1970s made it difficult for African countries to pull out of the economic stalemate against which they have been struggling.

Negative influences on Africa included the combined effects of inflation and slackening economic activity (stagflation) in the industrial countries. Indeed, the hike in oil prices led to a slowdown in the productive activity of industrial countries at a time when inflation was raging. As regards African countries, these conditions led to the collapse of their export commodity prices and to higher prices for their imports, resulting in the deterioration of their terms of trade and widening current account deficits.

The ambitious investment programs that some African countries initiated after becoming independent necessitated increased resort to external borrowing, thereby significantly increasing external indebtedness. African countries typically contracted most of their external loans as part of their investment program during the 1960s and 1970s, when the economic situation seemed to be favorable to the extent that lenders did not doubt the solvency of borrowing countries. Even the consequences of the first oil shock for the financial condition of developing countries in general, and African countries in particular, did not shake the confidence of lenders.

The current economic crisis, however, has led some African countries to experience payments difficulties so critical that these countries have been incapable of pursuing the development efforts initiated earlier, resulting in the thorny problem of mounting external debt service that these economies can no longer bear. This situation has jeopardized the access of most African countries to external capital markets, which, for some, are indispensable for financing their economic and social development.

In sum, the combined current account deficit of African countries worsened from some $6 billion in 1977 to over $10 billion in 1983. Foreign debt as a share of exports rose from about 140 percent (of exports) in 1977 to some 220 percent in 1983, while the debt-service ratio rose from 12 percent to 25 percent over the same period. To check the demand for foreign exchange, some countries adopted import restriction measures, thereby causing shortages of both consumer and investment goods. Scarcity of consumer goods aggravated domestic inflation, while scarcity of investment goods further contributed to the slowing down of domestic economic activity.

On the domestic front, it is necessary to underline the importance of structural obstacles and their aftereffects, which in turn derive from historical circumstances or from the physical environment, for example, human resource underdevelopment inherited from colonial training policies, economic confusion accompanying decolonization, the high cost of newly established institutions adapted to the new political realities and directed toward new requirements, harsh weather conditions, and internal economic dualism.

Some cyclical factors on the domestic front also need to be pointed out, since the high level of prices for basic commodities and minerals toward the end of the 1960s and the early 1970s moved many African countries into ambitious investment works. The shortfall in export revenue caused by declining prices of primary commodities and the rise of protectionism in industrial countries led to deficits not only in the balance of payments but also in the government budget, whose resources are drawn mainly from export and import duties. In most cases, budget and current account deficits have by now become structural. Indeed, with the evolution of institutions, population growth, and national security concerns, the burden borne by the government has become increasingly heavy.

In spite of the change in economic circumstances that reduced public revenues, the pace of public expenditure was not altered, hence significant new budget deficits financed through resort to domestic bank credit and foreign borrowings. Credit expansion engendered direct and unsustainable pressure on the balance of payments, while the often unrealistic repayment schedules caused serious foreign-debt servicing difficulties.

During the 1970s, several African countries resorted to the technical and financial assistance of the International Monetary Fund in an attempt to restore economic and financial equilibrium. Financial assistance to African countries by the Fund increased rapidly in three stages.

First, prior to the 1973 oil crisis, African countries had resorted to the Fund primarily under the compensatory financing facility created to finance temporary deficits in export earnings brought on by causes independent of the policies of the countries concerned. The second phase of intensive resort to the Fund related to the 1974–75 oil facilities, whose purpose was to finance deficits caused by the unexpected increase in oil bills, and to the Trust Fund, which used proceeds from gold sales to extend concessional credit to low-income countries for balance of payments adjustment.

The third phase of intensive resort to the Fund started at the end of the 1970s, in response to the second oil price shock and the subsequent world recession. At the end of 1979, a sharp increase in the Fund's assistance to African countries could be noted under the stand-by and extended facilities. African countries' share in Fund assistance under both these facilities reached 30 percent in 1979–80 against only 3 percent for 1970–78. The number of stand-by and extended arrangements signed by African countries rose to 53 percent of the total in 1979–80, against an annual average of 20 percent for 1970–78.

In accordance with its Articles of Agreement and subsequent convention, the use of some of the Fund resources provided under credit arrangements was subject to certain conditions.

Conditionality

The Fund's conditions take into account the revolving nature of its resources and its basic objective to promote international payments and trade. Resources extended by the Fund may be provided unconditionally, with low conditionality, or with high conditionality.

As regards drawings from the reserve tranche and uses of SDR assets, no specific condition is imposed on the member, who has merely to claim a need for balance of payments support. Low conditionality drawings have been financed by the buffer stock financing facility, the 1974 and 1975 oil facilities, the Trust Fund, drawings from the first credit tranche, the emergency aid facility, the supplementary financing facility, the enlarged access policy, and the compensatory financing facility.

Drawings by African countries after 1979 have been overwhelmingly of the high-conditionality type. High-conditionality drawings are subject to compliance with performance criteria and other conditions stipulated in the arrangement. These criteria and conditions, put together in a program of action, are related notably to domestic credit, public-sector financing, external debt, some key elements of the price system (including the exchange rate), interest rates, and prices of primary products.

The main characteristic of the conditionality imposed under arrangements relating to high-conditionality drawings is therefore the adoption of an adjustment program in which the implementation period is defined and limited. The size of drawings is preset, and drawings are made quarterly, provided the country complies with the performance criteria relevant to the previous quarter and the agreed schedule of policy measures has been maintained. Under the extended Fund facility, the Fund may grant financial assistance to member countries over a longer period than that provided under other drawing provisions. Credits under this facility are extended to some countries facing serious payments difficulties owing to structural distortions in production, trade and prices, when these countries agree to adopt a series of correction measures during the life of the agreements (typically two or three years). Any country applying for assistance under the extended credit facility must support its request with a program defining the objectives and policies it expects to achieve during the entire period it will resort to the facility.

Impact of Conditionality

In their attempt to embark on the economic recovery described earlier, African countries resorted to international financial assistance (particularly from the Fund). Recourse to the Fund's resources increased considerably following the first oil shock in the form of drawings under the special facilities, especially loans under the compensatory financing facility and the Trust

Fund. In principle, these low-conditionality drawings have not given rise to any particular problems.

As regards high-conditionality credit based on an economic and financial adjustment program, the typical case from 1979 onward, many African countries have been unable to use all the resources put at their disposal because of the severe performance criteria.

Conditionality provides a means of ensuring that the international adjustment process operates properly and benefits all member countries of the Fund. By linking adjustment to the supply of financial resources, the Fund tries to help member countries achieve a viable payments position in the medium term, that is, a position of sustainable current transactions, with reasonable price and exchange rate stability, an acceptable and sustainable level and rate of growth of economic activity, and a liberal international payments regime. Nevertheless, the Fund's policies in this area do not sufficiently take into consideration the peculiarities of African economies.

The unrealistic attitude that the Fund adopts at times has often led to the abandonment of programs implemented by African countries because of lack of compliance with the performance criteria set during negotiations. Indeed, out of the 20 African stand-by arrangements concluded with the Fund between 1982 and 1984, six were not totally used before the deadline or cancellation date, and two were canceled. Of the nine African agreements concluded under the extended Fund facility between 1975 and 1983, eight were not totally used at the deadline or cancellation date, and one was replaced by a stand-by agreement. Of the eight agreements not entirely used, five were canceled.

Consequently, the Fund has been criticized for its conditionality. In some cases, social tension has been created and economic growth has been checked because of the unrealistic measures taken with respect to major economic variables, particularly domestic credit, public sector financing, and external debt, as well as some elements of the price system, including exchange rates, interest rates, and, in some cases, commodity prices.

With undiversified economies based mainly on a few export commodities, most African countries often fall prey to external shocks. As a consequence of these structural realities, the type of adjustment often required by the Fund for the use of its resources entails loss of output and public revenues, with costs that, while possibly negligible in developed and more diversified economies, are considerable in Africa.

The limitation on aggregate credit expansion to achieve macroeconomic equilibrium often reduces considerably the share of credit devoted to financing productive activity. Limiting credit inhibits the expansion of supply and even reduces it when expanded supplies are required to improve the socioeconomic conditions of a country making the costly adjustment effort.

Devaluations, often part and parcel of the package of deflationary measures recommended by the Fund, have not always helped to achieve the desired objective, especially in terms of establishing a realistic and sustainable real exchange rate, transferring resources to specific sectors of the economy, particularly to the export sector, and restraining aggregate demand when other measures cannot be implemented simultaneously. In some cases, the economic situation of vulnerable countries, such as those of Africa, has worsened following devaluation.

Price liberalization that, in normal circumstances, is expected to lead to increased competitiveness and hence to lower prices through market forces has provoked social tension in cases in which the system of subsidizing some commodity prices and services was abolished before finding a valid substitute, notably a compensatory increase in salaries.

Liberalization of commercial transactions, expected to lead to harmonious world trade relations, does not seem to bring valid medium-term solutions for African economies. Their weak structure does not permit them quickly to measure up to the fierce competition of manufactured goods from industrial countries. Liberalization should be progressive, as a function of objectives to be achieved in the medium and long term.

As far as measures aimed at reducing the current account deficit are concerned, the Fund's conditions put excessive emphasis on regular debt-service payments, which at present absorb an excessive share of the external means of payment of African countries. This emphasis has led, in some cases, to a substantial reduction in the import of goods required for recovery and adjustment and has created further overall economic decline.

Ismail Sabri Abdallah, Chairman of the Third World Forum, notes that a developing country necessarily runs a balance of payments deficit due to imports of capital goods so that it needs an international banking system to help it bridge it over the fifteen to twenty years that are necessary to achieve a real growth of its exports. The current degree of external dependence in Africa, because of the specialization of production and consumption associated with foreign markets and because of the financing of this specialization through foreign capital, can only perpetuate and worsen the medium-term disequilibrium in external payments. In any case, the rate of growth of exports depends a great deal on the absorption capacity of industrial countries, which also determine most world prices. Moreover, the African industrial nucleus receives very little encouragement since public revenues are so dependent on foreign trade. Restructuring requires far more time and more fundamental change than is implied in the Fund's conditionality. There obviously remain conflicting points of view about ultimate structural objectives. Instead of granting financial assistance consistent with the magnitude of the required recovery and economic revival, the Fund offers a short-term regressive cure, followed sometimes by a few oxygen bottles. Herein lies the whole problem of striking a balance between adjustment and financing. The major basis of allocation, that is, quotas, limits the access of African members to Fund resources because it is biased from the start toward economically more important countries. The current policy of more restrictive access to Fund resources obviously does not favor an increase in financial flows to African countries either.

Conclusion

I have tried, in this short paper, to highlight the economic and financial problems of African countries during the last few years and to describe the approach generally adopted by the authorities who must deal with them. By the end of the 1970s, many African countries had asked for the Fund's financial assistance and, because of their urgent need, accepted conditions of which they did not always approve.

Indeed, while the Fund's assistance is certainly welcome—though its size and quality could be improved—recipient Africans deplore their subjection to socially costly reform of economic policies. We can cite the deflationary measures entailed by devaluations, the nonselective liberalization of producer prices, the tightening of domestic credit, and the readjustment of taxation that typically accompany the Fund's financial assistance.

Moreover, although it derives from a concern for enhancing efficiency in the use of resources, the idea of putting the economy into private hands, which has been advocated by the Fund, seems to reflect a preconceived notion of economic organization. However dynamic a role is attributed to the private sector and however efficient this sector may be, the solution lies not in adopting straightaway a "market solution" in all African countries, but rather in achieving, in accordance with circumstances, a good combination of private initiative and government action in order to reduce social inequalities and the deficiencies of the market.

To conclude, I believe that the International Monetary Fund should consider the following:

1. In view of the shortage of available external resources for supporting economic adjustment programs necessary for a durable economic recovery, the Fund should rapidly approve a new allocation of SDRs, the main part of which should be reserved for developing countries to finance their balance of payments deficits and particularly to settle their external debts. Such a decision by the Fund, whose major member states are official creditors of deficit developing countries, would allow the international community to move toward a lasting solution to the thorny problem of external debt in the poor countries.

2. The role played by the Fund in the renegotiation of the external debt of some of its members has become so important that creditors systematically require that these countries conclude stand-by agreements with the Fund before starting any discussions. The Fund should seize this opportunity to request that creditors set conditions that would encourage economic recovery in African countries and, more particularly, to insist that they provide new financial facilities to those countries that successfully apply substantial adjustment programs. Such financial support is fundamental to ensuring the smooth functioning of the economy and would allow recipient countries to continue to meet their external obligations.

3. The structural nature of the balance of payments deficits of most African countries requires substantial financial resources over several years. The present limitation on the use of the Fund's resources is not an answer to the needs and expectations of many, particularly African, member countries. The Fund should review its access policy. A lasting solution would be to enlarge the recurrent resources of this institution through increases in quotas and to reserve a substantial portion of this increase for countries with low quotas to allow them more access to resources needed to adjust their economies.

4. The international monetary system includes elements which need to be adapted to recent developments in the world economy. Since the reform initiated several years ago fell far short of meeting the needs of an important category of member countries, I emphasize that efforts at reform should be resumed and take into account the changes that have occurred since Bretton Woods. Doing so will enable the Fund fully to play the role expected by all its members, particularly in resource mobilization, economic adjustment, and supervision, with the objective of establishing an equitable sharing of the adjustment burden between the rich and the poor countries.

Comment

Kombo Moyana

Mr. Mawakani's paper cannot be adequately dealt with without referring to the broader paper prepared by the Director of the Fund's African Department, Mr. Ouattara. Since Mr. Ouattara set the broad parameters for the operations and actions of the Fund over the past few years, his paper assumes a certain importance as a reference point for our discussions. I should therefore like to consider the two papers together.

In the first place, I don't think that the two papers differ very much on the definition of the problems which the African countries face. But it is probably important to note, however, the different way the two papers deal with the problems and particularly with the question of productive capacity in Africa. Productive capacity is broadly defined not only as underdevelopment of human and natural resources, but also of a lower level of technology and an absence of the indigenous technological dynamism crucial for insuring productive efficiency over time.

We are all agreed, I think, that adjustment is necessary, but the question remains of adjusting to what. Are we adjusting in a context in which there is little productive capacity that is itself being eroded, or are we adjusting in a context in which that capacity is being created?

It seems to me that many problems facing African countries today are akin to the problems that faced Europe after the war, at the time of the Bretton Woods Agreement. Africa is probably not even at Europe's 1945 stage of development. We may be decades if not centuries younger in terms of historical development. It is important to note, with reference to Europe after the war, that the Fund was basically put on ice until the productive capacity of Western Europe was built up to a point where adjustment, in the Fund sense, became a sensible concept. It was not really until the 1960s that the Fund went into action there. By that time the European economies were performing in a way that they could have periodic adjustment problems. The Fund type of adjustment in Africa today is probably not a sensible form of adjustment. What is needed is another line of approach. The Fund will become relevant to the extent that it becomes a supporting institution for the type of effort in which the World Bank is the spearhead.

Mr. Ouattara and Mr. Mawakani agree that there are important external and internal causes for the problems of Africa and that the solutions have both an external and an internal dimension. They also agree that there is need for foreign adjustment as well as African adjustment.

Mr. Mawakani's argument differs from Mr. Ouattara's, however, in the degree and pace of adjustment that it maintains can be digested by a typical African economy facing the crises of drought, recession, and political and other constraints on policy action. Their arguments also differ in the extent to which they maintain adjustment should be shared between the countries at the center of the world system and the countries at the periphery of that system.

The developing countries themselves must decide on the appropriate modalities for finding solutions to their current problems. One approach has been to look inward at adjustment dynamics. That means compression of imports followed by reduced growth rates. Many other countries besides African countries are doing this. The other route, which is to go through the Fund (the two routes need not be mutually exclusive, and both routes are often combined), means that various conditions must be met. The conditions for Fund financing have ranged over a wide area, including limitation on public sector and fiscal deficits and on how they are financed. Other conditions involve limits on overall domestic credit creation for both the productive and the governmental (generally not directly productive) sector, limits on the size and nature of the external debt, and a wide range of pricing policies, on interest rates, agricultural products, and exchange rates.

On the question of the exchange rate, I would like to highlight several points. In many African countries, the data are generally unreliable, or incomplete. To measure inflation, many African countries use the consumer price index that, in many cases, unfairly reflects the cost of production. Often an exchange rate regime requires the maintenance of real effective exchange rates at a constant level during a program. If at the same time the Fund requires a reduction in subsidies, to the extent that price increases show up in consumer price index increases, that country must devalue even further. The Fund expects a full exchange-rate adjustment to correspond to the price differential between the country's economy and that of its trading partners. The Fund staff tends to be less geared to examining the reality of local situations and tends to use indices and formulae that may actually be meaningless.

Second, the nature of some world markets is such that an exchange rate change may result in a country's increasing the volume of exports without increasing export receipts and at times even experiencing reductions in foreign exchange earnings. Although the profitability of local enterprises may rise (a good thing in itself), this can be achieved through a different policy instrument if in other respects the exchange rate is appropriate. One needs to apply the right prescriptions to the right problems.

Liberalization of trading and monetary systems as part of conditionality also involves danger. Inadequate attention may be paid in Fund conditionality to the dynamic elements of comparative advantage and the infant industry argument for protection. It is sometimes suggested that dividends and profit remittances must be liberalized in order to attract direct investment. At a time when in the western economies themselves there is little investment because of world recession, however, investment may not come our way even after liberalizing. In this regard conditionality needs to be reexamined to take account of the real situation. Fund missions tend to be too worried about doing things only through market forces, almost to the exclusion of other forces, and this, at times, even in economies where the market does not exist or where market forces still have to be created. The balance between action in the public sector and action in the private sector has to be looked at.

If the developing countries face protectionism in the markets of the developed western economies, adjustment becomes difficult. Many countries in Africa, as well as in Latin America and Asia, besides reducing imports, took all sorts of measures to promote exports, only to find that the export markets in western industrial countries were in fact contracting.

Finally, there is the problem of access to Fund resources. The formula for access seems too rigidly based on the percentage of quota that a country can draw to finance a program. There is a problem, not only of adequacy of resources to achieve the so-called "adjustment," but also of the way in which these resources are distributed. Regional distribution between Africa and Latin America is somewhat unfair, as is the way access is geared toward different kinds of economy. In certain African countries, before adjustment is possible, capacity must be expanded, and that is a medium- to long-term problem. In other economies the capacity already exists and, with relatively modest resources, the economy can be stimulated, external imbalance overcome, and the budget problem resolved. (As the economy recovers, people pay more taxes and, if expenditures are kept within limits, this assists in solving the budgetary problem.) The quantum of funding should always be geared toward the size of the problem and the difficulties of the required adjustment.

Finally, a certain amount of flexibility and discretion is needed in the use of policy instruments. There is danger at times of too much emphasis by the Fund on a single policy element as a solution for all ills. Normally, this element is devaluation or budget and credit compression. It might be more useful if programs are designed to encourage countries to choose from three or four scenarios encompassing different policy packages and different instruments to realize those policies.

Alternative Approaches to Stabilization in Africa

John Loxley

The economic crisis in sub-Saharan Africa (SSA) is well documented (World Bank (1981, 1983, 1984)). Sharp falls in per capita income since 1980 have followed a decade in which growth per head was either negligible or, in the case of the poorest countries, negative. For many countries, chronic food shortages are the most serious aspect of the crisis and are the outcome of a failure of production to keep pace with population growth in the 1970s, and of a significant, largely drought-induced, fall in output since 1981. The result has been starvation in the extreme cases, widespread malnourishment, and a heavy dependence by most countries on food aid and other food imports.

The crisis has also been characterized by acute import volume compression or contraction, which many observers see as the principal cause of domestic difficulties in SSA (Green (1984)). A severe 10.6 percent cut in real imports in 1982 followed a decade of low import growth for SSA on average and of absolute reductions in imports for the poorest countries. Restricted access to imports has reduced output and caused excess capacity and rising unemployment in industry, agriculture, and services and a consequent deterioration in sales tax and income tax collections by governments. It has also undermined the export capability of many countries. Adverse trends in the availability of imports have been compounded by an instability in import supply which in turn, has been associated with poor growth performance in SSA.

Underlying the import problem has been a deterioration in the terms of trade stretching back, for non-oil producers, well into the past decade, which was of massive proportions (13 to 14.5 percent) in 1981–82. Export volume

---

Author's Note: Don Hurst assisted with background data, and Gerry Helleiner provided useful advice in the preparation of this paper, whose responsibility is the author's alone.

growth was also negative for SSA in the 1970s and markedly so during the recent global recession. Import problems would have been more acute, however, had foreign aid not risen over fourfold in nominal terms since 1970 (including a significant rise in export credits) and had SSA countries not drawn down their foreign reserves nor increased their import payment arrears over this period. An important characteristic of the current crisis is, however, the drying up of financing options. Foreign aid appears to have stagnated, foreign private investment has been halved, large debt services payments are falling due, reserves are at an all time low, and import arrears have probably peaked. The prognosis is equally grim. No dramatic improvements in the terms of trade are expected in this decade and, without emergency assistance, net capital inflows are likely to fall from $11 billion in 1980–82 to only $5 billion in 1985–87 (World Bank (1984)).

Nature of Fund Conditionality

It is in this context that both the need for Fund assistance and the appropriateness of the conditionality attaching to that assistance must be judged. Since 1979 no fewer than 27 SSA countries, or over 60 percent of the total of SSA members of the Fund, have turned to the Fund for emergency balance of payments assistance. Thus, a majority of SSA countries have had their economic policy shaped by the Fund through conditions attached to that assistance.

Fund programs have received careful scrutiny in recent years (Williamson (1983); Killick (1984); Helleiner (1983); Nowzad (1981)). In general, their objective is the "restoration and maintenance of viability to the balance of payments in an environment of price stability and sustainable rates of growth" (Guitian (1981)). While the detailed content of programs varies from country to country, some common elements are clearly discernible. They usually consist of a mix of demand restraint measures and of policies designed to "get prices right." Demand management usually implies restraining or reducing budget deficits by cutting expenditures, by abolishing subsidies on such items as urban food consumption, or by the raising of taxes or user fees on government services. Price adjustments entail introducing "realistic" exchange rates, "adequate" prices for producers and exporters, the reform of price-distorting tariff and subsidy schemes, the use of interest rates to mobilize savings and allocate investment and the "liberalization" or decontrol of exchange and trade systems.

While there seems to be little quarrel in SSA over the principle of conditionality, there have been major disagreements with the Fund over the nature and severity of conditionality in practice. President Nyerere of Tanzania has accused the Fund of excessive policy intervention and paternalism, and undoubtedly echoed the sentiments of other African governments who have found themselves in dispute with the Fund when he asked, "When did the IMF become an International Ministry of Finance? When did nations agree to surrender to it their power of decision taking?" (Nyerere (1980)). Also, a number of African scholars and officials were prominent signatories of the Arusha Initiative (1980), which rejected the Fund's approach to conditionality on the grounds that it is not "scientific," "objective," or "neutral."

In what follows, we shall examine some of the reasons for discontent with Fund conditionality and, drawing on these, attempt to sketch out in general terms what an alternative approach might look like. In fairness to the Fund, it is important to point out in advance that it does not accept many of the criticisms levelled against it (see Nowzad (1981), de Larosière (1984a), and Dale (1983)) and does not therefore share the enthusiasm of its critics for the reform of its approach to stabilization.

Practical Case for Alternative Approaches

The case for seeking an alternative approach to stabilization to that espoused by the Fund rests on both practical *and* theoretical grounds. The strongest practical argument is that the Fund's record in SSA is relatively poor. There is no evidence that the performance in the 1970s of low-income countries (most of which are in SSA) in terms of balance of payments, growth, inflation, savings, and investment was any better for countries with Fund programs than for those without (Loxley (1984a)). What is more, in a study of adjustment experience in 1980–81, the Fund itself admits that in only a minority of cases were its targets met by African countries. Growth targets were reached in only 5 out of 23 programs, inflation targets in only 13 out of 28, and trade targets in only 11 out of 28 (Zulu and Nsouli (1983)). What is more, between 1980 and 1982, there was a steady increase in the proportion of African programs breaking down in their first year from 36 percent to 58 percent. Though some of these were undoubtedly renegotiated, breakdowns are nevertheless costly in terms of disruption, frustration, and delay.

Although the record is quite clear, there is no agreement on the factors that explain it. The Fund argues that slippages in implementation were to blame for the poor performance and were the result of "the emergence of unforeseen developments, difficulties in mobilizing sufficient political support for the requisite adjustment measures, limitations in the administrative infrastructure, overoptimistic targets, and delays or shortfalls in net inflows of development assistance'' (International Monetary Fund (1983)). The Fund then argues that slippage could have been avoided if adjustment efforts had been intensified. In other words, it believes that policy failings of African governments were responsible for shortfalls in implementation. Yet even a cursory glance at the Fund's own explanations would suggest that the design of programs left much to be desired. They clearly imply that the Fund did not allow for flexibility in programs to accommodate ''unforeseen developments,'' and that programs were too ambitious relative to what was feasible in economic, administrative, and political terms.

Neither of the above studies addressed the question of what would have happened in the absence of a Fund program. In the past, the Fund has argued that even partial implementation of its programs was helpful in preventing ''the crisis situation that would have developed had no program been in effect'' (Reichmann (1978), p. 41); but a more recent study has concluded that there is at best, only ''a moderate connection between program execution and the achievement of desired economic results'' (Killick (1982), p. 38).

The practical case for alternative adjustment programs to those of the Fund rests therefore on the lackluster performance of African countries operating under Fund stand-by arrangements even when Fund criteria were met, and on the Fund's own explanations for the difficulties encountered in implementing its programs. It does not rest on complete counterfactual tests because we are not in a position to know how countries would have performed on alternative programs to those designed by the Fund.

Theoretical Case for Alternative Approaches

There are in addition, however, sound theoretical reasons why Fund programs might be expected not to work too well in this part of the world. SSA economies have a low capacity to adjust (Dell (1983) and Helleiner (1983)) because their problems are structural. This means that they are not particularly susceptible to treatment by an approach which is heavily oriented toward demand restraint and short-term adjustments. Since this structuralist critique is central to the case for alternative approaches to stabilization, it is worth discussing at some length.

To begin with, the most critical constraint on adjustment efforts in SSA is foreign exchange availability, but this is unlikely to be eased significantly by standard Fund measures. Domestic demand restraint can be expected to have little impact either by way of reducing import expenditures or by freeing up local goods for expanded export earnings because the substitutability of traded for nontraded goods is generally quite low in SSA; imports do not compete with goods produced locally, while exports are not usually consumed locally to any significant degree. The possibilities of improving the balance of trade through expenditure switching are, therefore, quite limited (Crockett (1981)).

Structuralists also tend to be less sanguine about the ability of large devaluations to stimulate improvements in the balance of payments. Individual SSA economies fit the ''small economy'' assumptions and can therefore generally export as much as they can produce at the going world price. In this situation the Marshall-Lerner condition for a devaluation to improve the balance of trade in foreign exchange terms is, quite simply, that the sum of the elasticity of supply of exports and the elasticity of demand for imports exceeds zero (Williamson (1983c)). Given these conditions, it is clear that a devaluation cannot cause a deterioration in the trade balance in SSA; but structuralists argue that there are grounds for believing that improvements may, at best, be minimal and may take time. Exports may not respond much to price incentives partly because of the limited opportunities for expenditure switching discussed above, but more especially because non-price factors are often the crucial constraint on their expansion. Thus, if incentive goods are not available to peasants or if intermediate and capital goods are in short supply, an increase in local prices paid to exporters may achieve little other than the worsening of inflationary pressures. This is, of course, not so much an argument against the use of price incentives as one against their being used in isolation from measures designed to solve the short-run ''goods famine'' that often hinders exports.

Expanding the capacity of tree crop or mineral exports also takes time so that output may respond only three to five years after the initial price stimulus. Promoting nontraditional exports, such as manufactured goods, requires much more than correct pricing incentives. It presupposes a reasonably well-developed manufacturing sector and an ability to penetrate foreign markets that implies overseas contacts, product quality, and appropriate credit systems. Few SSA countries could meet these requirements and certainly not within the one-year timeframe of most Fund programs.

On the import side, an adjustment in relative prices through devaluation may also fail to have the desired effect. Where imports are licensed, an increase in their domestic currency cost may succeed only in reducing the large rents accruing to license holders and have little impact on overall import demand. If, as in many SSA countries, excess demand for imports is large, if the state sector is a major importer, and if aid is important in total imports, then again price increases may have a negligible impact on overall import demand. In this connection, it is worth noting that non-food consumer imports are already quite low in most of SSA, being on average less than 10 percent of the total and as low as 5 percent for countries such as Tanzania (U.N. (1984)). The impact of import contraction, however induced, would inevitably fall, therefore, on intermediate and capital goods imports, thereby further disrupting current output or future growth.

For individual countries in SSA, export-supply elasticities and import-demand elasticities may, therefore, be quite low. Inflexibility and fragmentation remain the hallmarks of African economies. These characteristics have important implications for the speed with which adjustment to fundamental imbalances can occur.

The devaluation issue has been particularly controversial in SSA, and on this issue structuralists have disagreed strongly with the approach of the Fund. The Fund's preference for relatively large adjustments in advance of quite small amounts of balance of payments assistance is seen by some as a prescription for inflation and political instability. It is held that supply elasticities are such that price increases would rapidly erode attempts to depreciate the real effective exchange rate and that this raises questions about the usefulness of this instrument (Singh (1984)). Yet even critics acknowledge the case for devaluation where, for reasons of domestic inflation "the cost of production of a country's staple exports . . . ha(s) got seriously out of line with world prices expressed in terms of local currency at the prevailing rate of exchange" (Kaldor (1983), p. 36). A devaluation may also be justified if other attempts to raise export prices have led to large producer subsidies being granted from the budget of the government or parastatals. Thus the question to be faced by SSA governments experiencing overvalued real exchange rates is not *whether* to devalue but *how;* they must decide by what amount and over what period adjustments will be made. These decisions will be very much influenced by the amount and phasing of financial assistance available to ease supply inelasticities and by one's views of the capacity to adjust of SSA countries.

Structuralists would also question the preference of the Fund for the introduction of positive real rates of interest. It is argued that these too can contribute independently to both inflation and recession when interest costs are a significant proportion of total costs of production (Taylor (1981, 1983)). At the same time there is no evidence that real savings respond in a marked positive manner to increases in the rate of interest (Giovannini (1983)). There is some evidence from elsewhere that increases in interest rates cause financial savings to increase (Lanyi and Saracoglu (1983)), although sometimes the apparent increase represents no more than a shift from informal to formal markets (Wijnbergen (1982)). Fund analyses which postulate capital moving freely between SSA countries in response to differentials in real negative rates of interest seem, however, to be positively fanciful (Loxley (1981)). It should also be noted that even proponents of market rates claim no close association between increased financial saving and real growth (Lanyi and Saracoglu (1983)).

Those who emphasize the structural nature of the causes of crises would be less enthusiastic than the Fund about the need for, and possibility of, rapid adjustment. They argue that the shock treatment often involved in Fund programs "can seriously weaken the capacity for real adjustment" by preventing increases in production and required changes in the composition of output, as well as by prejudicing the political sustainability of programs (Nelson (1984)). Even though "it may sometimes involve rather high costs in terms of growth and employment" the Fund justifies this approach on the grounds that "it can be expected that important benefits will follow in short order, and over time the net benefits may be greater than if a more gradual course had been chosen" (Mookerjee (1982)). One will note that there is no claim that greater net benefits will inevitably flow from this approach.

It can be argued that SSA is less able than other parts of the Third World to absorb shock treatment because of its low absolute per capita incomes and, in the case of the poorest SSA countries, because per capita incomes have been falling steadily for over a decade now. The Fund itself claims to be sensitive to this structural reality and maintains that in its 1980–81 programs the emphasis was on gradual, medium-term adjustment, with allowance being made in a number of cases for deteriorating inflationary and balance of payments circumstances over the short run. In some cases, even budget deficits and domestic credit were allowed to expand (Zulu and Nsouli (1983)). It is difficult to deal with this claim without access to more information, but three comments would seem to be in order. To begin with, this picture of Fund approaches in Africa is incomplete because it excludes countries with which the Fund was not able to reach agreements. Thus, in Tanzania, the

Fund has been insisting since 1981 on shock treatment of a particularly severe kind, to a degree that might not have been sustainable politically. Second, there is evidence to suggest that quite large adjustments were indeed required of some SSA program countries in 1980–81. In some cases money supply growth fell significantly, by 20 percent or more, while at least two countries experienced extremely large devaluations (Uganda, 90 percent, and Zaïre, 40 percent, in terms of the dollar). Third, and perhaps most relevant of all for the purpose at hand, Fund conditionality has certainly been tightened up since 1981 (Williamson (1982)). Whether this is the result of a shift in the politics of the institution, as some claim, or whether it is merely a reflection of a more difficult global situation, including the Fund's own resulting resource constraint, as the Fund maintains, it is nonetheless a reality with which SSA has to live. One indication of this is to be found perhaps in the marked increase in the incidence of devaluation required of borrowers between 1981 and 1983.[1]

Critics of the Fund also complain about the inappropriateness of its performance indicators. They accuse the Fund of practicing pinpoint targetry in situations in which data deficiencies and shortages of skilled staff imply quite long time lags between the emergence of a problem and its identification (Helleiner (1983); see also Loxley (1979) for a practical example of data problems in Africa). They question the theoretical relevance of Fund performance criteria in terms of the strength of their relationship to real economic variables. Above all, they note that almost all the criteria are short run and demand oriented, notwithstanding the Fund's formal commitment to supply stimulation (Killick (1981) and Williamson (1982)). In defense, the Fund argues that its indicators are "subject to unambiguous reading" (Beza (1983)) and, in any case, cover variables that are monitored routinely by all governments.

The distributional implications of Fund adjustment measures have also been the subject of contention in SSA. Fund programs make no attempt to guarantee employment levels nor to preserve or extend the provision of basic needs (Brandt Commission (1980), pp. 215–17). They often have their most negative effects on low-income urban dwellers by raising unemployment, by cutting subsidies and government spending, and by raising inflation while restraining wage adjustments. But the rural poor may also be affected adversely by cuts in spending and may benefit little from changes in the inter-

[1]In 1981 devaluation was required of only 2 of the 10 borrowers which were not members of the French franc zone. In 1983 the equivalent figures were 7 out of 10.

nal terms of trade. In both groups, evidence is beginning to emerge that children and women are particularly vulnerable (UNICEF (1984), Green (1984)).

The issue of distribution is tied closely to those of shock treatment and political sustainability. Even where the economy as a whole is subject to only moderate reduction in growth rate as a result of austerity, this may be converted into a very significant proportionate decline for particular groups within the economy and, for this reason, may not be politically feasible.

The Fund's view is that income distribution is the clear political prerogative of member governments. Nevertheless, it maintains that, insofar as its measures shift the terms of trade toward the rural sector, they have a bias in favor of the poorer sections of society. Given the relatively low degree of differentiation in rural Africa, the argument has some merit, but it needs tempering to take into account the fact that urban/rural differentials appear to have narrowed significantly in SSA in recent years, and that the needs of both the urban and the rural poor are pressing in an absolute sense. The distributional impact of Fund programs is not estimated in advance and does not apparently form part of the negotiations with potential borrowers. There is no suggestion here that equity is a universal concern in SSA; unfortunately the reality is otherwise. Nor does one wish to imply the the Fund should press for greater equity where this is not a priority of governments; this would be as utopian as it would be fruitless. What is implied, however, is that the Fund be more open to negotiating the distributional impact of programs with governments for whom it is a matter of concern. What must be resolved in each concrete situation is the degree to which alternative distributional goals would "inevitably neutralize the effects one was seeking in the first instance" (Williamson (1982)).

Debate has also centered around the analytical, some would say ideological, preference of the Fund, for greater reliance on market forces in economic decision taking. Allowing domestic prices to move into line with world prices is one expression of this preference, but it also extends to liberalizing domestic markets in general. On efficiency grounds, therefore, the Fund presses for reductions in state intervention in the form of price, exchange and import controls, and of market-distorting tariffs and subsidies. The case against this emphasis is that market prices are suspect as guides to efficient resource allocation or optimal investment in a context in which social costs and benefits deviate from private ones, which is especially likely to be the case when far-reaching structural changes are taking place in the economy. Decisions based on market prices may also be unacceptable on distributional grounds or when markets are narrow and imperfect. Structuralists would argue there is a case for the use of controls or direct state intervention in SSA and that prices are so "profoundly important that markets cannot in general be trusted to set them" (Williamson (1983b)).

Thus, even if in the present circumstances it might make sense to move some prices in the same direction that the market is moving them, it does not follow that complete laissez-faire is the answer to SSA's problems.

The strategic thrust of Fund adjustment measures is toward integrating its members more fully into the world economy through trade and payments liberalization. In this respect, Fund conditionality is entirely consistent with the purposes of the Fund as laid down in Article I of its Articles of Agreement. On the trade side, the emphasis is very much on export promotion, while on the payments side Fund policies serve to enhance the internationalization of capital in the form both of bank debt and of direct investment. Indeed, the Fund goes so far as to argue that "(e)xpanded flows of direct investment to the developing countries are in everybody's interest . . . Thus the Fund is encouraging developing countries to remove obstacles to such flows and to place greater emphasis on policies designed to attract foreign private investment as part of their development strategy" (de Larosière (1984b)).

These strategic emphases may not be acceptable to all Fund members all of the time. Some SSA countries would take a much more cautious approach than others to encouraging foreign private investment, and for sound historical, ideological, and even narrowly economic reasons. Some might be quite skeptical that an open door policy would result in much of an additional capital inflow. Fund programs might, therefore, simply result in better terms being given to capital which would have flowed in anyway. More important (since there is little the Fund can do or would wish to do to impose private enterprise on unwilling member countries), the Fund's commitment to an outward-oriented growth strategy might also be found objectionable by some member countries. A strong case can be made that this underlying strategic thrust to Fund conditionality is not consistent with that prescribed by the Lagos Plan of Action (LPA) to which over 50 African governments are signatories. The LPA called for the design and pursuit of a uniquely African strategy based on "internally generated, self-sustained processes of development," and on "national and collective self-reliance." Central to this strategy is an explicit drive towards self sufficiency in food production, greater regional integration, and less reliance on traditional exports and markets

(O.A.U. (1981)). These strategic emphases are for the most part quite at odds with those of the Fund, and it is instructive that in the review of its own performance in SSA, the Fund apparently makes no mention of the LPA. This is perhaps not surprising since the literature on stabilization is remarkably silent on the issue of economic strategy, even when it is proposing alternatives to the orthodoxy (Stewart (1984)). It is almost as if the unwritten assumption is that stabilization measures are short-term adjustment measures applicable to any conceivable range of long-term economic strategies. Yet this may not be so. Short-run stabilization policies have important implications for the development of the economy in the long term. The redirection of incentives and institutions in the short term may lock countries into certain development strategies for many years.

Member governments will, of course, have differing degrees of commitment to alternative strategies, such as those outlined in the LPA, and hence differing degrees of difficulty in accommodating the strategic thrust of Fund stabilization programs. There is, however, no evidence that the Fund is in any way sensitive to the issue of alternative approaches to economic strategy in SSA or that the Fund adjusts its approach to accommodate governments pursuing quite different economic strategies from those it advocates. What is clear is that the approach of the Fund would only indirectly, if at all, address the strategic issues raised in the LPA and is more likely to entrench African integration into the World System as a whole than to encourage "inward looking" regional integration.

Two quite separate issues are involved in the discussion of strategic alternatives. The first is how efficacious different approaches are in meeting long-run development objectives. The second is national sovereignty. There is little doubt that the Fund would question the desirability of those that might not appear to be justified by immediate static comparative advantage or by reference to short-run efficiency considerations in general. Equally, the LPA arose out of frustration with the difficulties faced by SSA in its integration with the international trade and financial system as it now operates. There are therefore legitimate differences between the Fund and some SSA governments over what alternative strategies are likely to achieve in the long run. Since 1981, the export-oriented model of growth is looking much less like the panacea some thought it to be (Balassa (1982)). Its superiority seems to have been exaggerated theoretically (Streeten (1982)) and, for many countries, in practical terms (Cline (1982)). Now, more than ever, it seems appropriate to consider strategies that recognize the realistic limitations of export orientation for the poorest countries and which, at the same time, deal explicitly with the most serious problem facing most of SSA—the food problem.

There is therefore a strong case for the Fund to demonstrate more flexibility and sensitivity in its strategic prescriptions for SSA and to be more open to considering alternatives. Unfortunately, there is no evidence that the Fund is moving in this direction, and there are fears that instead it may use the considerable leverage it possesses by virtue of its role as lender of last resort to override the viewpoints of member governments. The issue of leverage and interference with national sovereignty is particularly live when the range of financing options open to governments is so severely restricted.

World Bank Approaches to Structural Adjustment and Conditionality

It has been suggested that some of the shortcomings of the Fund's approach to stabilization might be remedied if it was to adopt the type of conditionality attached by the World Bank to its structural-adjustment lending. This consists of a series of essentially supply-oriented policy conditions that borrowers must meet. The main emphasis is on price reform, raising institutional efficiency, reviewing investment priorities, and improving the management of foreign debt. The Bank avoids pinpoint targetry and reliance on a handful of demand oriented macroadjustments. In this respect, it is not dissimilar to the real-economy approach to conditionality advocated by the Overseas Development Institute (ODI) (Killick and others (1984)).

Despite these strengths, there are, however, a number of problems with World Bank conditionality in this form. To begin with, Bank conditionality is almost always superimposed upon Fund conditionality, subjecting borrowing countries to a double dose of external policy leverage. It is, therefore, not a substitute for Fund conditionality but a complement to it. This makes it even more demanding in political terms than conditionality alone, a factor acknowledged by the Bank in explaining why so few countries, and especially poorer ones, apply for or qualify for structural adjustment loans (World Bank (1984)). Furthermore, World Bank programs invariably follow Fund programs, and it could be argued that this is the reverse of what is desirable if structural issues are to be given the priority they warrant.

World Bank conditionality does not deal, however, any better with the strategic questions raised earlier. It is, if anything, even more explicit than the Fund in its advocacy of market-oriented and outward-looking strategies.

Environment > Policy factors
the cause of SSA crisis.

The Berg Report on which conditionality in SSA is apparently based, has been criticized by African governments for this emphasis and for uncritically extolling the virtues of expanding the private sector. Furthermore, critics have objected strenuously to the lack of emphasis by the Bank on food security (African Caucus (1982), Green (1983)), and to its apparent abandonment of a commitment to greater equity and the meeting of basic needs (Loxley (1984c)). Above all, African governments were especially disturbed by the basic assumption underlying structural-adjustment lending and the Berg Report, namely, that domestic policy shortcomings were the principal cause of the crisis in SSA. This finding is contradicted by a study commissioned by the Bank which found that ''environmental'' factors were more important than policy shortcomings (Wheeler (1984)). More recently, Bank publications have acknowledged the contribution of external shocks, played down the desirability of promoting greater rural inequity, and have addressed food problems more explicitly (World Bank (1983, 1984), but otherwise the Bank's policy prescriptions parallel closely those of the Berg Report and are entirely consistent with those of the Fund.

Financing versus Adjustment

Some critics of the Fund would argue that its stabilization programs involve a blend of finance and adjustment that is too heavily skewed toward adjustment. While the Fund has considerable discretion in determining this blend, it has opted, in recent years, to restrict the amount of finance it provides to countries undertaking adjustment programs. Thus, during the most recent economic crisis, the Fund chose not to reactivate special facilities such as the oil facility or to reinstitute Trust Fund loans; nor, since 1981, has it made further allocations of SDRs. In addition, while quotas were increased in 1983, the amount that could be borrowed from the Fund as a percentage of quota under normal circumstances was reduced. The net effect is that low-income countries can borrow, on average, 11 percent less than they could before quota revision (Loxley (1984b)), and SSA countries can borrow 8 percent less. The absence of special funding arrangements has also meant that the proportion of finance made available by the Fund on low or unconditional terms (excluding drawings in the reserve tranche) has fallen dramatically—from 76 percent in 1979/80 to almost zero in 1982/83 (Ibid.). Since 1983, the compensatory financing facility has also been converted into a high conditionality source of finance, and steps have been taken to neutralize the effect of the quota increase on members' ability to borrow from this source.[2]

The net effect of these developments has been that the Fund provided less than a fifth of the financing of SSA balance of payments deficits in 1982/83 at the peak of the balance of payments crisis, while in 1983/84 the net flow of Fund resources to SSA was almost nil.[3] Looked at from another point of view, net Fund credits were well below 10 percent of the impact of external shocks (terms of trade losses, reduce export growth, interest rate increases, and natural disaster losses) experienced by SSA after 1977. Despite assertions to the contrary by Fund staff (Zulu and Nsouli (1983)), there is also little evidence that Fund agreements have acted as catalysts in securing commercial bank loans for SSA (Loxley (1984a)).[4] Thus, an acute shortage of liquidity has forced SSA governments to run down their reserves and to fall into serious arrears on payments for imports. Above all, it has compelled them to adjust to the crisis by severe cuts in real imports.

A number of observers feel that the degree of adjustment required of SSA is both unwarranted and inequitable. It is the result of an approach to global equilibrium that places responsibility for adjustment almost entirely on the shoulders of deficit countries, since the Fund has little leverage to exercise over countries persistently in surplus. While this asymmetry was relaxed somewhat at the height of the debt crisis with the Fund pressuring creditors to cooperate in crisis management and advance more credit than they might have done otherwise, low-income countries were untouched by this development. Yet, many who feel that the crisis in SSA overwhelmingly results from external shocks also believe that the international community, and especially the international agencies, have an obligation to ease the burden of adjustment by the provision of much larger amounts of unconditional liquidity

[2]The changes in regulations converting the compensatory financing facility into a high conditionality facility have not been critical, since in 1982/83 all but 1 percent of drawings under this facility were by countries already pursuing Fund stabilization programs.

[3]Recent balance of payments data for SSA are difficult to come by. For 23 countries for which data were available in 1982/83, it appears that net Fund drawings were the equivalent of only 7.6 percent of total current account deficits. If Nigeria is excluded the proportion rises to 18.9 percent. It should be noted, however, that this excludes such large borrowers as Zaïre, the Sudan, and Uganda. Data derived from International Monetary Fund, *International Financial Statistics*.

[4]Fund agreements are, however, a prerequisite for the rescheduling of debts (including official export credits) through the Paris Club.

than has been the case in recent years. While the Fund acknowledges the need for greatly expanded concessional funding to poor countries, it does not believe it should be the source (International Monetary Fund (1982)); nor does it accept that the origin of disequilibrium in these countries should dictate the blend of financing and adjustment required. As Mikesell (1983) has put it, "(t)here is nothing in the cause of a country's payments imbalance that relieves it of the necessity for adjustment, given the limitations on the availability of external finance." It is, however, the view of critics that to a large extent the limits to Fund financing are self-imposed, though there is no evidence that the Fund and the major countries that control it are in disagreement on this issue.

Fund critics also bemoan the fact that the trend toward more conservative approaches to financing by the Fund has been accompanied by a retreat from lending under the extended Fund facility. This facility provides for drawings up to three years and allows longer repayment periods than normal stand-by arrangements. It was introduced to permit Fund programs to be explicitly supply oriented and although it was usually superimposed on traditional demand restraint approaches, often with even tighter credit ceilings than under stand-bys (Killick and others (1984)), it did hold out the promise of more enlightened adjustment strategies for a while. This promise was apparently realized with the Indian loan of 1981 which provided for adjustment with growth. It appears though that the United States felt that this type of assistance was not in keeping with the Fund's mandate as a lender of last resort, and hence from that time the Indian case has not been allowed to act as a precedent (Dell (1984)).

The one hopeful development on the financing side in recent years is the World Bank's "Joint Program of Action for sub-Saharan Africa." Originally proposed as a $2 billion a year additional aid package (World Bank (1984)) and now apparently scaled down to $1 billion, this proposal aims to mobilize funds from bilateral donors. Funds will, however, be made available only to SSA governments pursuing acceptable adjustment programs, and there are concerns that policy requirements will follow closely those outlined in the Berg Report and that donor leverage will be increased significantly. Also, in a World Bank paper outlining the possible impact of the Joint Program on specific SSA countries, all four case studies are countries with Fund programs in place or under discussion, which suggests that World Bank balance of payments funding will continue to be tied to Fund adjustment programs despite their shortcomings.

Obligation of African Governments

In arguing the weaknesses in Fund and Bank approaches to adjustment and the case for a less burdensome blend of financing and adjustment, it is not my intention to play down the responsibilities of SSA governments to meet their crises speedily and resolutely. Nor does one wish to absolve SSA governments from past errors of policy and from weaknesses in administration. SSA governments have undoubtedly often pursued policies that have exacerbated external shocks. There has been a pronounced anti-rural bias in policy and this has contributed to declining rural surpluses. Investment resources have been used unproductively with much lower growth rates than one might reasonably expect when investment rates exceed 20 percent, as they have on average in SSA in recent years. The export sector has been neglected and there has been a failure to recognize that this sector, traditional or otherwise, would necessarily have to be relied upon for many years to assist economic transformation. There has also been in many SSA countries an explosion of unproductive and expensive bureaucratization, and the expansion of state control and intervention to the very micro-level of the economy, with serious implications for efficiency and the surplus.

Recognition of these problems is essential if the crisis in SSA is to be dealt with effectively. The motive behind proposals for alternative approaches to stabilization and adjustment must not be to remove the obligation of SSA governments to "put their own house in order." Much of the diagnosis by the international institutions of domestic policy shortcomings in this part of the world has validity and must be addressed. For this reason, alternative prescriptions will unavoidably contain many similarities with those advocated by the Fund and Bank, so much so that the casual observer may conclude that "their differences are dwarfed by their commonalities" (Please (1984), p. 94). A central thesis of this paper is, however, that SSA governments can meet their obligations within the framework of approaches to adjustment that have quite different economic, social, and political implications from those of more orthodox approaches, although whether or not one describes them as "radically different" (Payer (1983)) is a matter of judgment.[5] We now turn to consider the possible content of such alternatives.

---

[5]Both Please and Payer were discussing the nature of the 1982 structural adjustment program of Tanzania which the author helped prepare. Some of the alternatives presented in this paper first found expression in this program which has not been fully implemented because of funding shortages due largely to a failure to reach agreement with the Fund.

Alternative Approaches to Stabilization

The justification for alternative approaches to stabilization lies, therefore, in the weak theoretical underpinnings of the Fund's current approach as well as in its indifferent track record in practice. Yet, the Fund is in no way restricted by its Articles or by any other legal requirements to one particular approach to stabilization. On the contrary, the 1979 guidelines on conditionality require the Fund to pay due regard "to the domestic, social and political objectives, the economic priorities and circumstances of members, including the causes of their balance of payments problems" and they allow the Fund to vary the performance criteria required of members according to the "diversity of problems and institutional arrangements" they face (Gold (1979)). These guidelines suggest that the Fund has much greater leeway in its approach to conditionality than it has chosen to exercise to date. Proponents of alternative approaches go further and argue that the various objectives of the Fund are themselves potentially contradictory and that on these grounds alone a strong case can be made for greater flexibility in the design of stabilization programs since ". . . a number of policy packages may be equally consistent with the Articles" (Stewart (1984), p. 203).

The lack of alternative approaches in practice reflects, therefore, neither an absence of need for them nor any legal or constitutional impediments faced by the Fund in considering them. Rather, it is explained in part by the Fund's commitment to a particular view of adjustment and in part by the absence of clearly articulated alternatives (Thorp and Whitehead (1980)). Of these two problems, that of Fund intransigence may be the more difficult to deal with since, on the rare occasions that they have been developed, the Fund has not been receptive to alternatives even when they appeared to be both internally consistent and feasible.

In outlining the nature of possible alternative adjustment programs one can be guided by the perceived shortcomings of Fund programs outlined above. To begin with, and in contrast to the Fund approach, the (essentially) structuralist critique does not provide a blueprint for adjustment to be applied in all circumstances. Rather, it suggests that alternative programs should be tailored to the structural characteristics of the country in question, to deal with the specific economic problems being faced at any particular time. Thus, programs could be expected to vary greatly between countries depending upon their economic structure and the precise causes of their instability. Likewise, the mix between finance and adjustment would also vary according to these factors to a much greater degree than it does now with relatively more finance being made available where exogenous shocks are clearly the major source of instability.

Member governments would be much more actively involved in the design of alternative programs than they appear to be at present. This would be justified on the grounds that "conditionality . . . must reflect the sovereign right of states to choose their own social and economic models and development paths" (Arusha Initiative (1980)). Moreover, without this enhanced involvement, the effectiveness of programs is likely to continue to be severely limited simply because programs that are imposed do not hold. Members would be free, of course, to call on assistance from outside agencies and individuals; the essential point is that governments would enter into negotiations with the Fund with their own clearly articulated, internally consistent, and feasible set of proposals to deal with instability.

Ideally, alternative programs should provide for adjustment with economic growth. They should recognize, therefore, that the import constraint is the single most important factor limiting both domestic and export growth in SSA economies. Accordingly, programs should provide for external assistance to as far as possible precede or, at worst, accompany, major policy changes. The argument for this is that unless consumer and intermediate goods are available, increased prices and other incentives will achieve little by way of stimulating exports or production in general and will tend, simply, to be inflationary. Yet there are time lags of several months between the receipt of foreign exchange assistance and the availability locally of incentive and intermediate products (three to four months in many cases). It will be much easier for an economy to absorb the strains of policy adjustment if programs are front-end loaded in terms of finance. While this reduces Fund sanctions over noncompliance with agreed-upon terms, it greatly reduces the risk of noncompliance in the first place. Alternative programs would therefore assume a very different phasing of both assistance and adjustment measures from those of the normal Fund programs.

Expanded imports resulting from an agreement would be allocated in a very selective manner to priority sectors and products using both market and nonmarket means, with the three principal objectives being restoring the output of crucial, locally produced basic needs or incentives goods, promoting exports, and raising production of important tax-revenue generating products.

Supply expansion would be the essence of alternative approaches and adjustment would focus on a limited number of key sectors and on selective, as opposed to economywide, policy initiatives (Foxley (1983)). Increased food security in terms of basic foodstuffs (as opposed to luxury products, such as wheat or sugar) would undoubtedly be a major preoccupation of SSA adjustment programs given the catastrophic situation in much of the continent. Indeed, it could be argued that this should be the prime focus of African adjustment efforts at this time, since success in this area would achieve multiple objectives; it would directly contribute to the meeting of basic needs; it would almost certainly be progressive in its distributional impact, given the structure of land ownership in most of SSA; it would reduce the import bill of many countries by between 5 and 25 percent and heighten self-reliance and national economic integration; it would contribute to growth and, in the medium term, would serve to reduce both inflationary pressures and the need for government subsidization of urban food consumption. Reliable food surpluses might also constitute a solid foundation for the growth of manufacturing industry (Adelman (1984)). No other sector is likely to offer such attractions to most SSA countries at this time. There are, therefore, compelling reasons for a food-security stabilization strategy in SSA, a strategy which would be entirely consistent with the Lagos Plan of Action.

Critics of this strategy, such as Chester Crocker, U.S. Assistant Secretary of State for African Affairs, would argue that "some old shibboleths badly need re-examination, including the notion that a country must physically produce its own food supplies, when in some cases it may be more efficient—and no less self-sufficient—to concentrate on cash crops and buy food with the money thus earned" (Browne and Cummings (1984), p. 55). While there is some obvious truth in this, the critique is oversimplistic in that it fails to appreciate the implications for food security of volatile cash-crop export earnings. Problems of planning, administration, and communications in SSA may also impede the conversion of cash-crop earnings into food consumption. At the same time, policies designed to expand cash-crop exports, and especially the "progressive" farmer policies advocated in the Berg Report, may have the effect of concentrating land ownership, thereby reducing the land entitlement, and hence the food entitlement, of former food producers (Sen (1981)). Efficient specialization may therefore be perceived to carry prohibitively high costs in enhanced food insecurity at both the personal and the national level.

In the context of SSA, there is also a widely held view that a people who cannot feed themselves is a people not in control of their destiny (Browne and Cummings (1984)). This view informed the Lagos Plan of Action and has undoubtedly been strengthened by the events of recent years. While seeking generally to redress the general bias against the rural economy, if there is any trade-off between promoting food production and promoting cash-crop exports, SSA adjustment programs should therefore err on the side of the former, since the potential human costs of a mistaken emphasis in the other direction are unacceptably high. This is not to say that food imports would be avoided at all costs; only that policy would aim for stable and reliable food supplies taking one year with another. Imports would still be drawn upon as a last resort, but to a much smaller extent and less frequently than at present.

In practical terms a food-security policy would involve not only correcting the bias against the rural sector in domestic terms of trade, but also developing an appropriate structure of relative prices between food production and export crop production. On the whole, both the Fund and World Bank programs have been much more concerned with the former than the latter. Little attention has been paid to the cross-elasticity of supply between food and cash exports and certainly no explicit weight seems to have been given to the desirability per se of food self-sufficiency in Fund and Bank adjustment programs. Both these weaknesses would require rectification.

Food-security policies could usefully draw on the deregulation emphases of orthodox adjustment programs—encouraging greater flexibility in food marketing at the local level by permitting small-scale private or cooperative traders and the free transfer of food within national boundaries. Where large, state-owned marketing boards have a poor record of efficiency, they might usefully restrict their involvement to managing strategic reserves and imports to ensure the availability of food for the urban population. Greater food security may, in addition, call for more unorthodox policy prescriptions. The redistribution of land holdings may be an essential, albeit politically difficult, prerequisite, while political campaigns to exhort greater food production in the national interest may be a useful complement to more traditional market incentives. It bears repeating that where market incentives are used to generate an increase in surplus, they will need to be preceded or at least accompanied by an increased availability of consumption and intermediate goods if they are to achieve their desired results.

It follows, therefore, that sensible alternative programs would in general avoid an across-the-board commitment to export promotion. Subject to the food self-sufficiency goal to be aimed at over a target number of years, these programs would, in common with orthodox programs, seek to restore existing export capacity by removing systemic bias against the export sector. They would achieve this by reducing or abolishing export taxes, by improving the efficiency of export marketing arrangements, and by channeling some state investment funds and scarce foreign exchange into export rehabilitation. In addition, producer prices would be improved by devaluation, but the approach to exchange rate adjustment would differ from that of the Fund. Adjustments would be smaller, more frequent, and subsequent to, or simultaneous with, the receipt of external assistance, and adjustments to prices set by marketing boards would be selective, varying from crop to crop and not necessarily proportionate to overall devaluation.

More caution would be exercised in the length of time over which the reversal of bias against exports would take place, recognizing that structural bottlenecks might prevent rapid supply adjustment to price incentives. The extent to which attempts would be made to offset past erosion of real producer prices would not be determined mechanistically by reference to prices prevailing in some arbitrarily chosen base year. Instead, careful consideration would be given to the market prospects for each commodity, the range of both price and nonprice impediments to production and the overall distributional implications of possible price adjustments. This may result in the use of multiple exchange rates, either explicitly or implicitly.

The emphasis would also be on selectively encouraging new export products, although the prospects for rapidly expanding earnings from new commodity exports are quite limited in SSA. Export demand prospects would be examined on a product-by-product basis, and incentives, such as export subsidies, rebates, differential exchange rates, and access to foreign exchange, tailored accordingly. This would help reduce the inflationary consequences of a more general approach involving large devaluations (Schydlowsky (1982)).

Alternative approaches would be premised on the assumption that rectifying the large ''structural'' external deficits (Williamson (1982)) of SSA countries will not be achieved quickly. Exports are generally in the range of between 40 percent and 70 percent of the import bill even after prolonged import contraction. In many countries imports are much less than required to maintain capacity production—often by as much as a third. Adjustment will need to take place over many years and will not be an easy task. It must be stressed, however, that adjustment is essential and it is not proposed here that the Fund bear the responsibility of financing Third World structural deficits. Adjustment will have to be achieved primarily through export growth rather than import contraction, although in some countries some limited potential still remains for restraining nonessential consumer imports and in all countries some restriction of imported investment goods would be beneficial. This latter may do little to ease the immediate foreign exchange shortage, since a good portion of such investment is aid finance, but it would reduce indirect import demands and, more important, would reduce the pressure on domestic resources and on the administrative capacity of SSA countries. What is called for is a significant scaling down of investment quantity and a much greater preoccupation with improving investment quality. In this respect, investment funds should be concentrated on expanding food supplies, on the restoration and rehabilitation of capacity, including the traditional export base, and on new projects that might quickly yield significant net foreign exchange benefits. To the degree that resources permit, some portion of investment should be reserved for strengthening national economic integration in areas other than food, where this is consistent with national policy. Ideally, governments should also seek to make a minimum annual commitment to projects that further regional cooperation within the continent.

Import constraint will for some time dictate the pace at which strategies of national economic integration and regional cooperation can be pursued. For this reason such strategies will, ironically, rely crucially on export recovery and expansion in the immediate future. What is required, therefore, is not a retreat into autarky or a sudden delinking of SSA from the world economy (Amin (1974)); this would be as impractical as all-out export promotion strategies are undesirable. Rather, there will need to be a delicate balance between objectives, with incremental resources increasingly shifted into other sectors as export earnings recover. The allocation of investment funds between a few high-priority sectors, with a focus on relieving crucial linkages will therefore assume paramount importance. Success in this approach will require tackling investment planning much more seriously and much more systematically than in the past.

SSA governments might also use the crisis to make virtue out of necessity and compensate for past errors by closing down uneconomic projects, such as those with excessive reliance on imported products, or by pressuring them to recast their operations to improve the net social benefits they offer over a predetermined time period. The emphasis throughout should be on improved investment performance within the given objectives of national economic policy.

This approach to investment will have far-reaching implications for aid policy. It suggests that SSA governments should consciously and deliberately set out to reduce their aid dependence in the coming years. In some countries an absolute moratorium on new project aid might be appropriate. This would permit SSA countries to regain control over their institutions of government and would facilitate macromanagement, both of which appear to have been undermined in recent years by excessive dependence on aid (Morse (1984)). At the same time, efforts should be made to switch a considerable proportion of aid, both bilateral and multilateral, from the form of project aid to that of balance of payments or import support. The attraction to donors would be that this type of quick-disbursing aid would increase the returns to past project aid and would have a high payoff in incremental output, exports, and government revenue. Import support could be phased out over a period of years as exports recover, and project aid could be phased back in, albeit perhaps at a lower real level than in past years.

In order to expedite flows of assistance, a strong case could be made for the Fund and the Bank helping member countries arrange a package of support funding from donors in anticipation of an agreement over the contents of an adjustment program; otherwise, the delay between a Fund agreement and a (hopefully much larger) inflow of aid-financed balance of payments support might be as long as a year. The greater the volume of aid funds that could be mobilized in this form, and the closer in time to a Fund agreement these fast-disbursing funds could be arranged to flow, the less painful would Fund programs need to be.

It is envisaged, therefore, that the international agencies could play an important catalytic role in arranging donor support for adjustment programs, in much the same way that the Fund deals with commercial bank consortia in large debtor countries. This type of initiative would be acceptable to many SSA governments, however, only if it complemented and supported alternative approaches to adjustment and, at the same time, recognized that the principal responsibility for aid coordination lies with recipient countries; otherwise it might serve only to increase external leverage over SSA in imposing an adjustment model that is, to say the least, contested. It might also undermine or preempt efforts of SSA governments to assert their aid-coordination responsibilities—an area in which there is much room for improved performance.

Alternative programs would explicitly outline their likely distributional implications. Generally, they would be accompanied by a clearly spelled-out incomes policy (Foxley (1983)) which would contain the government's view of how the burden of adjustment would be borne. Ideally, it should make provision for incentive programs so that urban workers could be encouraged to minimize cuts in real income through increases in their productivity. Those countries committed to ensuring greater equity might wish to safeguard a portion of the government budget committed to such basic expenditures as health, education, and water supply, and to monitor the impact of adjustment measures on the receipt of such services by those groups considered particularly vulnerable. The well-being of children should, of course, be of prime concern in this exercise, and concrete measures should be taken to prevent increases in the incidence of infant mortality, malnutrition, and deprivation of food, water, health care, and education. Efforts to reduce budget deficits would, as far as possible, therefore protect these expenditures and focus on restraining spending in other areas or on raising revenues. The less well-off sections of society might also be given a degree of protection against austere adjustment measures through the maintenance of limited subsidies on basic food items, through price control on, or rationing of, items important in their budgets or through increases in the minimum wage. Each of these is open to objections on efficiency grounds, but may be justified in terms of equity where it can be shown that their benefits accrue predominantly to the low-income target groups. The severity of the economic crisis in SSA is such that it would be impossible to protect all low-income groups fully from the impact of adjustment measures. The best that can be hoped for is a more equitable sharing of the burden and a concerted effort to prevent basic needs from being eroded altogether. In this respect, the restoration of positive per capita growth rates, and an unambiguous focus on expanded food production would greatly facilitate more equitable stabilization programs. By the same token, this approach suggests the removal of price control on all but essential goods and the focusing of (limited) subsidies on commodities consumed largely by the poor.

Alternative approaches to Fund stabilization would, therefore, be more supply oriented than are traditional Fund programs, would avoid shock treatment and provide for more gradual, longer-term adjustment with more sensitivity to distributional issues. Strategic implications of stabilization measures would be put much more to the fore, and an across-the-board commitment to export promotion would be avoided. Food security would be assigned first priority, and provision would be made for the pursuit of other strategies consistent with the Lagos Plan of Action. Nevertheless, increased exports would be encouraged since additional foreign exchange earnings would be needed to finance this eclectic strategic approach, to help pay off debt-servicing responsibilities and to help reduce dependence on external aid.

This approach places less reliance on market forces than would the Fund and envisages a blend of direct controls and state intervention together with enhanced use of the price mechanism in certain areas. The precise mix would again vary from country to country. Likewise, there is no a priori assumption in this alternative approach that foreign private investment is either necessary or desirable in the forms and amounts in which it is likely to appear. For most SSA countries it seems likely that shifting the composition of aid and arranging debt relief will be of more practical relevance than encouraging foreign private capital inflows, but there will undoubtedly be exceptions to this.

It should also be evident that this type of alternative approach would place less emphasis on short-run demand restraint than the Fund's usual approach. Supply expansion, especially when based on easing the import bottleneck, would in fact require an increase in working capital, and domestic credit should be expanded accordingly in the sectors concerned, or else recovery will be inhibited. Some degree of demand restraint will still be required on significant sections of society if expenditure switching and the income-redistribution implications of adjustment are to be allowed to proceed. In this respect, control over budget deficits will continue to be a major focus of stabilization although, even there, supply-led adjustment would put more emphasis on achieving this through expanded budget revenues than would an approach which focuses disproportionately on short-run demand restraint. Nevertheless, there must be consistency in macroeconomic policy to ensure movement toward both external balance (a situation in which exports fill the gap between trend-import needs and anticipated longer-term capital inflows) and internal balance over a reasonable period. Demand restraint will undoubtedly have some role to play; what is at issue is not so much the need for it as the degree, timing, and distributional impact of that restraint.

There would still be a need for performance criteria, but these would be designed to reflect the changed emphasis of conditionality. They would be more in the nature of contingent conditions than fixed requirements (Williamson (1982)) and would be adjusted without penalty in the context of unforeseen international developments that might disrupt adjustment plans, including unplanned rear-end loading of programs because of delays in receipt of financial assistance.

Finally, African programs should provide for the strengthening of the research capacity of African governments and for improvements in the quality and the coverage of the SSA data base. Fund positions are sometimes based on extremely dubious figures, and disputes about data have led to problems between the Fund and SSA governments in the past. The international institutions themselves might also usefully devote more resources to studying the adjustment capacities of SSA countries and especially the distributional implications of alternative approaches. Resources should also be made available to enable SSA governments to purchase advice and assistance from overseas to facilitate the preparation of adjustment programs where local technical capacity is inadequate. Provision should also be made for the arbitration of differences between the Fund and SSA governments where these have led to a breakdown in negotiations. These are not novel proposals (see, e.g., Helleiner (1983)), but they continue to be valid proposals.

Adjustment and Finance Revisited

It is evident that alternatives of the type proposed would require SSA adjustment efforts to receive more financial support than they have up until now. The emphases on reducing supply bottlenecks, on gradualism and long-term programs, on equity, and on national economic integration would all imply greater demands on external financial assistance than would orthodox adjustment programs. If the Fund is to consider altering its approach along these lines it would also need to reassess its policies with regard to financing. A structuralist response to external shocks will inevitably require more financing than orthodox responses. The case for allowing poorer countries access to more liquidity—through allocations of SDRs, expanded quotas, or larger borrowing limits relative to quota, through a liberalized compensatory financing facility—is a powerful one, but it has met with little sympathy from the Fund and the countries that control that institution. The result has been that programs inevitably entail more shock treatment than many governments can sustain politically. Alternatively, and as the international institutions themselves admit, current programs in SSA can offer only partial recovery and face a high risk of collapse, even when governments possess the political determination to implement the required adjustments (World Bank (1985)). The creation of the World Bank's Joint Program of Action for SSA is a step in the right direction. Its effectiveness will depend crucially, however, on the extent to which it can mobilize further net new funds from bilateral donors and, above all, on the willingness of both the Fund and the Bank to be more flexible in their approach to conditionality.

References

Adelman, Irma, "Beyond Export-Led Growth," *World Development* (Oxford), Vol. 12, No. 9 (September 1984), pp. 937–54.

African Caucus, Memorandum of the African Caucus of the World Bank and the International Monetary Fund on the World Bank's Report entitled "Accelerated Development in sub-Saharan Africa: An Agenda," in *The Lagos Plan of Action vs. The Berg Report*, by Robert S. Browne and Robert J. Cummings (Washington: Howard University, 1984), Appendix 3.

Amin, Samir, "Accumulation and Development: A Theoretical Model," *Review of African Political Economy* (Sheffield), No. 1 (1974).

The Arusha Initiative, *Development Dialogue* (Uppsala), No. 2 (1980), pp. 10–23.

Balassa, Bela, "Structural Adjustment Policies in Developing Economies," *World Development* (Oxford), Vol. 10, No. 1 (January 1982), pp. 23–38.

Beza, Sterie T., Comments in *IMF Conditionality*, ed. by John Williamson (Washington: Institute for International Economics, 1983), pp. 589–93.

Brandt Commission, *North-South: A Programme for Survival: Report of the Independent Commission on International Development Issues* (Cambridge: Massachusetts Institute of Technology, 1980).

Browne, Robert S. and Robert J. Cummings, *The Lagos Plan of Action vs. The Berg Report* (Washington: Howard University, 1984).

Cline, William R., "Can the East Asian Model of Development be Generalised?" *World Development* (Oxford), Vol. 10, No. 2 (February 1982), pp. 81–90.

Crockett, Andrew D., "Stabilization Policies in Developing Countries," *Staff Papers*, International Monetary Fund (Washington), Vol. 28 (March 1981), pp. 54–79.

Dale, William B., "Financing and Adjustment of Payments Imbalances," in *IMF Conditionality*, ed. by John Williamson (Washington: Institute for International Economics, 1983), pp. 3–16.

Dell, Sidney, *On Being Grandmotherly: The Evolution of IMF Conditionality*, Essays in International Finance, No. 144 (Princeton, New Jersey: Princeton University, 1981).

________, "Stabilization: The Political Economy of Overkill" in *IMF Conditionality*, ed. by John Williamson (Washington: Institute for International Economics, 1983), pp. 17–45.

———, "Conceptions and Misconceptions of Adjustment," in *Adjustment with Growth: A Search for an Equitable Solution*, ed. by K. Haq and C. Massad (Islamabad: North-South Roundtable, 1984), pp. 217–28.

Foxley, Alejandro, *Latin American Experiments in Neo-Conservative Economics* (Berkeley: University of California Press, 1983).

Giovannini, Alberto, "The Interest Elasticity of Savings in Developing Countries: The Existing Evidence," *World Development* (Oxford), Vol. 11, No. 7 (July 1983), pp. 601–607.

Gold, Joseph, *Conditionality*, IMF Pamphlet Series, No. 31 (Washington: International Monetary Fund, 1979).

Green, R.H., "Incentives, Policies, Participation and Response: Reflections on World Bank Policies and Priorities in Agriculture," *IDS Bulletin* (Brighton, Sussex), Vol. 14, No. 1 (January 1983), pp. 30–38.

Guitian, Manuel, *Fund Conditionality: Evolution of Principles and Practices*, IMF Pamphlet Series, No. 38 (Washington: International Monetary Fund, 1981).

Helleiner, Gerald K., *The IMF and Africa in the 1980s*, Essays in International Finance, No. 152 (Princeton, New Jersey: Princeton University, 1983).

International Monetary Fund, *Annual Report of the Executive Board for the Financial Year Ended April 30, 1982* (Washington, 1982), p. 55.

———, "African Adjustment Programs," *IMF Survey* (Washington), August 22, 1983, p. 244.

Kaldor, Nicholas, "Devaluation and Adjustment in Developing Countries," *Finance and Development* (Washington), Vol. 20, No. 2 (June 1983), pp. 35–37.

Killick, Tony, "IMF Stabilisation Programmes," *Overseas Development Institute Working Paper* (London), No. 6 (September 1981), pp. 1–56.

———, "The Impact of IMF Stabilisation Programmes in Developing Countries," in *Overseas Development Institute Working Paper* (London), No. 7 (March 1982), pp. 1–40.

———, ed., *The IMF and Stabilisation* (London: Heinemann, 1984).

———, and others, "The IMF; Case for a Change in Emphasis," in *Adjustment Crisis in the Third World*, ed. by Richard E. Feinberg and Valeriana Kallab (Washington: Overseas Development Council, 1984).

Lanyi, Anthony and Rusdu Saracoglu, "The Importance of Interest Rates in Developing Countries," *Finance and Development* (Washington), Vol. 20, No. 2 (June 1983), pp. 20–23.

de Larosière, J., *Does the Fund Impose Austerity?* (Washington: International Monetary Fund, 1984a).

———, "Stability and Sustainable Growth," *IMF Survey* (Washington), March 26, 1984b, p. 84.

Loxley, John, "The Behaviour of the Tanzania Money Supply, 1966–70, and the Use of Monetary Indicators," *Papers on the Political Economy of Tanzania*, ed. by Kwan S. Kim and others (London: Heinemann, 1979), pp. 133–42.

———, *The IMF and the Poorest Countries* (Ottawa: North-South Institute, 1984a).

———, *External Finance and Structural Adjustment in Third World Countries* (Ottawa: North-South Institute, 1984b).

———, "The World Bank and the Model of Accumulation," in *The Politics of Agriculture in Tropical Africa*, ed. by Jonathan Barker (London: Sage, 1984c).

Mikesell, Raymond F., "Appraising IMF Conditionality: Too Loose, Too Tight or Just Right?" in *IMF Conditionality*, ed. by John Williamson (Washington: Institute for International Economics, 1983), pp. 47–71.

Mookerjee, Subimal, "Countries Tackling Large Payments Imbalances Often Need a Medium-Term Adjustment Strategy," *IMF Survey* (Washington), Vol. 11 (August 30, 1982), pp. 274–79.

Morse, Elliot R., "Institutional Destruction Resulting from Donor and Project Proliferation in sub-Saharan African Countries," *World Development* (Oxford), Vol. 12, No. 4 (April 1984), pp. 465–70.

Nelson, Joan M., "The Politics of Stabilization," in *Adjustment Crisis in the Third World*, ed. by Richard Feinberg and Valeriana Kallab (Washington: Overseas Development Council, 1984), pp. 99–118.

Nowzad, Bahram, *The IMF and its Critics*, Essays in International Finance, No. 146 (Princeton, New Jersey: Princeton University, 1981).

Nyerere, Julius Kambarage, ''No to IMF Meddling,'' *Development Dialogue* (Uppsala), No. 2 (1980), pp. 7–9.

Organization for African Unity, *The Lagos Plan of Action for the Economic Development of Africa, 1980–2000* (Geneva: International Institute for Labor Studies, 1981).

Payer, Cheryl, ''Tanzania and the World Bank,'' *Third World Quarterly* (London), No. 5 (October 1983), pp. 791–813.

Please, Stanley, *The Hobbled Giant—Essays on the World Bank* (Boulder: Westview Press, 1984).

Reichmann, Tomás M., ''The Fund's Conditional Assistance and the Problems of Adjustment 1973–75,'' *Finance and Development* (Washington), Vol. 15, No. 4 (December 1978), pp. 38–41.

Schydlowsky, Daniel M., ''Alternative Approaches to Short Term Economic Management,'' Center for Latin American Development Studies, Discussion Paper No. 50 (Boston: Boston University, 1981).

Sen, Amartya Kumar, *Poverty and Famines: An Essay in Entitlement and Deprivation* (Oxford: Clarendon Press, 1981).

Stewart, Frances, ''Alternative Conditionality,'' *Development* (Rome), No. 1 (1984), pp. 64–76.

Streeten, Paul, ''A Cool Look at Outward-Looking Strategies for Development,'' *The World Economy* (Oxford), Vol. 5 (September 1982), pp. 259–69.

Taylor, Lance, ''IS/LM in the Tropics: Diagrammatics of the New Structuralist Macro Critique,'' in *Economic Stabilization in Developing Countries*, ed. by William Cline and Sidney Weintraub (Washington: The Brookings Institution, 1981), pp. 465–506.

________, *Structuralist Macroeconomics: Applicable Models for the Third World* (New York: Basic Books, 1983).

Thorp, Rosemary and Lawrence Whitehead, eds., *Inflation and Stabilisation in Latin America* (London: Macmillan, 1979).

United Nations, *1982 Yearbook of International Trade Statistics*, Vol. 1, Trade by Country (New York: United Nations, 1984).

UNICEF, *The Impact of World Recession on Children* (New York: UNICEF, 1984).

Wheeler, David, "Sources of Stagnation in Sub-Saharan Africa," *World Development* (Oxford), Vol. 12, No. 1 (January 1984), pp. 1–23.

Wijnbergen, Sweder van, "Stagflationary Effects of Monetary Stabilization Policies: A Quantitative Analysis of South Korea," *Journal of Development Economies* (Amsterdam), Vol. 10, No. 2 (April 1982), pp. 133–69.

Williamson, John, *The Lending Policies of the International Monetary Fund* (Washington: Institute for International Economics, 1982).

________, ed., *IMF Conditionality* (Washington: Institute for International Economics, 1983a).

________, "A Comparison of Macroeconomic Strategies in South America," *Development Policy Review* (London), Vol. 1 (May 1983b), pp. 22–33.

________, *The Open Economy and the World Economy* (New York: Basic Books, 1983c).

World Bank, *Accelerated Development in Sub-Saharan Africa* (Washington: World Bank, 1981).

________, *Sub-Saharan Africa: Progress Report on Development Prospects and Programs* (Washington: World Bank, 1983).

________, *Toward Sustained Development in Sub-Saharan Africa: A Joint Program of Action* (Washington: World Bank, 1984).

Zulu, Justin B., and Saleh M. Nsouli, "Adjustment Programs in Africa," *Finance and Development* (Washington), Vol. 21, No. 1 (March 1984), pp. 5–9.

Comments

Azizali F. Mohammed

I have two preliminary difficulties in commenting on Professor Loxley's paper. First, it is such a cornucopia of ideas about the Fund, some rather critical, that it is difficult to know where to begin. Second, he is so fair minded that for almost every criticism he also supplies the counter-arguments. I find this particularly true in the case of the alternative strategy that he proposes when he states that much of the diagnosis on domestic policy shortcomings has validity, must be addressed, and for this reason, "alternative prescriptions will unavoidably contain many similarities with those advocated by the Fund and the Bank."

Now, as one looks at the alternative program, one major characteristic stands out. All alternatives presented, whether they emphasize the reduction of supply bottlenecks, gradualism in adjustment, longer-term programs, or more equity-based programs, imply greater demand "on external financial assistance than would orthodox programs." I would suggest that here the basic issue is joined. One cannot fairly compare two programs, one of which assumes a larger supply of finance than the other. The question therefore becomes, "What are the possibilities that one could evoke larger amounts of finance?" Professor Loxley has asked this question quite fairly, and I propose to answer it with equal honesty because I feel that the financial constraint is the fundamental constraint within which the Fund operates.

If one were starting with a clean slate for individual countries, this issue could perhaps be addressed in a far more constructive way, but it so happens that we are in the middle of an ongoing process. We have had four years of substantial injections of Fund money—SDR 4.4 billion into sub-Saharan Africa. The total amounts outstanding are SDR 6.1 billion at the end of 1984. If you look at the relationship between credit outstanding and Fund quotas—and I am including here all use of Fund resources, conditional credit, the compensatory financing facility, and the Trust Fund—for country after country the percentage of Fund credit extended relative to quota is already high. It is over 200 percent in most cases and in some cases approaches 400 percent. There are "track records" and institutional memories. There have been problems of arrears with certain countries. It becomes difficult to speak of larger financing flows when there is a perception in the institution that very large sums have already been committed and that therefore the prospects of continuing to make commitments on the same scale are not practical.

I would go a step further. Not only can we not expect to continue to provide resources on the same scale: it is probable that resources will be injected on a reduced scale in the coming years. This is reality. And one must accept this reality because one is also facing, at this time, a growing sense of uneasiness on the part of the countries that finance the Fund. The creditors of the Fund look at the figures of rising arrears, for instance. They look at what they call "prolonged use" of the Fund's resources, where one program follows another year after year, and they ask, "How can we regard the resources we have provided to the Fund as part of our liquid reserves?" When one talks about putting in larger amounts for longer periods of time, one is talking about a fundamental change in the character of the institution. I do not venture to ask whether that change should or should not take place. I am merely pointing out that the creditors of the institution are faced with a major issue of how the Fund will develop. Will it remain a monetary institution? In that case, it will continue to get support. Or will it become a surrogate long-term lender? In that case, the risk becomes real that the Fund will be unable to raise quotas or even to obtain larger resources from existing quotas or lines of credit such as the General Arrangements to Borrow. I am sure that over the next few years the Fund will continue to provide additional amounts in individual cases, but the chances that it may be unable to do so in all cases should be taken into account in recommendations made for its future development.

This leads to a second point. If one cannot think of the Fund providing a substantial part of the financing, then one must look more carefully at the catalytic role of the Fund, the ability of the Fund to influence donors and creditors to provide more resources. Here I would agree with Professor Loxley that where large changes in policies are being made, particularly in exchange rate policies, it is essential that resources be available, preferably in advance, to make sure that the framework of incentives created through the exchange rate change will be supported through larger imports that remove supply bottlenecks and strengthen and reinforce the creation of new capacity.

As a practical matter, one must look carefully at the modalities of the "gap-filling" exercises in which the Fund has been engaged in the past two or three years to draw lessons out of this experience. Occasionally these exercises have involved commitments by donors that have not always led to disbursements in the period promised. We need to be thinking carefully about how to plan these gap-filling exercises prudently so as to ensure that the resources that are committed will, in fact, disburse in the periods assumed in the programs. This applies not only to the timing but also to the quality of disbursements. It is no use obtaining funds to aid projects if one is looking at the moment to commodity aid or program assistance. This is another area in which one must use the Fund as well as one's own relationships with donors in order to get the right quality and quantity of external resources.

Third, there is the question of the timetable of Paris Club and London Club debt reschedulings. These timetables can slip, and when they slip, programs may fall out of line. Here again it is important to be quite sure that one is correctly planning these debt reschedulings and the bilateral agreements that follow the multilateral minute in the Paris Club, to be sure that one is getting the right amounts at the right times.

Finally, in all these matters, one must be quite sure that the commitments the country itself has made will materialize on schedule and on the terms envisaged in the program. Otherwise, one is not only risking the credibility of the country, but also the credibility of the institution that provided the judgment on the correct balance between financing and adjustment, determined the size of the gap that had to be filled, and specified the type of resources that would be required from other lenders or donors. If the adjustment is not forthcoming, the gap becomes larger. Clearly one loses credibility. And here one must look at this question of how far one can push the Fund into this catalytic role without, at the same time, becoming responsible for protecting its credibility. Credibility cannot be protected through public relations or image building by the institution itself. The image of the institution remains in the hands of its members.

Let me move on to another major issue raised by Professor Loxley—the distributional consequences of Fund programs and the apparent lack of sensitivity on the part of the Fund. May I suggest that distributional issues are so highly political that for an international institution to seek to influence these issues would be regarded by most, if not all, governments as an intolerable violation of national sovereignty? There is simply no way that a Fund mission chief could say to national officials that they should protect the salaries of their teachers and cut down the salaries of their policemen or that they should do something to reduce defense expenditures. The Fund staff would be told immediately that "this is not part of your mandate; please stick to the macroeconomic issues.'' Finally, I must say that there exists a basic misunderstanding between us on the Fund staff and Professor Loxley regarding his sense of Fund programs being somehow imposed. There is no way that can be done. The Fund staff is dealing with countries on the basis of clearly established rules and on the basis of the decisions of our Executive Board. In that Executive Board, every member country is represented. When negotiation for the use of Fund resources takes place, the Executive Director is often present. He is aware of all precedents; he is aware of how other countries have been treated in similar circumstances; and he is going to fight for the country during the negotiations and in the Executive Board. Let us not depreciate the important role that our Executive Directors play in this negotiating process, and let us not ignore the fact that the Fund is here dealing with a sovereign member government that knows its business, that knows its priorities, and that knows precisely how it wishes to use the Fund at a particular time. All this talk about impositions strikes me as totally surreal. After all, it is the national officials who are putting their careers on the line. It is they who are making the difficult decisions. It is they who will face the political consequences of either success or failure. Hence, there is a basic difference between us on the question of what role the Fund can play in distributional issues and on the general issue of how programs are developed and how programs are implemented.

Julio Jimenez

In these remarks, I would like to address some of the practical problems of Fund missions and Mr. Loxley's suggested new approach. After many years of reviewing developments in Africa, I have difficulty in generalizing experiences from country to country. I was glad this morning that Professor Loxley advised us that his paper had Tanzania as its point of departure. I think, however, he errs in generalizing this experience to represent the experience of sub-Saharan Africa. For example, many stand-by arrangements in this region of Africa have not included exchange rate alterations. By and large, each country provides a different set of problems deserving a separate approach.

Programming for a stand-by arrangement is a race between adjustment and available resources plus debt service. Within this overall limitation, the approach is flexible. We have been reminded that in 1981–82 many stand-by arrangements, or rather an increasing proportion of stand-by arrangements, faced difficulties. Many of these had to be scrapped and begun again. This observation is true enough, but it does not represent the whole picture. Reference should be made to what these years reflected in the world economy. Few could, and few did, estimate the depth of the recession at that time or the magnitude of the fall in commodity prices. It is, however, a sign of the flexibility with which the Fund has approached these problems that many programs were reinstated after close consultation with the authorities.

The figures of the resource flows from the Fund to sub-Saharan Africa deserve a comparative look. Net flows from the Fund to sub-Saharan Africa during this period represented close to one third on average of the financing of the overall deficits of these countries. While it is difficult to measure exactly what other catalytic effects Fund programs may have produced, one item can be identified, and this is the relief that sub-Saharan countries gained from rescheduling. Rescheduling, on average, financed another 30 percent of the overall deficit. Resources from the Fund and financing made available by rescheduling probably provided about 15 percent greater inflow of imports than would have been available without these two sources.

The Fund staff must work within the realities of the world economy and certainly within the guidelines set by the Governors and the Executive Board. One of the problems in the negotiations of stand-by arrangements is estimating available resource flows. It is common to find authorities overoptimistic about the likely flow of resources, as well as about their ability to negotiate loans and make use of them within a given period. Stand-by arrangements must have a balance of resources to be successful. These arrangements are always reviewed several times, when problems can be discussed afresh and, most important, include a consultation clause of benefit both to the country and to the Fund. At any moment if authorities, for any reason, feel that the stand-by arrangement they have entered into has become unrealistic, they can call for a consultative review. It is, of course, better if these consultations are held before a major departure from the objectives of the stand-by arrangement.

During this symposium, I have heard unwarranted statements about the weakness of many African economies. We hear of disjointed economies and the lack of supply response, and I think perhaps we are misjudging these economies. As for the integration, it is only necessary to see how efficient parallel markets can grow in cases of disequilibrium and how quickly these parallel markets can reflect factors of scarcity and factors of risk. Economies respond to proper incentives. The comments of the Governor of Ghana contain an adequate estimate of how quick the response is to proper policies. A characteristic of countries in disequilibrium is a substantial shortfall in production. Proper incentives would allow this unutilized capacity to be brought on stream once more. In effect, even with some tree crops, such as tea, proper incentives have allowed increased fertilization and plucking of leaves to increase the productivity of the planted acreages. Viewing events in Africa, I think it is unrealistic to deny that peasant farmers react swiftly to incentives. Peasant farmers also respond quickly when incentives are not correct by not producing up to expectations.

We have, on various occasions, talked about the speed of adjustment and its relationship to access to the Fund. The Fund is realistic in believing that many of the deep-seated problems cannot be resolved in one year. Some countries have been in stand-by relationships for three or four years because they have made progress in adjustment, allowing the Fund to continue to provide the needed financial support. In other parts of the world—Mexico, for example—a quicker response has been expected from the economy and a shock treatment was given. The type and magnitude of policies applied in Mexico are not the sort that we would be applying to our African members. Policies must be proportioned to current disequilibria.

It is wrong to view Fund programs as simply concerned with financial matters. Most Fund programs include from the beginning a long series of supply-oriented measures. Such measures as adequate pricing, reduced public sector deficits (both in the government budget and public enterprises), and improved financial savings help transfer increased financial savings to more productive uses. Financial matters are, of course, closely monitored. Why? Because the Fund does not want inadequate financial policies to destroy the progress being made under the supply-oriented policies. Certainly, you can set up adequate producer prices, but if you have inadequate financial policies, you will find that they will quickly fall out of line and require additional changes. It is an inadequate interpretation to say that Fund conditionality is "pinpoint" conditionality. Credit limitations and budgetary objectives are outer margins. A country can fall anywhere outside these limits and have no difficulty in meeting the targets.

J.S. Addo

Instead of commenting on Mr. Loxley's paper directly, I would like to tell the story of Ghana, because I believe that in the process I may be able to illustrate some of the points that he has raised.

I would like to start by giving you a brief idea about the history of the country. Ghana was, during the late 1950s and the 1960s, the world's leading producer of cocoa. We produced 500,000 tons of cocoa annually. The industry comprised mainly peasant farmers. There was no state participation. Ghana in the 1960s was also the fifth or sixth most important gold producer in the world. The situation in 1981–82 was, however, as follows. GDP declined in 1982 by 6.4 percent; population increased by nearly 3 percent. Our export proceeds declined from just over $1 billion to just under $600 million. Our budgeted deficits constituted 4.4 percent of GDP, and we had an inflation rate of 122 percent. We had a regimen of controls: price controls, import controls, distribution controls. The list was so long as to cover almost every item.

The actual situation (and I have lived through it) in 1982 and the early part of 1983 could be briefly described as follows. We had to queue for days for oil, for food items, for soap, for toilet paper, in fact, for everything. We had to walk long distances because there were no vehicles, either because they had no tires or batteries, or because we could not get petrol. Food could not be brought into the cities from the rural areas for lack of transportation. Farmers had no fuel for tractors nor could they buy fertilizers. In the export sector we had overvalued the currency for a very long period. We had arrived at a stage where even for timber and gold the export proceeds converted into the local currency at the overvalued exchange rate were insufficient to cover the producer costs. The economy was spiralling down, but we had subsidies on petrol and other items, even though they were not available. We reached a stage that we had to barter goods.

We explored various avenues for addressing the situation and finally in late 1982 we decided to go to the Fund. We negotiated with the Fund. The resulting program was not imposed on us, because we went through it in detail. In some cases we rejected or argued against the Fund's proposals; I will cite only two instances—interest rates and wages—where we disagreed with the Fund, and after some discussion our point of view prevailed.

In April 1983 we entered into the first stand-by arrangement with the Fund. We have the usual Fund conditions, which I am not going to go over, and we complied with them. We adjusted the exchange rate in one year by 91 percent. We liberalized prices and distribution and we continued to reduce the arrears position. We eliminated subsidies. We were able to perform satisfactorily under the first stand-by, so we entered into the second stand-by last year. The program is on track, and by the end of 1983 we achieved growth in GDP of 0.7 percent. In 1984 we had a growth of 7.6 percent.

Inflation has been reduced—we have the rate of inflation down to about 36 percent—and we have been able to give price incentives to farmers. At the same time as the drawings on the Fund, the World Bank gave us a quick-disbursing facility for the reconstruction of import credits to help improve supply, particularly in the productive sectors, namely agriculture, transportation, and timber.

By the end of 1984, we had improved our agricultural production. We were able to increase production of maize, for instance, so as to export 20,000 tons to neighboring countries. For 1985 we projected a GDP growth rate of 5.5 percent and a budget deficit ratio to GDP of 2 percent, with an inflation rate of 20 percent.

The strategy of the program was, first of all, to fill the gap in the balance of payments position; second, to rehabilitate the export and the agricultural sector so that we could stabilize export capability in the short run. As a result, we have already seen an improvement in cocoa production despite the fact that it is a tree crop. We expect this year a significant improvement in timber exports, and we think that the improvement in agricultural production will continue. The program I tried to describe briefly has had the support of the World Bank, of the donor community, and of other multilateral financial agencies. We think that with satisfactory performance we should be able to succeed.

The point I would like to emphasize here is that the alternative approaches suggested by Professor Loxley's paper do not constitute a package. Some countries are already implementing some of the individual measures he recommends, but probably not in the degree he would wish. For the type of problem we have, we need a complete package of macroeconomic measures. The macroeconomic measures cannot solve the rural problems, and I would suggest strongly that we look at every possible alternative to the conventional Fund program. If we can design one ourselves, we will be in a better position to suggest improvements in the existing methods of operation of the Fund.

The responsibility for the Fund program is ours, and its management is also ours. After a program with the Fund has been agreed upon, we implement it. In the course of implementation there may be problems, such as administrative bottlenecks and physical constraints, which in the end may undermine the success of the program. Managing the program is consequently important. I think that Governors should look at this aspect seriously, because all the economic and financial problems of the country surface in our offices. If, in implementing a program, we do not anticipate the changing situation and do not design systems to enable us to respond to developments, we may find it difficult indeed to implement the program successfully. This requires effort on the part of all economic units in the country, and there is need for coordination at the country level in implementing a program. We Governors have the responsibility, the management responsibility, and this is an aspect that I, for one, want the Fund to reexamine. In regard to failed programs, they may not wish to tell us here, but we should be able to tell whether the fault is ours as managers of the program, or if it is the Fund's, or that of somebody else.

John Williamson

My first comment relates to what Mr. Mohammed said on the difficult question of income distribution. Is it a fact that the Fund never adopts an attitude on what particular programs should contain? Do food subsidies never come in for particular criticism? Is the claim of Fund "neutrality" true or not true? I think we have to ask that question. Second, a comment on national sovereignty. Clearly there is a problem here; it would be unrealistic, even if one thought it appropriate, for the Fund to start trying to tell a country whether it should be policemen or teachers whose salaries are to be cut. Nevertheless, there is surely an intermediate stage at which the Fund should attempt to estimate the distributional impact of the program decided by the country and to pass on the estimate to the Executive Board with the observation that "if the generals go on living well, the populace won't." Maybe some countries wouldn't like to see a program with that sort of implication going up before the Executive Board. Maybe it would help a little bit without in any way curtailing national sovereignty.

Reply

John Loxley

For those who came to this symposium seeking a genuine dialogue, the vigor with which Fund staff defend the status quo must be a source of great disappointment. The Fund apparently sees no need to change its approach to stabilization in Africa; this is evident from the focus of staff papers and commentaries on what the Fund considers its success stories. But surely this is only part of the total picture. Is there nothing to be learned from the large number of Fund programs that have failed, including those that have resulted in political upheaval for member countries, or from experiences with countries with which the Fund has been unable to reach agreement? Surely a dialogue requires an even-handed assessment of Fund experience.

Mr. Mohammed, for example, is not prepared to consider any changes of Fund policy even when these could be accommodated within the Fund's financial constraints. Thus, while agreeing that front-end loading of finance is desirable to facilitate policy adjustments by member countries, he suggests that such financing be found from sources other than the Fund. Likewise, both he and Mr. Jimenez avoid dealing with the critique that a series of one-year stand-by arrangements has quite different policy and planning implications from those of a single loan for the same overall period under the extended Fund facility. The former inevitably focuses on adjustments that can be made within a year and therefore disproportionately on demand adjustments. The latter would involve no additional financial commitment, but would permit a more gradual and a more supply-oriented adjustment. Other proposals that could be accommodated within the existing level of resources are those of greater involvement by member countries in the design of alternative programs; greater selectivity in allocating foreign exchange to imports and in the design of export incentives; a greater emphasis on food security; a less dogmatic faith in market forces; a shift of emphasis in the nature of performance criteria and a greater awareness of distributional implications. This list is not exhaustive but suggests ample scope for alternative approaches that do not necessarily imply the need for greater financial commitment by the Fund.

At the same time it is interesting to note that the staff faithfully reiterate the Fund's position that its resources are rigidly restricted at this time. Given widespread excess capacity in the Third World and elsewhere, a strong case can be made for an expansion of Fund resources. Expanded allocations of SDRs would be the ideal method of seeking to inject further resources into the poorer countries of the Third World; the creation of special concessional funds through expanded quotas would be a second best method, while a revitalized compensatory financing facility or larger borrowing limits relative to quota would also be helpful. Third World countries continue to press for such reforms in the face of determined monetarist opposition from the Fund and the major powers that control it, because their perception is that the Fund is not now fulfilling its mandate. It is a moot point whether proposals for expanded funding are any less practical than the Fund's insistence that the current crisis in the Third World can be met by more assiduous application of austerity programs. If, as one strongly suspects, current Fund approaches fail to contain the African economic crisis, then the politics of disaster may force the Fund to consider more expansionary approaches.

Mr. Mohammed states that the Fund does not seek to influence distributional issues as this would constitute "an intolerable violation of national sovereignty." This is a remarkable statement. Fund conditionality affects income distribution both directly and indirectly. The abolition of urban food subsidies, restrictions on the growth of urban money wages, the imposition of user fees for government services, and the raising of export producer prices, for instance, all directly affect income distribution. What is more, it is through the distributional impact of such measures that resources are reallocated or demand is restrained. That the Fund undertakes no comprehensive accounting of the full distributional impact of its programs does not make that impact any less real. It is difficult to see how a proposal for a clear spelling out of the likely distributional implications of adjustment programs in the context of incomes policies articulated by member governments themselves could in any way be said to breach national sovereignty. On the other hand, it could be claimed with some justification that member governments are frequently not aware of the full distributional consequences of programs designed by the Fund and are not, therefore, in a position to propose alternatives.

Furthermore, while it is true technically that the Fund does not impose its programs on member governments, it is equally true that the Fund is a lender of last resort. In a generalized crisis, such as that now faced by Africa, the options facing member countries are limited. It is precisely now that the inflexibility of the Fund, and especially its take-it-or-leave-it attitude toward governments with which it disagrees, is particularly costly for African governments.

I disagree with the Governor of the Bank of Ghana that my alternative proposals do not constitute a package. Indeed, I would argue that they present a more comprehensive package than the one he outlines. In this connection, I am particularly struck by the absence of any mention by him of food production and the distributional implications of recent programs. Moreover, I do not share his optimism about the recovery of traditional exports since it seems that the recovery of cocoa output has precipitated a fall in world prices.

He is correct, however, in stressing, as Mr. Jimenez does, that there is some supply elasticity in most African economies. My point is that there are clear limits to that elasticity, limits set in part by import constraint and in part by the structural nature of obstacles to both output and export expansion. Once the immediate slack in the economy has been picked up, and this can only be achieved by a significant capital inflow, it becomes more difficult to expand output or exports, and it certainly takes time.

External Debt Management in the African Context

Eduard H. Brau

The widespread and prolonged debt-servicing difficulties among African countries are the financial reflection of the disappointments and problems encountered in many sectors of the real economy. Policies directed at achieving sustained improvement in underlying economic trends are therefore prerequisite to improving the debt-servicing capacity, and hence the creditworthiness, of many African economies. But such policies alone are insufficient to deal adequately with existing debt-servicing difficulties or to establish a framework for improved policy on external indebtedness.[1]

This paper focuses on external debt management issues that also must be addressed, after first highlighting in a series of tables the distinctive features of external debt in the African context. It then discusses objectives, constraints, and operational problems in alleviating service payments on existing external debt. This discussion is followed by suggestions for improving the framework within which future credit flows should be managed. An annex lists technical assistance made available to African countries by the Fund and World Bank in external debt management.

Principal Features of External Debt in Africa

Statistical material on the external debt and debt service of African countries from a variety of perspectives is contained in the Annex. The key features that seem to define the African context may be summarized as follows:

1. In comparison with low-income countries in Asia, African countries have a relatively high share of debt to private financial institutions in their

[1]For a discussion of these issues, see *External Debt Management*, ed. by Hassanali Mehran (Washington: International Monetary Fund, 1985).

outstanding public external debt (Tables 1 and 2). The ratio of external debt to GDP and of external debt to exports of goods and services has been rising very fast for sub-Saharan Africa (Table 3), substantially because of a slow increase in export earnings by sub-Saharan African economies.

2. Substantial arrears on commercial payments, as well as on debt-service payments, are relatively frequent (Table 4), and a large number of African countries have already sought a rescheduling of debt-service obligations with commercial banks and with official creditors, mainly through the Paris Club (Table 5).

3. There is a sharp rise in scheduled debt-service payments on the existing stock of external debt for nearly all countries in 1985–86, mainly on account

Table 1. Africa's External Debt, 1975–84
(billions of dollars)

	1975	1980	1981	1982	1983	1984
Africa[1]	**22.7**	**77.2**	**83.9**	**94.5**	**101.3**	**104.3**
Medium- and long-term	22.6	73.2	80.0	83.9	92.6	96.8
Of which (percent share):						
Multilateral	14	14	15	16	17	18
Bilateral	41	35	36	40	40	41
Financial institutions	21	35	34	33	32	30
Other	24	16	15	12	11	10
Short-term	. . .	4.0	3.9	5.2	8.7	7.5
North Africa	**7.3**	**29.9**	**30.0**	**30.7**	**30.5**	**30.7**
Medium- and long-term	7.3	27.8	28.2	28.0	27.9	28.0
Of which (percent share):						
Multilateral	7	5	6	7	9	9
Bilateral	35	26	28	31	32	33
Financial institutions	33	50	47	45	44	44
Other	25	19	18	16	15	15
Short-term	. . .	2.1	1.7	2.7	2.7	2.7
Sub-Saharan Africa	**15.4**	**47.3**	**53.9**	**63.9**	**70.8**	**73.6**
Medium- and long-term	15.3	45.4	51.7	61.4	64.8	68.8
Of which (percent share):						
Multilateral	17	20	20	19	21	22
Bilateral	44	40	41	43	44	45
Financial institutions	16	26	27	28	27	25
Other	23	14	13	9	9	8
Short-term	0.1	1.9	2.2	2.5	6.1	4.8

Source: International Monetary Fund, *World Economic Outlook, April 1985.*
[1] Excludes Libyan Arab Jamahiriya and South Africa.

Table 2. Average Terms of Public External Borrowing, Africa and Low-Income Asia, 1975–84

	1975	1980	1981	1982	1983	1984
Africa[1]						
Interest (percent)	6.5	8.3	7.6	9.2	8.1	8.5
Maturity (years)	15.8	13.9	16.0	13.9	16.7	13.8
Grace period (years)	4.4	4.4	4.5	4.0	4.4	3.4
Grant element (percent)	21.6	12.0	17.8	8.3	15.9	13.0
Low-income Asia						
Interest (percent)	4.2	5.2	4.5	4.8	4.2	3.0
Maturity (years)	23.7	20.7	22.6	25.1	28.1	30.9
Grace period (years)	6.1	5.5	5.8	6.1	6.6	7.2
Grant element (percent)	41.8	34.1	40.0	40.8	45.8	55.1
Low-income Asia						
Interest (percent)	2.5	2.8	4.0	4.4	5.4	3.7
Maturity (years)	31.9	32.4	30.2	32.1	30.1	34.5
Grace period (years)	8.2	7.9	7.3	7.5	7.3	7.9
Grant element (percent)	59.5	58.3	49.5	48.8	39.5	53.5

Source: World Bank, *World Debt Tables;* and Fund staff estimates.

[1] Excludes Libyan Arab Jamahiriya and South Africa.

of principal repayments on borrowing from private markets. For Africa as a whole, the ratio of debt-service payments to exports of goods and services doubled to over 30 percent in 1984 from about 14 percent in 1980; for sub-Saharan Africa, the ratio reached 27 percent in 1985–86 (Table 6). At the same time, there is a decline in the amount of debt service eligible for rescheduling, as repayments to multilateral development institutions rise along with repayments of previously rescheduled debt service.

4. In addition, and reflecting relatively high recourse to Fund credit in the early 1980s, repurchase obligations to the Fund in 1985–87 will average $1.25 billion annually (Table 7).

The recent and current debt-servicing difficulties of African countries are clearly widespread and reflect deep-seated economic and financial problems. Moreover, a significant increase in scheduled debt-servicing obligations is in prospect in the near term, at a time when decisive and immediate improvements in the debt-servicing capacity of the African economies are unlikely, even if necessary economic policy reforms are widely introduced. While it is not the purpose of this paper to trace the macroeconomic causes leading to past and present debt-servicing difficulties, a consensus seems to be emerg-

Table 3. Developing Countries: External Debt[1] Relative to Exports and to GDP, 1977–86
(percent)

	1977	1982	1983	1984	Estimates 1985	Estimates 1986
Ratio of external debt to exports of goods and services[2]						
Indebted developing countries	126.7	148.0	157.9	151.3	148.5	141.5
Small low-income countries	207.7	315.5	330.8	341.5	349.1	346.4
Sub-Saharan Africa[3]	120.0	199.8	216.6	223.2	230.7	230.9
By region						
Africa	112.2	145.6	160.4	161.7	162.8	154.6
Asia	87.5	85.7	90.4	85.5	86.3	84.7
Europe	117.8	121.5	129.1	127.0	121.4	110.9
Non-oil Middle East	165.7	151.4	173.6	175.6	183.6	181.9
Western Hemisphere	191.8	270.7	294.1	280.0	269.6	257.6
Ratio of external debt to GDP[2]						
Indebted developing countries	24.9	32.9	35.6	36.3	36.7	32.5
Small low-income countries	32.2	44.4	45.8	47.7	49.9	46.9
Sub-Saharan Africa[3]	33.8	49.7	54.2	62.6	68.9	68.0
By region						
Africa	31.4	37.2	38.8	39.8	39.9	35.8
Asia	17.2	21.3	22.6	23.7	25.4	24.9
Europe	21.6	29.2	34.4	38.4	35.7	33.5
Non-oil Middle East	53.0	60.0	57.7	58.3	57.9	43.4
Western Hemisphere	29.0	42.0	47.6	46.0	45.6	36.9

Source: International Monetary Fund, *World Economic Outlook, April 1985.*

[1] Does not include debt owed to the Fund.

[2] Ratio of year-end debt to exports of goods and services or GDP for year indicated.

[3] Excludes Nigeria and South Africa.

ing among observers that inadequate policies on resource allocation, relative prices, and demand management—aggravated by negative external economic influences—are at the root of the problem. In addition, weaknesses in external debt management policies proper were prevalent and often included the following:

- absence of effective centralized control over the authorization of external borrowing by the public sector;
- absence of adequate procedures to establish proper selection of projects financed by external borrowing;

- absence of purposeful control over the maturity and other terms of debt incurred;
- and for countries that had incurred relatively high shares of commercial debt, extraordinary rapidity in the rise of such commercial debt in a procyclical manner during periods of strong primary-commodity prices.

Table 4. Estimated African External Payments Arrears, 1980–84
(billions of dollars)

	1980	1981	1982	1983	1984
Africa[1]					
Amount	4.2	4.6	9.7	9.3	9.4
Number of countries	20	21	19	18	16
North Africa					
Amount	...	...	...	...	...
Number of countries	...	...	...	...	...
Sub-Saharan Africa					
Amount	4.2	4.6	9.7	9.3	9.4
Number of countries	20	21	19	18	16

Source: Country authorities; and Fund staff estimates.
[1] Excludes South Africa.

Table 5. Official Multilateral and Commercial Bank Debt Reschedulings, African Countries, 1980–84
(millions of dollars)

	1980	1981	1982	1983	1984
Central African Republic					
Paris Club	...	72	...	13	...
Commercial banks	...	...	...	...	...
Côte d'Ivoire					
Paris Club	...	...	...	...	356
Commercial banks	...	...	...	...	...
Equatorial Guinea					
Paris Club	...	...	...	...	...
Commercial banks	...	...	...	...	...
Liberia					
Paris Club	35	30	...	17	17
Commercial banks	...	...	30	...	...
Madagascar					
Paris Club	...	140	107	...	89
Commercial banks	...	147	...	...	195

Table 5 (continued). Official Multilateral and Commercial Bank Debt Reschedulings, African Countries, 1980–84
(millions of dollars)

	1980	1981	1982	1983	1984
Malawi					
Paris Club	...	...	25	26	...
Commercial banks	...	...	...	57	...
Mauritania					
Paris Club	...	...	...	...	...
Commercial banks	...	...	...	...	...
Morocco					
Paris Club	...	...	...	1,489	...
Commercial banks	...	...	...	...	...
Mozambique					
Paris Club	...	...	...	...	404
Commercial banks	...	...	...	...	213
Niger					
Paris Club	...	...	...	36	26
Commercial banks	...	...	...	...	26
Nigeria					
Paris Club	...	...	...	...	...
Commercial banks	...	...	...	1,935	...
Senegal					
Paris Club	...	75	74	72	...
Commercial banks	...	...	...	...	78
Sierra Leone					
Paris Club	37	...	...	...	25
Commercial banks	...	...	...	...	25
Somalia					
Paris Club	...	...	...	...	...
Commercial banks	...	...	...	...	...
Sudan					
Paris Club	...	...	80	536	269
Commercial banks	...	498	55	790	838
Togo					
Paris Club	...	232	...	300	75
Commercial banks	69	...	...	84	...
Uganda					
Paris Club	...	30	19	...	...
Commercial banks	...	...	...	...	...
Zaïre					
Paris Club	...	500	...	1,497	...
Commercial banks	402	...	...	58	64
Zambia					
Paris Club	...	...	...	375	253
Commercial banks	...	...	...	...	73

Source: Fund staff estimates.

Table 6. External Debt Service, 1980–86
(billions of dollars)

	Actual			Scheduled	
	1980	1983	1984	1985	1986
Africa[1]	10.9	14.1	17.4	19.2	18.9
Interest	4.7	5.5	6.5	6.8	6.6
Amortization	6.2	8.6	10.9	12.4	12.3
As percent of exports of goods and services	13.9	25.5	30.3	32.4	30.0
North Africa	5.5	5.7	7.4	8.3	8.2
Interest	2.1	2.0	2.2	2.1	2.1
Amortization	3.4	4.7	5.2	6.2	6.1
As percent of exports of goods and services	26.2	35.0	38.4	40.6	37.8
Sub-Saharan Africa	5.5	5.8	10.0	11.0	10.8
Interest	2.6	3.5	4.3	4.8	4.6
Amortization	2.9	3.9	5.7	6.2	6.2
As percent of exports of goods and services	9.5	20.6	26.2	28.1	26.0

Source: International Monetary Fund, *World Economic Outlook, April 1985.*
[1] Excludes Libyan Arab Jamahiriya, and South Africa.

Table 7. Use of Fund Credit and Scheduled Repurchases, 1980–87
(billions of dollars; end of period)

				Scheduled Repurchases[1]		
	1980	1983	1984	1985	1986	1987
Africa[2]						
Net purchases	0.4	1.4	0.6	1.0	1.3	1.4
Outstanding use of Fund resources	2.3	6.0	6.3	...	...	...
North Africa						
Net purchases	0.1	0.1	0.1	0.1	0.3	0.2
Outstanding use of Fund resources	0.3	0.9	0.1	...	...	...
Sub-Saharan Africa						
Net purchases	0.3	1.3	0.5	0.8	1.0	1.2
Outstanding use of Fund resources	2.0	5.1	5.3	...	...	...

Source: International Monetary Fund, Data Fund.
[1] On purchases outstanding at end of 1984.
[2] Excludes South Africa.

Issues in External Debt Management

The existing and prospective debt-servicing difficulties of African countries confront both creditors and debtors with delicate issues whose resolution will require a patient and long-term perspective on both sides. Creditors, for example, could be inclined to view the serious debt-servicing difficulties as largely a manifestation of basic underlying economic difficulties and to doubt the desirability of advancing additional net financial assistance to help resolve those underlying difficulties. Debtors, on the other hand, could feel inclined to view the necessity of honoring external debt obligations as hampering the recovery of their economies; in particular, they might doubt the practicality of their efforts to provide for some service on external debt if the prospects for further net financial assistance seem unpromising. The overall task is well described in the April 1985 *World Economic Outlook* (p. 14) prepared by Fund staff:

> Debtors and creditors will have to work together, both bilaterally and with agencies such as the World Bank, to ensure that viable projects are identified, that suitable financing is made available, and that the adjustment efforts required for the poorest countries are not made unrealistically large by the debt-service burdens resulting from earlier borrowing at unsustainable rates.

Because achievement of the development aspirations of African economies will continue to depend on access to foreign savings, it is essential that African policymakers deal with their debt-servicing obligations in a manner acceptable to the international financial community. This does not mean, of course, full service of external debt when this is not possible; it does mean, however, the pursuit of policies promising ultimately to restore full debt-servicing capacity. The whole range of economic policies to this end are considered in other papers in this volume. Only if there is a prospect of eventual improvement in the debt-servicing capacity of an economy could creditors be expected to continue to provide the new financial assistance (mostly on concessional terms), even while full debt service on existing debt is suspended. While, in the near term, the need for increased concessional financial assistance is paramount, it is highly important that policymakers in debtor countries keep in mind that actions unacceptable to the international financial community will jeopardize their access to credit markets in the long term. It cannot be in the African countries' interests, by any actions in the current crisis situation, to cut themselves off from capital market access in the longer run. The aim is to grow out of aid dependency.

In this connection, and as noted earlier, for many African economies, debt rescheduling in the period ahead will be a significant, but declining, source of external financing, as an increasing share of debt-service obligations is ineligible for rescheduling by normal standards. A key aim in the numerous prospective refinancing or rescheduling operations relating to accruing debt-service obligations is to follow, to the maximum extent possible, procedures protective of new financing flows. In other words, the close connection between alternative modalities of debt rescheduling and the possibilities for obtaining access to new financing must be recognized. In particular, there are considerable costs associated with incurring arrears on short-term obligations and with seeking a rescheduling of short-term obligations falling due, or with pursuing unilateral rather than cooperative methods of resolving debt-service difficulties.

Debt rescheduling and new financing, on appropriate terms, will jointly be needed in many African countries to support policy reform. This paper does not comment on the needed size or the possible sources of such new financing flows, as these matters have to be considered on a country-specific basis. In any case, a World Bank report[2] outlines the key issues. Likewise, the paper will not address the related topic of the methods used to coordinate the elements of financing packages for African countries, namely, the sum of financial assistance made available from possible debt rescheduling, new bilateral and multilateral lending flows, and Fund assistance.

The central issue addressed below is the need to adopt financing procedures that are supportive of economic adjustment required and pursued in African economies, and to do so in a manner avoiding repetition of errors of past years in external debt management. Two questions are therefore addressed in the remainder of this paper. What implications for financing policy reforms arise from the existing stock of external debt and its rising debt servicing (how is any "overhang of debt" dealt with)? Within what improved debt management framework, embodying what principles, should new financing flows to African economies take place?

Difficulties in Meeting Debt-Service Obligations

Arrears on commercial payments

An essential priority, if commercial arrears exist, is to eliminate them as fast as possible. As is well known, commercial arrears are expensive to a coun-

[2]World Bank, *Toward Sustained Development in Sub-Saharan Africa: A Joint Program of Action* (Washington: World Bank, 1984).

try, as most imports will be priced with a significant risk premium whose annual aggregate cost to the economy may, in some cases, exceed the actual stock of outstanding commercial arrears. The methods of clearing commercial arrears range from cash settlements to refinancing through a loan or, in some cases, rescheduling.[3] The latter method is often employed in the Paris Club framework in the case of arrears on short-term commercial credits insured by official export-credit agencies. Nigeria, with the help of merchant bank advisors, rescheduled its arrears on uninsured commercial payments in 1984. Turkey adopted an innovative and successful scheme (in 1980) that was distinctive in tailoring options to the varied interests of foreign suppliers. Most other countries strive to clear uninsured commercial arrears through cash payments as rescheduling or refinancing often cannot be obtained, partly because of large-scale practical problems arising from the presence of many, at times small, uninsured suppliers. The benefit in clearing commercial arrears as quickly as possible is the opening of the way toward renewed access of the economy to regular short-term trade finance, including that insured by official export credit agencies in industrial countries. Fund-supported adjustment programs, in all instances in which commercial arrears are present, have as one of their aims the elimination of commercial arrears according to a defined schedule along with a reconstitution of gross foreign exchange reserves to levels adequate to cushion against short-term payments fluctuations.

Restructuring debt-service obligations

There are some similarities between the experiences of African countries rescheduling debt-service obligations falling due to banks and reschedulings in the major bank-debt countries, notably those in Latin America—broad coverage of medium-term debt service due, the exclusion of short-term trade-related debt when feasible, and avoidance of formally rescheduling interest payments due. But the African cases differ in one key respect. While there have been more than a dozen African reschedulings with bank creditors during 1980–84 (see Table 7), in only one case—that of the Côte d'Ivoire in 1984—could banks be persuaded in the context of a Fund-supported adjustment program to provide new money to the country and, in that case, only

[3] For a discussion of experiences in rescheduling the debt of several countries, see *Recent Developments in External Debt Restructuring* by K. Burke Dillon and others, Occasional Paper No. 40 (Washington: International Monetary Fund, 1985), Appendix III, pp. 34–39.

with great difficulty. In all other instances, the bank-debt rescheduling was confined to a rollover of amortization payments due, with interest payments normally to be made as scheduled without the help of new money. At the request of the member countries, Fund staff have explained the policies of African member countries to their bank creditors, as part of the negotiations leading to Fund-supported adjustment programs. As in other cases, the Managing Director has only presented a program to be supported by use of Fund resources for the consideration of the Executive Board after having received prior assurances that sufficient financing would be available, including, when needed, refinancing of obligations falling due to banks. In other instances, including those of Morocco and Madagascar, the Fund has, again at the request of the member country and with the consent of bank creditors, extended its good offices to help resolve particular issues arising between the member country and its bank creditors.

There has been, to date, no case of multiyear bank-debt rescheduling for an African country; nor does such restructuring appear to be under active discussion for any African country at this time. As exemplified in the cases of Ecuador, Mexico, and Venezuela, multiyear bank-debt restructurings have been agreed in principle only for those borrowing countries that have already achieved substantial adjustment in their external current accounts, thereby reducing their need for net new financing flows from private sources to relatively small amounts. At the same time, however, these countries face a "hump" in gross amortization payments to banks, and these payments cannot be refinanced in normal market fashion. The stretching out of this hump in amortization payments to banks through a multiyear restructuring paves the way for restoring more normal capital-market access for these countries.

In the African context, reduced indebtedness to private capital markets and increased concessional assistance are needed. Even if it is feasible to obtain new money from commercial banks in the context of rescheduling, which is highly improbable given the loan provisioning already made for many credits to African countries by commercial banks, such new money could aggravate debt-servicing burdens. Thus, the outlook is mostly for a continuation of rollover of principal, where necessary, with, in some cases, a gradual repayment of principal. As noted above, scheduled repayments of principal to banks will peak in 1985 and 1986 and continue at a high level in 1987.

Because the largest share of outstanding debt of most African countries represents official credits from abroad, the Paris Club has been the major forum for debt-rescheduling exercises involving African countries. As is well recognized, governments participating in the Paris Club have been willing to consider a rescheduling of arrears on debt-service payments or of principal and interest payments falling due only when the debtor country has in place a Fund-supported adjustment program. To a growing degree, Paris Club creditors have adjusted the scale of debt relief to amounts necessary to support adjustment programs, but, of course, only within limits. These limits are defined primarily by the desire of creditor governments to protect the financial integrity of their official export credit insurance agencies. Nevertheless, in some recent cases, de facto debt relief approached 100 percent, with the rescheduled debt to be serviced over a period well in excess of ten years. Actual experience with many recent reschedulings for African countries has been disappointing from the creditors' viewpoint, however, because of failures by debtor countries to make timely payments as required under the rescheduling agreements. Partly in consequence, Paris Club creditors, in certain instances, have established special accounts into which they have asked the debtor country to make regular progress payments during the year. In a limited number of cases in which very extensive relief was agreed, creditors have been especially disappointed that even purely token payments under rescheduling agreements have not been made.

It has frequently been suggested that the essentially year-by-year nature of Paris Club reschedulings is not suited to the needs of African countries where policy reform and its financing must be placed in a medium-term framework. Paris Club creditors should grant debt relief once and for all over the medium term, it has been suggested, with many possible variations of detail in the modalities, including the linking of debt service due after rescheduling to commodity-price movements. Creditors typically recognize the need of countries to seek debt relief for a number of years and agree that policy planning must be put in a medium-term framework, but they do not generally consider their procedures as standing in the way of such necessary and desirable planning. In fact, the documentation provided to the creditors by the Fund, World Bank, and UNCTAD makes the medium- or longer-term nature of many problem cases explicit. For these cases, creditors point to the fact that they have extended debt relief to a relatively large number of countries year after year, provided they were assured at annual intervals that the country in question continued to pursue appropriate adjustment policies. Creditors have expressed their continued willingness to refinance by explicitly indicating, during each annual rescheduling exercise, their readiness to meet again to consider a further rescheduling request. It would appear therefore that no procedural obstacles exist for debtor countries in obtaining debt relief over the medium term when this is necessary. On the contrary, a well-defined and credible economic policy plan, set in a realistic time frame, is welcomed by creditors as evidence of the debtor country's commitment to adjustment and facilitates the extension of debt relief on an annual basis over an extended period.

The suggestion has also been made that in certain cases the rescheduling terms of the Paris Club are inadequate, and that both longer grace and maturity periods and lower interest rates are needed. Concessional rescheduling is complex. Many low-income countries clearly need increased concessional assistance. In rescheduling debt service due on development assistance loans, creditors generally maintain the original concessional interest rate; if more concessional terms are needed, an instrument for converting aid loan obligations into grants is readily available (see below). In addition, of course, the Paris Club procedures do not stand in the way of donors providing additional new concessional assistance. In rescheduling debt service due on commercial loans, creditors generally apply market interest rates. Paris Club procedures have evolved with debt service on commercial loans extended or insured by official export credit agencies in mind, and this continues to account for the vast bulk of the "eligible" debt service of the Paris Club. It is highly questionable whether debtor countries, if they were to gain concessional treatment of rescheduled commercial debt service, could regain access to commercial loans after a rescheduling, since a concessional rescheduling would involve considerable financial loss for the export credit agencies. Borrowers currently in difficulty must keep in mind that the resumption of commercial lending to the more creditworthy countries in Africa is normally only possible with the insurance provided by official export credit agencies.

Except in the case of the Côte d'Ivoire (1984), official creditors have not insisted that banks provide new money to African countries to establish comparability in rescheduling exercises. (Both principal and interest payments due are rescheduled in the Paris Club framework, whereas banks reschedule only principal payments.) In the African context, an issue of increasing importance to official creditors has, however, been the comparability of treatment for governmental creditors not participating in the Paris Club framework. Under usual Paris Club accords, the rescheduling country agrees to obtain rescheduling from governments not participating in the Paris Club on comparable terms and agrees not to grant more favorable terms to them. Especially in cases in which debt relief on generous terms (by Paris Club standards) was anticipated, a close examination of the prospective contributions of other governments has been made by the Paris Club creditors. In instances of apparent noncomparability revealed ex post, subsequent reschedulings have confronted serious obstacles.

Conversion to grants

A number of governments have converted existing development-assistance loans into grants, sometimes in line with their more recent policy of offering mainly grants to low-income countries. This policy will continue to be of help in individual cases, but not all governments have adopted this policy, and those that have appear largely to have exhausted all scope for further conversion to grants, having already converted the bulk of existing loan obligations to grants.

Improved Debt-Management Framework for New Credit Flows

If debt service on the existing stock of debt is dealt with, new credit flows should take place on terms, and within a debt-management framework, that gives highest assurance that resources will be used effectively and that payments associated with the new flows will be made in a timely manner. It is not the purpose of this paper to discuss the general macroeconomic policy conditions that must be fulfilled in order for an effective external debt management policy to be feasible. Without realistic exchange rate and interest rate policies, however, effective external debt management is rarely possible. Indeed, evidence about the detrimental effect of inappropriate exchange rate and interest rate policies on efficient resource allocation is now persuasive. Likewise, the capital flight that was encouraged in the late 1970s and early 1980s by policies of maintaining overvalued exchange rates and negative real interest rates has been documented not only for certain Latin American countries, where it occurred in large absolute amounts, but also for some African countries.[4]

The present debt-management framework in a number of African countries appears seriously deficient. The attainment of the development aspirations of African countries can be significantly furthered by sustained access to, and prudent management of, foreign savings. No one can make a credible case for additional financial assistance in instances in which even such

---

[4]Glynn, Lenny, and Peter Koenig, "The Capital Flight Crisis," *Institutional Investor* (New York), November 1984, pp. 109–119.

basics as reasonably complete data on existing debt and scheduled debt service are unavailable. Yet, in a number of countries, a central unit to advise the authorities on external debt management, to control the contracting of loans, and to administer existing debt is either nonexistent, not fully functioning, or lacking in the appropriate powers. Such a central unit has three purposes: (i) to administer the existing public external debt and discharge debt service on it, monitor private sector borrowing, and keep information on all external borrowing readily available; (ii) to assist the authorities in centralizing approval authority for contracting new external loans by all public sector entities; and (iii) to provide the authorities with analyses and policy recommendations about alternative borrowing proposals.

With respect to the second function of assisting authorities in authorization procedures, three aims should dominate: to centralize loan contracting authority, to help provide proper screening of projects, and to control the composition and terms of new credit flows. Experience strongly indicates that a lack of centralization of loan-contracting authority contributed not only to undisciplined contracting of external loans on inadvisable terms, but also to the initiation of projects of insufficient merit. Without effective central authority for approving public sector external borrowing and, in particular, borrowing by all public sector enterprises, there can be no external debt management.

Concerning the aim of project screening, it may be sufficient to refer to a key conclusion of the World Bank's report on sub-Saharan Africa which states that "the heart of Africa's economic crisis is the low rate of return on its capital investment. Much of this failure comes from investment programs that have been extensively financed from external sources."[5] Because of the need to employ future external resources with much increased efficiency, improved procedures for screening externally financed projects are essential. World Bank expertise in this field will be of critical importance to African countries.

With respect to the control of the composition and the terms of new debt-creating flows, it is evident that a central authority is needed to help ensure an appropriate level and composition of debt-creating capital flows. The aim for most African countries at this juncture will be to secure adequate conces-

---

[5]World Bank, "*Toward Sustained Development in Sub-Saharan Africa: A Joint Program of Action*" (Washington: World Bank, 1984), p. 41.

sional assistance in support of their policy reforms and to contract commercial loans, when available, only after the strictest of checks. For this function, as for the previous ones, any debt-management unit needs the full support of the highest authorities who determine the guidelines under which the unit is to function. The rejection of external loans that promise short-run relief, but are offered on terms inconsistent with the economic interests of the country, is among the hardest of tasks.

As far as analysis and policy recommendation by a central external debt management unit is concerned, the aim is to provide authorities with advice on the medium-term implications of their borrowing plans. For this purpose, a comprehensive medium-term sectoral and macroeconomic analysis, with particular focus on balance of payments implications, needs to be undertaken and regularly "rolled forward" in light of experience and new information. For many African economies, a procedure distinguishing core and non-core external borrowing may be helpful. Core borrowing, financed from bilateral and multilateral development loan sources and perhaps, to some limited extent, through foreign official export credits and other commercial credits, would relate to the external finance of undertakings in a national development plan. Barring severe shocks, other policies of the government would seek to protect this core program from disturbance. Non-core borrowing (which may or may not be tied to projects) would relate mainly to smoothing out, to some degree, fluctuations in commodity prices or other temporary payments influences.

A key feature of the analysis to be provided to the authorities would be to establish a normative framework for taking on external loans, which, in light of medium-term aims of the authorities, is judged realistic and feasible. When developments deviate from this medium-term framework, economic adjustment policies would be initiated and no recourse would be had to external borrowing beyond that set in the normative framework by the authorities. One purpose of such a framework is the avoidance of procyclical borrowing on the strength of commodity price booms, as happened so often in the past at great subsequent cost to the African economies. Indeed, some non-core borrowing might be repaid during commodity price booms. A borrowing margin must be preserved for a time when the ability to borrow is needed most, namely in periods of temporarily increased payments deficits. All too often in the past, the ability to borrow abroad was nonexistent precisely when its contribution to maintaining high-priority development was indispensable.

Role of the Fund

To establish an improved debt-management framework such as that suggested above, technical assistance is available from several sources, including the World Bank and the Fund (see Annex).

The Fund has, for many years, attempted to assist African member governments in their external debt management. In regular Article IV consultations with members, continued attention has been paid to countries' external borrowing policies before debt-servicing difficulties arise, and suggestions have been made for improving the management framework. In recent years, Fund missions have discussed explicit medium-term balance of payments scenarios with authorities in the context of consideration of adjustment and financing policies. Moreover, the Fund will continue to play a catalytic role in helping African member countries obtain the necessary financing for their adjustment efforts, in addition to the assistance made available by the Fund itself. For this purpose, the Fund has supported the rescheduling requests of countries in the Paris Club framework as well as those to commercial banks, and has participated in Donor Group meetings, usually chaired by the World Bank. It has also taken the initiative in mobilizing exceptional quick-disbursing balance of payments assistance to countries with adjustment programs.

Repurchase obligations to the Fund on the part of African countries will fall due in 1986–87 in amounts averaging about $1.25 billion per year (including Sudan). These repurchase obligations reflect the substantial net assistance, totaling some $4.4 billion, made available by the Fund in 1981–83 (Table 6). In 1981–82, net Fund flows to sub-Saharan Africa were equivalent to about a quarter of total official development assistance. Responding to drought conditions in Africa, nearly $1 billion was disbursed in 1983 under the compensatory financing facility. The gross repurchase obligations of African member countries must, of course, be seen in conjunction with the continued assistance the Fund will make available to African countries in accordance with its policies, if suitable adjustment policies can be agreed with the member countries concerned. Nevertheless, it is clear that a number of African countries may have to make net repurchases to the Fund in the period ahead. It is essential that the scheduled repurchases take place in order to preserve the revolving character of the Fund's financial resources. Only if it is respected as a monetary institution rather than an institution offering development finance will the Fund be able to continue its function as a catalyst, inducing additional finance from official and private lenders, partly through reschedulings.

Annex

Technical Assistance on External Debt Management to African Countries by the Fund and the Bank

As pointed out above, the Fund has, for many years, discussed external debt with authorities of its members within the context of its regular Article IV missions, and the World Bank has assisted countries in establishing a data base on external debt as part of its work on the Debtor Reporting System. As the need for a comprehensive and systematic approach to external debt management has become pressing for many countries, however, both the Fund and the Bank have in recent years instituted technical assistance programs specifically tailored to the needs of member countries regarding external debt.

This assistance has been provided in three different forms, corresponding to different needs and objectives. First, both institutions have provided in-house training for officials of member countries in seminars on external debt. Second, the World Bank has provided teams of professionals for short missions. Third, both institutions have assisted countries through the assignment to the host country of resident experts for longer periods of up to two years.

Fund assistance

The technical assistance programs of the Fund were extended to include external debt in December 1982. The program is administered by the Fund's Central Banking Department.[1] The technical assistance provides experts

[1]A description of technical assistance by the Fund can be found in *Technical Assistance and Training Services of the International Monetary Fund*, IMF Pamphlet Series, No. 43 (Washington: International Monetary Fund, 1985).

Table A1. Technical Assistance to African Countries by the World Bank and the Fund on External Debt, 1981–84

	World Bank		Fund	
	Field Missions 1981–84	Advisor Year Started	Advisor Year Started	Length of Stay (months)
Benin	2	1982		
Burundi	1			
Central African Republic	2	1981		
Cameroon	5	1982		
Cape Verde	1			
Congo	4	1981		
Côte d'Ivorie	4		1983	24
Equatorial Guinea	?	1984[1]		
Gambia, The	2		1984	6
Guinea	1	1985[2]		
Guinea-Bissau	1			
Kenya	4	. . .[3]		
Liberia	3		1983	14
Madagascar	1			
Malawi	4	1984[4]	1984	1
Mali	2	1985[1]		
Mauritania	3		1983	6
Mauritius	1			
Niger	1	1984[1]	1983	16
Nigeria	3	1985[2]		
Rwanda	?	1983		
Senegal	8	1981	1983	24
Sierra Leone	1		1984	6
Somalia	5		1984	12
Sudan	4		1984	28
Tanzania	4			
Togo	3	1984		
Uganda	4		1983	24
Zaïre	1	1981[5]		
Zambia	3		1983	12

[1] Credit signed.
[2] In preparation.
[3] Financed by the United Nations Development Program (UNDP).
[4] Second credit.
[5] Originally funded by UNDP; by World Bank since 1982.

from its panel of highly trained professionals. As shown in the attached table, seven experts on external debt were assigned to African countries in 1983. Another five African countries requested and received experts in 1984, and technical assistance in this field is expected to continue at this level over the next few years. The period of assignment was generally up to two years, with shorter assignments being the exception.

Bank assistance

During the past four years, the number and scope of regular debt missions from the World Bank has increased rapidly to an average of 19 missions each year. Twenty-eight countries have been visited. These missions were generally of short (two to four weeks) duration and were usually designed to assist countries with the solution of a particular problem, such as the preparation of debt rescheduling negotiations. The Bank has also provided credits for and assisted in the selection of resident experts in 14 countries.[2] This level of technical assistance is expected to continue over the next few years.

Most assignments aim to set up permanent machinery for the collection, classification, and analysis, as an integral part of the host country's institutions, of data on external debt. Since a reliable and up-to-date data base is essential for the analysis and management of external debt, the first steps toward such a system consist of making a complete inventory of existing debts, setting up an accounting framework for the collection and centralization of debt statistics, and establishing regular reporting procedures to keep the data base current. The expert can assist the country in this task by tailoring to the specific institutional arrangements of the host country procedures that have proved useful elsewhere. The computerization of debt statistics is often an integral part of such a system. Here technical experts can advise on options for putting in place the appropriate information system. In many cases, technical assistance has expanded upon this basic need for data and has included support in the design and the implementation of analytical procedures and information systems needed to adequately manage external debt.

A crucial element in the expert's assignment is the training of local counterparts. The expert's terms of reference almost always include a clause em-

[2]In the case of the assistance by the Fund, the financial costs are largely borne by the Fund.

phasizing this important aspect of his responsibility. The need for an assignment is considered to last until a local officer can take over without relying on further outside support. This training aspect of technical assistance has proven to be the most valuable contribution to many member countries in their efforts to improve the management of external debt.

Comment

C.M. Nyirabu

I find Mr. Brau's paper interesting, although its scope is somewhat limited. It is less a discussion of African external-debt problems than a discussion of some limited aspects of management of the debt problem.

There is little to disagree with in what he says. His figures on debt, however, are official figures that underestimate the debt, particularly short-term debt and arrears; even the Fund debt is excluded from the data in his paper. Some analysts have concluded that total debt is in the order of $130 billion in sub-Saharan Africa, perhaps about $190 billion for the entire African continent, excluding South Africa.

On the relationship between creditors and debtors, I think creditors in other contexts usually take the view that helping to overcome debt-service difficulties is prudent and that providing new money to pay interest is a way to minimize losses.

On the question of arrears, I find the discussion admirable in principle, but somewhat unreal. The paper suggests how commercial arrears can be paid off quickly. It assumes that the clearing of commercial arrears would automatically open the way to renewed access to regular trade finance, including that insured by export credit agencies. While this sounds theoretically logical, in practice care should be taken not to assume that new money will be advanced in all cases where arrears are cleared. Many export-credit agencies are not providing new cover to exporters to restore that previously offered when arrears are paid. Therefore, rather than merely paying off all short-term arrears, methods of reducing trading arrears in exchange for incremental support should be seriously considered. In this context, paying arrears, which in some countries are equivalent to a whole year's export earnings, within a short time is impracticable. Using the whole of the Fund's drawings for this purpose would be a questionable allocation policy and would not suffice to clear arrears anyway. In any event, three years later it would be likely to cause the emergence of either commercial arrears or arrears in Fund repurchases. I do not have an answer to these problems, but I think the proposal by Mr. Brau is not possible. Perhaps selective payments tied, if possible, to prior agreements with suppliers of potential imports might be a priority. Perhaps also conversion of arrears into local currency for investment in the country may be an alternative—or even allowing creditors to purchase some nontraditional exports to promote new items.

I agree that the Paris Club reschedulings have, in general, provided adequate relief for sufficient periods for stabilization and export recovery to have a reasonable chance of success. Typical balance of payments projections have had three characteristics: optimistic export growth forecasts, assumed import growth rates well below those of GDP, even though GDP was constrained by import levels, and large "other items," which in effect might more accurately be entitled "resources yet to be located." A rolling annual rescheduling is not an adequate substitute for, say, five-to-seven-year rescheduling for the following reasons. First, we are constantly asked to make medium-term plans. As a prudent banker, I feel unable to budget future reschedulings dependent on future negotiations. I believe many of my colleagues feel likewise. Second, the amount of time high-level staff of central banks and economic ministries have taken up by the annual debt reschedulings is a serious misallocation of scarce resources. We in Tanzania sometimes find that we spend infinitely more time—weeks on end—negotiating with the Fund, the World Bank, and creditors than with working to put things right. To increase still further the allocation of time to negotiations, leaving less time for formulating and implementing policy, cannot, in my view, be efficient.

Few reschedulings in Africa can hope to succeed without injections of new concessional loans or grants. Creditors have powerful leverage over the performance of debtors through year-to-year rescheduling. They can cut off the new money. Thus the year-to-year approach seriously misallocates our scarce personnel time and gives scope for additional surveillance or leverage powers to the creditors. Surely, these are the hallmarks of a cost-inefficient approach or a negative sum game. Paris Club negotiations have, in general, not been adequately focused on a total improvement in resource availability, from rescheduling plus new grants or new money, sufficient for stabilization and adjustment programs to succeed in Africa. Of course, in principle, they can. My concern is that they usually seem not to do so.

Mr. Brau's paper mentions central coordination and approval of external borrowing as having been weak—a missing link in African external-debt management. I think this is an important but insufficient condition to avoid overborrowing. We in Tanzania have practiced centralization of this type for over 20 years. Also weak is the analysis of the viability of macroeconomic projects, that is, whether a project can pay for itself in terms of foreign exchange. Another problem is our inability to forecast how global economic swings might affect the viability of any project by imposing constraints on the rate of growth of the economy as a whole. A third problem is adequately forecasting how rapidly the external environment can improve and therefore when and to what extent our use of external credit to sustain private and public fixed investment in a downswing was prudent.

In my view, the worst problem has been a forecasting failure, and I am not sure we know enough to avoid it again, except by assuming all downswings will be so long and severe that virtually no additional medium-term external credit should be drawn on. I fully agree that debt on unsustainable terms or conditions should not be incurred, whatever the source. I agree that prudent debt management requires avoiding the use of moderate or higher interest rate, short- to medium-term loans, except on specific projects that generate net foreign exchange earnings year by year equal to debt service once they enter production. General use of money at, say, 9 percent, and the repayment of three years of borrowing over the subsequent three to six years is excessively imprudent; but this leads me to wonder whether Fund drawings beyond the first credit tranche and perhaps the compensatory financing facility themselves are consistent with prudent debt management in a low-income country, when a reasonable estimate of the length of the period required for stabilization or adjustment is about seven or eight years. Certainly, if we used other sources of credit, such as export or suppliers' credits, on similar terms, we would rightly be accused of grossly imprudent debt management and virtually disqualified for consideration for World Bank structural-adjustment lending on these grounds alone. I quite agree that when the economy and external balance are strong, one should reduce, rather than increase, external borrowing, and should build up external reserves. As noted earlier, however, we are no longer sure we can accurately enough forecast how long a downswing will last to know when and to what extent it is prudent to raise external borrowing above budgeted levels.

The World Bank in Adjustment and Economic Growth in Africa

Luis de Azcarate

It should be clear that the subject—the role of the World Bank[1] in adjustment and growth in Africa—cannot be adequately covered in a paper of this kind. I have chosen to look at it mainly from one angle and to discuss the evolving role of the Bank in the hope that what is being lost in detailed analysis of the Bank's activities in the present difficult period will be compensated by some gain in historical perspective. One of the more interesting and perhaps useful aspects of the Bank's role has been the effort of the Bank to adapt to changing and different conditions in member countries and to learn from experience. Whether such efforts have been successful is not for me to judge, even though the paper will point to some successes and to some problems.

The first part presents the background of Bank activities during what I call the first period, that is, from the initial operations in Africa (the first IBRD loan was made to Ethiopia in 1950; the first IDA credit to Sudan in 1961) to the turbulent period of the late seventies. The second part reviews the impact of the shocks of the seventies, whose combined outcome has created new and more difficult conditions for development, and the countries' policy responses. The "new development agenda" that the countries and the aid community, including the Bank, face together since the beginning of this decade is the subject of the third and longest part of the paper.

[1]Throughout the paper "the Bank," unless otherwise specified, refers to the International Bank for Reconstruction and Development (IBRD) and the International Development Association (IDA).

Supporting Growth: The First Period

This part presents a sketch of the conditions and problems faced by African countries at the time of their gaining independence, around 1960 for the majority of sub-Saharan countries, and the main currents of thought that provided the intellectual underpinnings for development policies and aid. It then reviews the main aspects of the World Bank's activities during the period and finally assesses some of its achievements and weaknesses.

Initial conditions

At the time of independence a quarter of a century ago, the countries of sub-Saharan Africa presented a new challenge to the international community. All these countries were unmistakably poor, although in very different degrees. Per capita incomes in some better endowed countries of the West African coast, for example, were probably five or six times higher than those of the Sahelian region. Infrastructure was embryonic, and the levels of literacy dramatically low. Social conditions reflected in the lowest life-expectancy rates in the world were, to say the least, unsatisfactory.

But the challenge was not seen as overwhelming. Africa was, after all, a continent of immense untapped resources; no major macroeconomic imbalances obtained; export activities were well developed, and the demand for African primary commodities was expected to grow in line with the overall fast expansion of the industrial countries. Public aid would provide the additional financing necessary to sustain the growing volume of imports needed for the "modernization" of the young economies of the continent; direct private foreign investment would eagerly compete to develop the natural resources, especially minerals, that required large, lumpy amounts of investment to encourage the required technology and management skills. Foreign private industry would also seek to share in the expansion of domestic markets through direct investment in manufacturing. Private bank lending on the other hand was not expected to play a great role, except of course for normal external-trade financing.

No one expected development to take place rapidly and everywhere at once. The agenda was daunting since income levels were so low, but it was also clear and had a dominant imperative: investing for growth.

Evolving thinking on development

Development strategies were hotly debated in the fifties and sixties, and the economics profession thrived on the production of innumerable formal or informal models of growth and development. Africa was rarely the region of reference; Asia or Latin America were. Thinking on development evolved as follows.

The dominant theme was that growth is determined by capital formation (or rather by the stream of income from a growing capital stock). But there were variations on this theme. The "first-things-first" view held that there was a natural sequence in capital formation starting with infrastructure or as it was often called, "social overhead capital," as a precondition for more directly productive capital. Another view suggested the need to advance on all fronts at the same time ("balanced growth") in order to create simultaneously incomes and markets and to do it fast ("big push") in order to avoid freezing the economy in lines of production corresponding to a state of comparative advantage that might entail deep and prolonged dependence on external trade and foreign capital.

Gradually the role of human capital came to be recognized as a critical ingredient of the production equation, and education and health came to be considered not only, as in established national-accounting principles, as a form of consumption but also as productive "assets." Related to this view, although not directly emanating from the same intellectual current, concern for poverty alleviation became a dominant feature of development literature and, among policymakers, dissatisfied both with the state of the low-income countries of Asia and Africa and with the persistence of large segments of absolute poverty in the more rapidly growing economies of Latin America, Southern Europe, or East Asia. Here also a virtuous association between poverty alleviation and increased productivity was found to exist, or at least was thought to exist, with the implication that more productive assets had to be allocated to the poor.

Foreign capital in general and public aid in particular were seen in the main current of economics as potentially playing a dual beneficial role. Since investable resources, at low per capita incomes, were insufficient, foreign savings would complement domestic savings and increase the rate of capital formation. At the same time they would relieve the foreign-exchange bottleneck that was considered as an additional and separate scarce resource. Indeed, in addition to large aggregate savings, developing countries could not afford economically to produce certain goods, especially capital goods and other specialized inputs that could only be imported. An inflexible and undiversified structure of production required a complementary, specific factor, namely foreign exchange. This was the essence of the ''two-gap'' models of growth on whose basis many projections of capital needs were made and the analytical justification of international aid was built. The Bank was seen then as ideally suited to provide much needed untied foreign exchange. It was also to be a source of technical assistance, although this function was not much emphasized in the early periods of the Bank.

Role of the Bank

When the Bank began its assistance activities in the newly independent states, the ''product'' (as we called it these days) had been shaped by 15 years of experience in other developing areas as well as by the intellectual currents just mentioned.

Thus, as they did in other parts of the world, economic missions from the Bank sought to assess countries' creditworthiness, that is, their capacity to borrow and service debt on IBRD terms (the interest rate on IBRD loans gradually moved from 4.5 percent in the 1950s, to 7 percent in 1970, and to 8 1/2 percent in 1975), or alternatively, their eligibility for IDA, as well as to determine their capital requirements in light, among other things, of the availability of other official development assistance, and identify sectoral investment opportunities.

Lending was almost exclusively for specific projects, and the well-established ''project cycle''—identification, appraisal, negotiation, supervision—was faithfully adhered to as it had proven its worth in many other countries in ensuring sound technical, financial, and economic standards for Bank-financed operations.

The evolution of lending to Africa is shown by sectors in Tables 1 and 2 for the period 1965–84. During the period 1965–80 there was, first, an uninterrupted progression of lending resulting in more than a fourfold increase in nominal terms between the two quinquenniums, corresponding to an average annual growth rate of about 10 percent over the 15-year period. More than half (52 percent) of total lending in the initial stages (1965–74) was for infrastructure (transportation, telecommunications, and energy, which, at that time, was almost exclusively electric power). This proportion fell to one-third, however, in the next five years. Concomitantly, lending for the main, directly productive sectors (agriculture and industry) increased sharply from 30 percent to 43 percent of the total. This movement, in turn, reflected two

Table 1. World Bank Lending to Africa by Purpose, FY1965–84
(millions of U.S. dollars)

	Average 1965–74	Average 1975–80	1981	1982	1983	1984
Agriculture/rural development	87.2	510.2	782.1	587.0	631.4	785.7
Education	36.2	158.1	249.7	130.7	202.3	24.9
Energy	61.0	209.0	153.5	362.4	309.5	521.3
Industry[1]	41.3	267.9	265.3	481.8	483.2	731.6
Nonproject	11.0	67.1	277.0	220.0	210.9	471.7
Population, health and nutrition	2.7	5.0	12.5	23.0	21.8	30.5
Technical assistance	...	8.8	113.6	56.7	36.5	93.9
Telecommunications	12.7	29.8	15.2	173.7	22.0	128.0
Tourism	5.5	26.0	...	...	...	...
Transportation	145.7	370.3	507.1	366.2	375.1	463.7
Urban development	2.9	44.7	51.0	120.0	154.0	117.0
Water supply and sewerage	15.0	109.8	157.6	181.5	154.2	376.9
Total	421.4	1,807.7	2,584.6	2,703.0	2,600.9	3,645.2
Of which:						
IDA	171.0	653.1	1,151.2	839.8	1,230.9	1,212.9
IBRD	250.5	1,154.6	1,433.4	1,863.2	1,370.0	2,432.3
North Africa	97.7	682.0	772.2	901.5	807.3	1,276.9

Source: World Bank Data Files.
[1] Including Development Finance Companies.

new but interrelated directions in the Bank's assistance strategy that broadly paralleled and in some cases spearheaded the evolution of development thinking.

First, with at least most components for the basic infrastructure in place, there was a need for more forcefully pushing material production or, in modern parlance, effecting a shift from the nontradables to the tradables sectors, that is, toward exportables and import-substitutes. This shift was especially needed after the first oil price increase of 1973–74 to pay for the much heavier import bill of the oil-importing countries (i.e., all sub-Saharan countries except, at that time, Nigeria, Gabon, and the Congo). Higher non-oil commodity prices gave impetus to this movement in the mid-seventies.

Second, there was growing concern for issues of employment and poverty. This led the Bank to focus attention on these problems in its economic and

Table 2. World Bank Lending to Africa, by Purpose, FY1965–84
(percent)

	Average					
	1965–74	1975–80	1981	1982	1983	1984
Agriculture/rural development	20.7	28.2	30.3	21.7	24.3	21.6
Education	8.6	8.7	9.7	4.8	7.8	0.7
Energy	14.5	11.6	5.9	13.4	11.9	11.6
Industry[1]	9.8	14.8	10.3	17.8	18.6	20.1
Nonproject	2.6	3.7	10.7	8.1	8.1	12.9
Population, health and nutrition	0.6	0.3	0.5	0.9	0.8	0.8
Technical assistance	...	0.5	4.4	2.1	1.4	2.6
Telecommunications	3.0	1.6	0.6	6.4	0.8	3.5
Tourism	1.3	1.4	...	...	...	...
Transportation	34.6	20.5	19.6	13.5	14.4	12.7
Urban development	0.7	2.5	2.0	4.4	5.9	3.2
Water supply and sewerage	3.6	6.1	6.1	6.7	5.9	10.3
Total	100.0	100.0	100.0	100.0	100.0	100.0

Source: World Bank Data Files.
[1] Including Development Finance Companies.

sector work and to direct lending toward medium- and small-scale enterprises, which typically employ more workers per unit of capital invested, through loans usually providing finance as well as technical assistance through intermediary institutions (development finance corporations). Indeed, much of the six-and-a-half-fold increase in the volume of lending under "industry" between 1965–74 and 1974–80 reflects this new orientation. But more important, following Mr. Robert McNamara's Nairobi speech of 1974, lending for rural development assumed top priority in Bank operations in general and for Africa in particular. Together with more traditional lending (i.e., for commercial export-oriented projects), the agricultural sector became, and has remained, the largest single beneficiary of Bank lending, reaching a peak of 30 percent, in dollar terms, in FY1981. Within the sector, the most ambitious integrated rural-development projects sought to reach the majority of the rural population of the designated area through provision of credit, inputs, extension services, marketing facilities, as well as needed infrastructure (such as feeder roads) and a minimum of social services (including maternity care and functional literacy programs). The objective was to intensify farm and nonfarm rural employment, foster cash crops as well as food crops within the existing farming systems, and generally enhance the quality of rural life, thereby reducing, but not arresting, the flow of rural emigration. Not all rural projects had such extensive attributes, but the thrust of the operations was certainly directed toward fulfilling a multiplicity of objectives involving small farmers. Such complex projects needed strong management and effective monitoring. This was provided for, in these projects, through the creation of autonomous management units, often with rather strong doses of expatriate technical assistance.

Rural development projects have been implemented in 20 sub-Saharan countries in a variety of contexts, in Nigeria and practically all the Sahelian countries, in Malawi and Rwanda, in Kenya and Sierra Leone, and elsewhere.

Also related to concerns over employment and poverty were the Bank's attempts at innovation in urban projects. These were designed to create jobs in the so-called informal sector, through simple credit cum technical assistance operations, and to provide housing (''sites and services''), water supply, and sewerage facilities at costs sustainable in terms both of users' charges and of capital requirements from central and local governments.

Similar principles guided the Bank's work in education where gradually greater priority was given to primary or basic education. While the share of this sector in Bank lending to Africa had remained modest (below 10 percent), training components included in other projects (agriculture, industry, energy, transport, technical assistance) together represented (and still represent) amounts at least equivalent to those involved in direct education lending. The effort toward developing ''human capital'' was therefore commensurate with the promotion of infrastructure and production, although it represented only a modest contribution relative to the needs of a rapidly growing population. Other sources of official and private assistance and most important the governments themselves were extremely active in developing education at all levels. The real progress achieved in this area has been noted in several Bank reports on sub-Saharan Africa and in the *World Development Report* of 1980. No less remarkable have been the educational achievements of North African nations.

Achievements and weaknesses

The Bank's assistance to Africa during the first years emphasized investment projects, microeconomic institutions and gradually more directly productive activities and the alleviation of poverty, with the reasoned expectation that the latter two objectives could be effectively combined. There is no reason to doubt that, in some unmeasurable way, Bank lending contributed to African growth and was instrumental in building a stronger institutional base. But there have been some serious weaknesses and in retrospect it appears to a certain extent that we did not help prepare the countries well enough for more difficult times.

First, we were not very good at predicting the turbulences of the seventies—not the drought, of course, but also not the oil price increases, not the commodities price fluctuations, not the recession, not high interest rates, not the evolution of aid itself. In this, we were perhaps no worse than others, but not distinctly better either. We were not therefore in a good position to advise borrowing governments on policies that would have permitted them to adapt better to the changing external environment.

Second, in the course of our operational activities (including technical assistance which first appeared as a lending operation in FY1976 in East Africa and in FY1977 in West Africa) we were not very good at strengthening the macroeconomic managerial capacities of our borrowers, whether in terms of institutional reforms or training and human resource development in general. Institution building was essentially project specific, not always effective at that and too loosely linked to existing public institutions.

Third, our economic and sector work often lacked robust analytical underpinnings, policy focus, relevance, or practicality. It was oriented mainly at providing the Bank with needed information on general economic conditions, creditworthiness, IDA eligibility, overall capital requirements, and main sectoral-investment needs; it was much weaker in providing relevant analysis of the policy framework for lending.

Fourth, and closely linked to the above, the policy dialogue with governments was rather unspecific and above all not fully integrated into the Bank's country-assistance strategy except in a basic sense through our assessment of the country's creditworthiness—but even this did not necessarily mean an effective dialogue with governments when issues arose.

Finally, despite the careful process of selection, design, and supervision, the projects financed by the Bank have not always withstood the erosion of time or the turbulence, domestic or otherwise, of the environment. This is an aspect which would require careful evaluation by country and by sector (and which is carried on in the Bank by the Operations Evaluation Department), well beyond the scope of this paper. Suffice it to say for our purpose here that the "stock of assets," whether physical, human, or institutional, built through a cumulated amount of lending in excess of $15 billion up to FY1980 for about 800 projects was not as robust as one would have wished, even if possibly stronger than would have been the case in the Bank's absence. In some important areas, particularly rural development and livestock, the rate of absolute failure, that is, zero or negative economic rates of return (ERRs), or only relative success, that is, ERRs significantly below appraisal but still positive, is much higher in sub-Saharan Africa than for the rest of Bank borrowers. Perhaps this is because too much was expected in too short a period, because not enough attention was paid by the Bank to the maintenance and operating capacity of borrowing entities, or because the projects supported by the Bank did not always fully reflect governments' real priorities. Probably the cause is a combination of all these factors.

******

Despite these and other problems the first period of Bank involvement, corresponding to what may perhaps be called the formative years of the newly independent nations of Africa, was one of reasonable progress for many African countries. Growth of GDP exceeded 4 percent in all countries except in the low-income semi-arid group (see Table 3), quite a respectable achievement considering initial conditions. The Bank was instrumental in contributing to expansion of the physical and human capital base and in building up development institutions. The Bank very much contributed, I believe, to introducing the ''project'' and the ''project cycle'' concepts, even though, as noted above, this approach had its own weaknesses. At the same time, independent African development was beginning amidst a favorable environment of rapid growth in industrial countries, rapidly expanding world trade, and widespread support for foreign aid and multilateralism.

These achievements and these factors, however, proved insufficient to help African countries withstand without much damage the assaults of a world environment turned more hostile.

Shocks, Reactions, and Policy Responses

For most African countries the turbulent period from the first oil shock of 1973–74 to the second large price increase of 1979–80 and the 1980–82 world recession has been devastating. The upturn in industrial countries since 1983 has had little positive effect on the continent, among other reasons because

Table 3. Growth Rates of GDP in Africa, 1960–83
(percent)

	Average				
	1960–70	1970–80	1981	1982	1983
Low-income countries	4.0	1.9	1.1	0.5	2.7
Low-income semi-arid	2.4	3.2	1.8	0.1	2.0
Low-income others	4.2	1.8	1.0	0.6	2.7
Middle-income oil importers	4.3	4.8	2.0	3.5	0.1
Middle-income oil exporters	3.7	4.9	- 3.7	- 1.1	- 2.1
All Africa	3.9	4.2	- 0.1	0.9	0.0
All except oil exporters	4.0	3.2	1.9	1.8	1.8

Note: Figures include Egypt, Morocco, and Tunisia, and exclude South Africa. The figures, which are weighted by GDP, also exclude the three higher-income oil exporters, Algeria, Gabon, and Libya, whose combined GDP is 25 percent of total African GDP despite constituting only 5 percent of the total African population.

commodity prices have generally remained depressed. And the current drought has added untold human suffering in more than a dozen countries. More than ever, in contrast to the large low-income countries of Asia, let alone the most dynamic economies of East Asia or Latin America, Africa stands out as a special case.

A serious understanding of the impact of exogenous shocks and the policy response can only be expected from a country-by-country study. Such an analysis cannot even be attempted here. I will only offer what, I believe, are a few valid generalizations on both the main problems and the policy responses. In doing so, I will abstain also from any systematic review of statistics, which can be found elsewhere, and use numbers only by way of illustration.

Drought, food, and the agricultural problem

The great drought of 1972–74 and the even more terrible current one have dramatized the food problem of Africa. The first Bank report on sub-Saharan

Africa and the two subsequent reports[2] have noted the generally declining per capita food production and the rising trends of food imports over the last 15 years or so. At the same time the volume of African agricultural exports has marginally declined between 1970 and and 1982 (by about 10 percent), and so has their share in world markets.

Aside from the climatic factors, which are obviously of major importance, but also still poorly understood, the underlying issues seem to be technical, human, institutional, and economic, often all at the same time. Summarily stated, the constraints by now well identified are the following.

At the technical level no satisfactory, proven technical packages adapted to local conditions, for example, drought resistant varieties, have been found for the Sudano-Sahelian zone. Neither have water retention systems nor livestock development systems been found that would both be more productive than traditional forms of husbandry and as well adapted to local conditions.

The human problem has several dimensions. Continued population growth in rural areas has resulted in growing demand for social services which is not being met. One of the consequences of unsatisfactory living conditions in rural areas is the emigration of the younger, more dynamic, entrepreneurial members of the community. Increasing land scarcity, given the state of technnology, is observed in both the drier Sahelian zone and in the more ecologically favorable coastal regions and highland areas where settlement densities are greatest, although there are great intercountry variations; hence shorter fallow periods, deforestation, erosion, lower yields, and growing conflicts between herders and farmers. Finally, agricultural projects suffer from scarcity of managerial and technical skills to which technical assistance has sometimes provided only a transitory solution, and sometimes not even that. Most seriously, failed agricultural schemes have developed farmers' resistance to change rather than acceptance of it.

Institutional weaknesses have emerged in essentially two areas. First, central ministries in charge of rural development are still too often the weakest ones in organization, staffing, policy design, and finance, and they have remained too far removed from, in some cases unconcerned by, the projects being supported by foreign aid both because of their own weakness and because of external donors' excessive emphasis on autonomously managed op-

---

[2] *Accelerated Development in Sub-Saharan Africa: An Agenda for Action* (Washington: World Bank, April 1983); *Sub-Saharan Africa: Progress Report on Development Prospects and Programs* (Washington: World Bank, July 1983); *Toward Sustained Development in Sub-Saharan Africa: A Joint Program of Action* (Washington: World Bank, August 1984).

erations. Secondly, inefficient marketing and input delivery systems continue to result in high intermediate costs and lower than economically justified farm-gate prices. Marketing boards and similar agencies in charge of export crops, which could be and often have been efficient, have tended to become bloated bureaucracies. Government monopolies or quasi-monopolies of trade in domestic food (especially cereals) have almost universally proved either coercive or ineffective as they attempt to buy and sell at administratively fixed prices unrelated to underlying market conditions. Lack of financial means has prevented them from effectively dampening sharp market price fluctuations through timely purchases and sales.

For a long time the most pervasive economic issue in agriculture has been the persistence of distorted incentives. This has been abundantly illustrated and discussed in Bank reports and many independent analyses. Such distortions extend from overvalued exchange rates that favor imports and depress producer prices, through excessively subsidized inputs and credit which result in de facto rationing (since supplies are limited by the amount of subsidization that budgets can afford) and therefore inequitable and inefficient allocations.

But the task of setting prices at more economic levels has been made more difficult since the mid-seventies by the erratic behavior of world prices. This has had a number of adverse consequences. Thus, the sharp increases in prices of imported cereals coinciding with the severe drought of 1972–74 made it extremely difficult, until food aid began to flow, to regulate domestic markets. Boom and bust periods in coffee, cocoa, and tea prices led to sudden unanticipated revenue windfalls followed by no less abrupt declines in a period of only three or four years, greatly complicating fiscal and investment policy in the countries concerned.

External shocks and policy response

All African countries are small and open (with external trade sectors typically representing 20–40 percent of GNP) and therefore particularly vulnerable to external shocks. Vulnerability is aggravated by structural factors, that is, a narrow export base and an infant industrial sector, as well as by persistent policy factors such as those discussed above, that is, overvalued exchange rates and other price and quantitative distortions that almost universally create an anti-export bias.

The magnitude of the shocks (understood the movement in terms of trade and the slowdown of foreign demand for the country's exports)[3] has been estimated, according to one methodology,[4] to have been equivalent in 1973–78 to a 4.4 percent loss in GNP for the oil-importing countries of sub-Saharan Africa (with variation of between 8.8 percent for the middle-income countries of Eastern and Southern Africa (excluding South Africa) and 0.5 percent for the corresponding group in Western Africa). The shocks were, as expected, favorable (+ 12.4 percent) for the oil-exporting countries of the region. They were generally most severe and also more uneven during the 1979–82 period, ranging from adverse impacts equivalent to 10–15 percent of GNP for Kenya, Côte d'Ivoire, or Tanzania to mildly positive impacts again for the oil exporters.[5] Morocco also was seriously affected (– 7 percent).

Only specific country studies could do justice to the complexity and diversity of the initial situations, the impact of the shocks on various parts of the domestic economies, whether favorable or unfavorable, or the different policy responses. But here also I will venture some stylized facts which, in my view, reflect the essence of the policy responses and explain much of this episode's outcome. These facts relate to debt, the public sector, and pricing.

The debt explosion

The growth of sub-Saharan African debt after 1975 has been quite extraordinary, as shown in the following table, and reflects two kinds of policy reactions, which in many countries happened in sequence.

Initially, as part of the so-called "recycling process," international private capital became much more easily available and African countries that enjoyed a commodity boom (including oil), as well as others not so fortunate, were seen as new, attractive borrowers. Most countries took advantage and borrowed. Commercial banks and suppliers' creditors, with or without back-

---

[3]These estimates do not include the impact of events such as drought or political disturbances.

[4]See B. Balassa *Adjustment Policies and Development Strategies, 1973–1978*, Discussion Paper, Development Research Department (Washington: World Bank, November 1982). The "impact" on GDP in this and the study cited below refers to changes in GDP relative to the historical trend, had this trend continued. These estimates do not include the impact of events such as droughts or political disturbances.

[5]See B. Balassa and D. McCarthy *Adjustment Policies in Developing Countries 1979–83, An Update*, World Bank Staff Working Paper, No. 675 (Washington: World Bank, 1984). The measurement methodology between the two periods varies in some respects, and the numbers given here should be taken as orders of magnitude.

Debt of Sub-Saharan Africa

	1972	1983
Medium- and long-term debt		
(*billions of dollars*)	11.1	79.8
Of which (*percent*):		
Financial markets	14.5	36.2
Suppliers' credits	14.3	4.4
Nonconcessional bilateral	5.2	12.2
Total nonconcessional *(percent)*	34.0	52.8

Source: Kathie L. Krumm, *Sub-Saharan Africa Debt*, CPD Discussion Paper (Washington: World Bank, January 1985). Numbers are from the World Bank Debt Reporting System and cover 39 countries. The figures do not include short-term debt (trade debt), which according to the Bank for International Settlements increased from $2.6 billion in 1977 to $6.5 billion at end of 1983.

ing from export credit agencies, competed to provide funds. Countries that had hardly ever borrowed from private sources also succumbed or were led to succumb. Subsequently oil-importing countries, doubly hit by the second round of oil price increases and the collapse of commodity prices (Côte d'Ivoire's terms of trade, for example, declined by 25 percent in 1979–81), not unnaturally chose to borrow more. Presumably, this was done because of expectations that export prices would recover, or because adjusting to the new situations seemed a less politically and socially attractive alternative than foreign borrowing. When it appeared that the external environment was not improving, and it did not improve until 1983–84, the borrowing policy of many countries turned out to have created more problems for the future than it had solved in the short run. The debt problem is therefore to a large extent the result of failure, quite understandable, to anticipate major and rapid changes in external conditions. The pace of increase in total debt in the second half of the seventies and the associated hardening of terms should in themselves, however, have been warning signals of possible future difficulties. There were also complicating factors in other areas to which I now come.

The public sector expansion

The period also witnessed a rapid expansion of the public sector in Africa. While total public expenditures of central governments alone in 36 sub-

Saharan African countries increased from 16.5 percent of GDP in the mid-sixties to 29.5 percent in 1981, the real growth spurt occurred in 1974–80. Other measures of the public sector (e.g., investment and employment) show the same pattern of expansion since the mid- seventies. The point here is not whether such a trend is good or bad in principle, but rather that some aspects of this rapid structural change had negative implications.

First, there is the crude fact that expenditures increased much more than resources, resulting in growing public-sector deficits (including those of public enterprises), which in turn were reflected in greater inflationary pressure from accommodating monetary policies and were ultimately translated into unsustainable external deficits.

Second, the pace of expansion stretched the public sector's managerial capacity, with adverse effects on implementation as too many projects were attempted simultaneously (an effect felt on numerous Bank-supported projects).

Third, and perhaps most damaging in the long term, the quality of public investment, and public expenditure in general, declined badly. In particular, new investments undertaken with commercial-bank financing and suppliers' credits were often of weak intrinsic economic merit, overdesigned, and overpriced. This is one of the factors behind the declining return on investment highlighted in the recent Bank report on sub-Saharan Africa. Other forms of incremental public expenditure included accelerated expansion of government employment and more subsidies.

Price distortions

While admittedly it is difficult to measure price distortions, that is, the distance between actual prices and prices that reflect opportunity costs (as reflected, for example, by import and export prices at the border), that such distortions increased after 1974 is suggested by two interrelated observations. One is the acceleration in inflation rates and the other the movement of real effective exchange rates.[6]

[6] It is well known that price indices are deficient for most countries, but the *movement* of prices is inescapable in whatever statistics exist. The real effective exchange rate is here measured as import-weighted change in bilateral nominal exchange rates, adjusted by the ratio of the domestic price index to the import-weighted combination of consumer price indices in the trading partners.

Inflation was not historically a general problem in Africa. The average rate of consumer price increase was less than 3 percent a year in 1960–70, but grew three times faster in the following decade with periods of markedly accelerated growth in 1975 and again in 1981 (see Table 4). Rapid inflation is never uniform across or within sectors and is always a source of distortions. One reason is that bottlenecks appear in the short term, raising the price of specific goods or factors of production relative to their long-run scarcity value. Another reason is that governments try to maintain prices of basic necessities (food) or ''strategic'' goods, such as energy or transport, as low as possible, making them artificially cheap relative to the general price level. In effect, this means imposing administrative rationing and more often than not encouraging parallel markets, that is, different prices for the same good, one of them often being foreign exchange.

Overvalued exchange rates had been identified in several African countries well before the shocks of the seventies, but they appeared more or less tolerable in the presence of low inflation and abundant aid inflows. After 1974, however, the general tendency was toward further appreciation of real exchange rates because inflation was not offset by compensating changes in nominal rates. Thus, the study of the African Center for Monetary Studies cited in the first *Bank Report on Sub-Saharan Africa* of 1981 found that in 18 out of 19 countries reviewed, the real exchange rate had increased between 1963 and 1977–78. Another study for broadly the same period found 19 cases of real exchange appreciation out of 27 countries. The real exchange rate also appreciated for Egypt and Morocco. While changes in the upward direction have been much less general in the more recent years, between 1980 and 1983 there was still further appreciation of the real effective exchange rates in 16 sub-Saharan countries, of which 9 appreciated by more than 20 percent. Real depreciation on the other hand has occurred in 16

Table 4. Inflation Rates,[1] 1973–82
(percent)

	1973	1975	1977	1979	1981	1982
Africa (non-oil)	9.3	15.4	18.1	17.8	20.4	15.9
All Africa	7.6	19.2	17.1	14.3	18.6	12.2

Source: International Monetary Fund, *International Financial Statistics Yearbook*, 1984; World Bank Data Files.

[1] Weighted by GDP in U.S. dollars for the corresponding years.

countries, mainly those belonging to the franc area and those where the degree of overvaluation was highest in the seventies (e.g., Ghana, Uganda, Zaïre).

Real appreciation over time does not necessarily imply overvaluation. Overvaluation has to be demonstrated at each point in time. The presumption, however, is that one leads to the other when, as in the case of African countries, appreciation is associated with widening current account deficits. The extent of overvaluation from the point of view of balance of payments sustainability is a matter for the Fund in which the Bank is not institutionally expert. There are at least two reasons, however, why the Bank is concerned by exchange rates and why, therefore, I mention them as a problem here. One is precisely because of their impact on the balance of payments and therefore on the need for external financing, of which the Bank is a source. The second is because exchange rates affect relative prices, that is, domestic versus foreign prices and ultimately prices of tradables versus nontradables (the relative price which many economists nowadays call the ''real exchange rate''), and thereby resource allocation, which, of course, is of concern to the Bank.

******

A general consequence of these developments—the debt explosion, the public sector expansion, and the pricing distortions—has been the creation of greater rigidities in the economies concerned. These rigidities complicate the task of policymakers at a time when adjustment is to be the order of the day.

Rigidities were created in at least five ways. Additional debt, first, has imposed new contractual obligations that cannot be modified except through rescheduling exercises. Rescheduling thus becomes a (painful) part of the adjustment process. Second, to the extent that a number of low-priority projects were financed during this period, economies were burdened with operating and maintenance costs, without corresponding economic benefits, and these costs are difficult to compress or eliminate, especially when it involves laying off workers. In some cases, costly transformations of plants have to be undertaken; in other cases, the solution may be privatization (more easily said than done) or introduction of protective measures to keep the operation alive, again at a real though less visible cost to the community. Third, increased recruitment into the public sector cannot be easily reversed; hence the commonly observed excessive wage bills in government budgets relative to expenditure on material inputs and equipment. Fourth, equally difficult to reverse are the consumption or input subsidies introduced or increased when finance became more abundant during the short-lived export booms of the seventies or when inflation accelerated. Fifth, but not the least of all, severely overvalued exchange rates are notoriously difficult to correct, for political and other reasons.

A New Agenda

At the outset of this decade, then, we faced a set of problems more complex than ever before. The world depression that lasted until 1983 represented an additional shock, and so did the decline in oil prices for the oil exporters. The new agenda for Africa is more difficult and also more compelling.

The new agenda is a difficult combination of immediate and longer-term issues, some of which have begun to be seriously tackled while others remain almost untouched. This section highlights its main dimensions and then reviews the Bank's response.

Growth and adjustment

The problem in 1980 was not just growth but also adjustment. Adjustment in the first instance meant reducing external current account deficits, which totaled about $4–5 billion in 1980 (excluding Nigeria, which then had a surplus), to sustainable levels. This usually meant a relative reduction of rather enormous proportions since current-account deficits had typically increased by three or four times relative to their "normal" levels of before 1975. In the second half of the seventies they varied between 6 and 20 percent of GNP, even more in a few cases. As for the growth objective, it was not just a matter of continuing unfinished business. It was rather reestablishing the conditions for resumption of growth where the process had been interrupted; creating such conditions for growth in the semiarid areas in particular, where there had been very little growth before; and reversing declines in a few cases where the combination of adverse factors and ill-conceived policies had been particularly damaging.

What has happened in the course of the last five years is significant, but it has not fundamentally changed the task ahead. In brief, the process of adjustment has begun in earnest almost everywhere on the continent, but it is far from complete. The growth record, on the other hand, has been poor, and prospects are not bright. The agenda remains.

In its simplest macroeconomic terms, the implication of having to face massive adjustment problems while the growth objective remained so necessary was—and to a large extent still is—that external resources have gone to finance balance of payments gaps rather than investment. Of course, external capital always helps the balance of payments, by definition, and is not antithetical to capital formation. The point is that the bulk of external resources over the last few years had to be used to maintain essential imports of food, energy, and current inputs for agriculture, for industry, and for the maintenance of infrastructure. Even so, all requirements have not been fulfilled, by a far stretch. Indeed, real imports (excluding food aid) have declined. In the meantime, new investment has suffered.

As can be seen from Table 5, the rate of gross domestic investment in the 1960–70 decade was fairly uniform across the various groups of (sub-Saharan) African countries at close to 16 percent of GDP. It went up to nearly 19 percent in the first half of the 1970s, again without great variation among countries. The differentiated impact of the investment boom can be seen for the period 1975–80 with rates among countries between 18 and 28 percent. By 1983 the (estimated) average was down to 12.5 percent. (Strangely enough the investment rate seemed to be highest in the semi-arid, low-income countries.) It is unlikely that these rates increased in 1984.

Not surprisingly, GDP growth rates (see Table 3) have fallen dramatically from around 4 percent for the whole of Africa in each of the two decades up

Table 5. Gross Domestic Investment in Africa, 1960–83
(annual average, as percentage of GDP)

	1960–70	1970–75	1975–80	1981	1982	Estimate 1983
Low-income countries	14.1	16.9	17.8	17.7	9.3	10.6
Low-income semiarid	14.5	17.8	20.5	17.9	19.0	19.2
Low-income others	14.2	16.8	17.4	17.7	8.7	10.2
Middle-income oil importers	16.0	20.8	23.0	22.8	22.2	17.9
Middle-income oil exporters	16.5	20.2	26.6	27.2	26.1	18.0
All Africa	15.7	19.4	23.7	24.0	19.8	14.8
All except oil exporters	15.1	18.8	20.2	20.0	14.0	12.5

Source: World Bank Data Files.

to 1980, to virtually zero since 1980. Declines in per capita incomes and consumption are, of course, the consequence.

At the same time, resource gaps and current account deficits of oil-importing countries following adjustment programs have been reduced to about half their peak levels of 1980–81. The costs of adjustment in terms of capital formation and growth have been severe, but given the dimension and unsustainability of external deficits, the trade-off was essentially unavoidable.

The agenda for the future therefore clearly includes a need to re-establish investment levels and to improve returns on capital.

Population

The issues of fast and accelerating population growth have been dealt with extensively elsewhere (see, for example, the *World Development Report,* 1984) and need not be discussed here in any detail. But it would be a serious mistake to think or pretend that these issues are not at the heart of the current problem of adjustment and growth. In that sense the term "crisis" so often cited in regard to Africa is misleading if it evokes only an image of a sudden and brutal phenomenon. Population growth never appears as a problem in any one year, and it has been very generally and conspicuously absent as well from the traditional five-year framework used by planners all over Africa.

It is well to remember that from the first oil shock, to take a convenient date, to today, the population on the African continent has increased by about 25 percent, or 100 million people. Continuation of the same rate of demographic expansion will mean an addition of 125 million people over the next ten years. The frightening power of compound interest is perhaps a cliché but it is not a worn out one!

The central concern, of course, is not with population density and availability of land on the continent as a whole. Indeed, larger populations would be ultimately desirable for several little-populated countries. However, the question of excessive settlements does arise in the semiarid zones. The consequences—deforestation, shortened fallow periods, herder-farmer conflicts, soil erosion, and rural emigration—have been mentioned earlier. And even in the humid, coastal countries availability of good, easily accessible land is no longer a factor of growth; deforestation there is also a problem.

The main concern is with the pace of population increase—at 3 percent a year or more, the highest in the world—and with the growing proportion of children and job-seekers that such an increase implies. The problem is the attendant social costs to the country in terms of health, education, and urban facilities requirements. Hence, at a time of constrained domestic and external resources, virtually all African countries face a painful trade-off between meeting the basic needs of a growing population and investing in directly productive capital formation. The trade-off would be much easier over the long haul if significant declines in the demographic growth rates were achieved. In the meantime, elements of a solution have to be sought, among other means, through improved agricultural techniques and more effective, low-cost health and education systems.

Use of national assets

A further general problem has emerged in the course of the last crisis decade: the deterioration of African nations' assets. The issue has already been touched upon, but it merits separate mention here because of its implications for future growth and thereby also for current domestic policies and the direction of aid.

Natural resources, man-made capital, and human capital are all at stake. While there is no precise estimate of the magnitude of the resulting loss in productive value—of any of the major components just mentioned, let alone any aggregation for any particular country or region, there are some partial direct or indirect estimates[7] which are easily corroborated by simple observation in country after country. They all point to a serious problem.

The factors at play are essentially three. Population growth, as already mentioned, puts pressure on natural resources in an obvious manner. It also affects, though more indirectly, social infrastructure resulting, for example, in a lowering of education standards (at primary as well as in some cases higher levels) which in turn means a deterioration of human capital. Second, as previously noted also, the declining rates of gross domestic investment

[7]For example, Food and Agriculture Organization (FAO) and Bank studies have found that potential accessible domestic supply of fuelwood in the Sahel is only 20 percent of the natural forest cover (i.e., the volume of wood that can be cut annually without depletion of the capital) creating a large gap between demand and supply which is in fact covered by abusive woodcutting. By the turn of the century, demand (35 million m^3 of firewood) will be more than twice sustainable supply (15 million m^3). In other studies the FAO has estimated that deforestation destroys 3.6 million hectares a year in Africa.

must imply net disinvestment, overall or in some sectors, in probably all countries where such rates are below 12 percent of GDP. Third, even when total investment levels implied maintenance of existing capital stock and even some net additions, common observation confirms that current maintenance expenditures on roads, buildings, plants, and machinery, have long been neglected and have recently been among the first victims of budget cuts. Fourth, both governments and aid donors have traditionally favored new projects rather than financing rehabilitation of existing assets. Finally, foreign exchange constraints that have limited imports of current inputs have resulted in vast unused capacity in industry. (In extreme cases, such as Ghana until the recent past, average utilization rates were as low as 20 percent.) When such situations persist, existing assets inevitably deteriorate.

As emphasized in successive Bank reports on Africa, maintenance and rehabilitation should attract top priority in public expenditure programs. When applied to all but strictly nonviable projects (which should be scrapped) such expenditures yield the highest economic returns.

External resources and debt

Gross disbursements to sub-Saharan Africa from all sources increased steadily from the 1960s until 1977, approaching $5 billion at that date. They increased massively in 1978, to somewhat under $8 billion, on account of a doubling of private loans (in excess of $4 billion) and have hovered between $9 and $10 billion since then; that is, they have declined marginally in real terms over the five years to 1983. In net terms, that is, after repayment of principal, the amounts were at historic highs because of the generally favorable terms of official assistance and small volume of private debt. This situation has also changed since 1978. Repayments in 1978–83 have on average represented 20 percent of gross disbursements and will be a significantly greater proportion in 1984–87, in part because of the accumulation of previously rescheduled debt. Interest payments, also a small item in the typical African balance of payments until the late 1970s, have grown even more as average terms of debt have hardened.[8] Thus, debt service ratios—estimated at 16 percent for all of sub-Saharan Africa in 1983—represent a relative burden (with respect to exports) more than twice the level before 1974 on aver-

[8]The grant element of total public and publicly guaranteed debt declined to 15 percent in 1982 against a 38 percent average for the period 1970–74. See the Bank's *Sub-Saharan Africa Report*, 1984, Table 17.

age; and reflect serious servicing difficulties for about 15 countries that have had to reschedule debt. In the absence of further reschedulings African debt service in the second half of this decade would jump to levels well in excess of 20 percent of projected exports *on average*, again signifying much higher levels for some of them.

The debt management problem in the African context is treated in detail in a separate paper[9] and does not need further comment at this point. I shall simply conclude by noting that the agenda here includes two closely interrelated aspects: the debt problem which needs a country-by-country approach as situations vary widely (but should not exclude some commonality in approaches) and the general issue of shrinking net resource flows to Africa at a time when policy reforms are taking hold throughout the continent and external support is more needed and deserved than ever.

The Bank's Response

The previous section has highlighted some of the central problems needing priority attention from both the African countries and the aid community, noting further that while these issues have come to the fore since the beginning of this decade, and despite some progress in various areas they are all still with us. Indeed, the prospects for easy solutions are simply not there: the possibility of recurrent spells of drought in the course of, say, the next ten years cannot be ruled out; the possibility of much enhanced export revenue is not consistent with the rather mediocre outlook for commodity markets; the difficulties in mobilizing concessional aid are well known; renewed commercial lending is problematic in view of the continuing debt difficulties of several countries and not desirable in any significant degree for countries with limited creditworthiness; policy reforms undertaken by many African governments will take time to yield results; and meanwhile population will continue to increase.

The Bank for its part has tried to respond flexibly and in a variety of ways: by diversifying its lending instruments, through shifts in sectoral allocations and types of projects, by intensifying its catalytic role in mobilizing resources and through intensified cooperation with other agencies, notably the Fund, and through a more systematic exchange with governments on policy issues. In these various undertakings we have had to capitalize on past experience—both successes and failures.

[9]By Mr. Brau of the Fund.

Resource transfer

I would like to review here three questions: commitments, disbursements, and additional resources.

For Africa as a whole, as shown in Table 1, the level of Bank group commitments has approximately doubled between the 1975–80 average and 1984 to more than $3.6 billion. The proportionate increase has been quite similar for IBRD and IDA, though obviously IDA is much smaller (about one-third of the total in FY1984) in absolute terms because of well-known resource constraints. Sub-Saharan Africa[10] receives much higher levels of IDA credits on a per capita basis than other low-income recipients (the main ones being India, China, and Bangladesh): about one-third of all IDA funds have been directed to sub-Saharan Africa under the last two and the current (FY1985–87) replenishments, whereas Africa has only about one-fifth of the IDA-eligible countries' population. The situation is quite different for the IBRD in which none of the recipient African countries is a major borrower; the prime constraints on further flows to Africa from the IBRD are creditworthiness, policy, and performance. These also apply to IDA countries.

Resource constraints, creditworthiness, and policy considerations will result in a sharp drop in total Bank commitments for FY1985. A small decline of only about $100 million may occur on IDA lending as every effort has been made to protect current levels (and a somewhat increased share) for Africa, but a $1 billion drop in IBRD lending is a likely outcome, mainly affecting sub-Saharan Africa.

Disbursements of IBRD and IDA together have increased at almost the same pace as commitments between 1978 and 1983 (1984)—to nearly $1.3 billion. However, as past IBRD loans continue to be amortized there is a danger of rapidly diminishing net disbursements in the event new IBRD lending does not resume its previous pace. While it is of course in the nature of the normal "debt cycle" that eventually all borrowers should have net outflows, it is clear that this stage should not yet have been reached anywhere in Africa (although such episodes as "oil booms" have created transitory capital surpluses).

In order to assist countries facing serious financial constraints, both external and domestic, the Bank initiated a special action program in March 1983. This effort did not involve new resources but aimed at accelerating disbursements on ongoing projects and through new operations to countries where

---

[10]North Africa comprises IBRD borrowers only.

the execution of priority public investment programs was threatened by foreign exchange and public revenue shortages. Eligibility naturally required that the countries themselves make their best efforts to mobilize resources and apply them to priority projects only. For ongoing operations, the program involved restructuring of projects to reduce costs, provision of revolving funds, increased cost sharing by the Bank and IDA, "front loading" of disbursements relative to original plans, and supplementary financing for groups of projects in difficulty. It involved also more or larger new lending operations with quick disbursing characteristics (see following section).

Over its two years of implementation the program has been quite successful, and it is estimated that the consequent net increase in disbursements for IBRD and IDA worldwide has been about $1.6 billion in FY1984 and will probably be $3.5 billion for FY1984–86. The amounts involved, however, have gone primarily to IBRD borrowers, while IDA beneficiaries have for obvious reasons continued to be constrained. Nevertheless, in terms of countries (25) and number of operations (75), sub-Saharan Africa has been the primary beneficiary. Thus, while the special action program has not resulted in large increases in disbursements to Africa, it has been instrumental in protecting priority projects from unusual financial difficulties and has thereby assisted in the adjustment process.

Finally, the Bank's efforts in mobilizing additional funds for sub-Saharan Africa have met with success with pledges of at least $1.1 billion (of which almost $700 million are in direct contributions to the new facility) obtained at a recent (early 1985) conference in Paris. The facility came to operation by July 1, 1985, and its resources are intended to be fully committed in a matter of three years (on IDA-type terms). No precise allocation procedures have been designed yet, but the overall objective is clearly to provide fast-disbursing financing in support of reform programs undertaken by African governments along the lines indicated in the Bank's recent report on sub-Saharan Africa.[11] While the amounts involved are significant and most certainly needed, the new facility approximately corresponds to no more than restoration of IDA VII at its originally intended minimum level of $12 billion, assuming a one-third share for sub-Saharan Africa. Since the facility is therefore only one element in the total resource effort, other flows of official development assistance and, in some cases, commercial lending will need to be expanded.

---

[11] *Toward Sustained Development in Sub-Saharan Africa* (August 1984).

Diversifying lending instruments

The first structural adjustment loan, approved for Kenya in FY1980 (an IDA credit of $55 million), marked a sharp, qualitative reorientation from pure project lending which generally, and in Africa almost exclusively, characterized previous Bank lending there.

In fact, there has been a remarkable diversification of Bank lending instruments over the last five years in response to both changing needs of borrowers resulting from the unusually difficult times and adjustment efforts by governments. In an effort to classify operations the Bank has recently determined five principal categories that apply equally to IBRD loans and IDA credits.

1. Specific investment loans
2. Sector operations
    a. Sector involvement and maintenance loans
    b. Financial intermediary loans
    c. Sector adjustment loans
3. Structural adjustment loans and program loans
4. Technical assistance loans
5. Emergency reconstruction loans

In effect, these categories cover a continuous range, and specific operations may share in characteristics common to two or more categories.

Africa as a whole has received loans or credits under all categories. Table 6 lists, in chronological order, those operations which form the more novel part of the Bank's activities in the continent. As can be seen from the list, more than 30 operations, in five years, for 19 countries, the coverage has been wide and the amounts, approaching $1 billion in FY1984, as well as the proportion, increasing from 8 to 27 percent of total lending to Africa, have been quite significant.

This set of operations, comprising structural adjustment loans to six countries and a variety of sectoral loans to others, does not by any means exhaust the range of activities through which the objectives of overall adjustment and growth are being pursued. It includes, however, those where the interrelationship between the two goals is closest as a result of two principal characteristics of the operations in question.

The first is the quick-disbursing character of these loans. Whereas regular loans (i.e., categories 1, 2a, 2b and 4 of the list above) typically disburse in five to seven years as the physical execution of the project advances, the structural adjustment loans (SALs) and sector loans take only between a few weeks

Table 6. Sector, Structural Adjustment, and Reconstruction Loans in Africa, 1980–85

Year	Country	Name of Loan/Credit	IDA/ IBRD	Amount (millions of dollars)	Percentage of Total Lending
1980	Kenya	SAL I	IDA	55.0	29
1980	Sudan	Agricultural rehabilitation	IDA	65.0	38
1980	Uganda	Reconstruction I	IDA	72.5	100
1981	Malawi	SAL I	IBRD	45.0	38
1981	Mauritius	SAL I	IBRD	15.0	50
1981	Senegal	SAL	IBRD/IDA	60.0	58
1981	Tanzania	Export rehabilitation	IDA	50.0	54
1981	Zimbabwe	Manufacturing rehabilitation	IBRD/IDA	65.0	100
1981	Zimbabwe	Transport rehabilitation	IBRD	42.0	
1982	Côte d'Ivoire	SAL I	IBRD	150.0	40
1982	Uganda	Reconstruction II	IDA	72.0	66
1983	Ghana	Reconstruction import	IDA	40.0	55
1983	Kenya	SAL II	IBRD/IDA	130.9	68
1983	Malawi	Fertilizer credit	IDA	5.0	9
1983	Sudan	Agricultural rehabilitation II	IDA	50.0	38

1983	Togo	SAL	IDA	40.0	49
1983	Uganda	Agricultural rehabilitation	IDA	70.0	71
1983	Zimbabwe	Manufacturing export promotion	IBRD	70.6	29
1984	Ghana	Export rehabilitation	IDA	76.0	61
1984	Cote d'Ivorie	SAL II	IBRD	250.7	100
1984	Malawi	SAL II	IDA	55.0	54
1984	Mauritius	SAL II	IBRD	40.0	66
1984	Morocco	Industrial trade policy	IBRD	150.4	57
1984	Nigeria	Fertilizer imports	IBRD	250.0	57
1984	Sierra Leone	Agricultural sector I	IDA	21.5	100
1984	Uganda	Reconstruction III	IDA	50.0	41
1984	Zambia	Export rehabilitation	IBRD	75.0	77
1985	Burkina	Fertilizer project	IDA	13.7	. . .
1985	Guinea-Bissau	Reconstruction imports	IDA	10.0	. . .
1985	Madagascar	Industrial assistance	IDA	40.0	. . .
1985	Zambia	Agricultural rehabilitation	IDA	25.0	. . .

Summary:	1980	1981	1982	1983	1984
Total Amount	192	277	222	406	969
Percentage of Bank lending to Africa	8	11	8	16	27

and, say, 18 months.[12] They will also finance either a broad range of general (but priority) imports not specified in detail (not "appraised") in advance, under SALs and some of the sector loans (those for Morocco and Uganda, for example), or a short list of specifically needed inputs for a sector (fertilizers as in Nigeria, or replacement parts and pieces of simple machinery for Ghana and Zimbabwe).

These financial characteristics clearly make these loans a form of balance of payments support. Indeed the size of each particular loan is, within the overall programing constraint, geared to the foreseeable foreign exchange needs of the country. But a caution is in order here: these operations are not intended as "gap-filling" exercises, in connection, for example, with debt rescheduling, any more than are disbursements under regular projects. They are part of medium-term country assistance programs designed by the Bank with the governments concerned, and disbursements will be made only when conditions agreed under the loan are fulfilled.

This latter point relates to the second characteristic, which is the policy reform program in support of which the loan is made. The scope, detailed content, and timing of the policy measures vary greatly. SALs to Africa, as to other countries, however, in varying degree all cover five main areas: medium-term public investment programs (size, composition, and programing systems); the external trade regime (usually seeking to correct the anti-export bias implicit in overvalued exchange rates and protective systems by moving toward a more uniform level of protection of domestic activities and by removing quantitative restrictions); resource mobilization (including such varied aspects as level and administrative management of foreign debt, cost recovery systems for public services, interest rates, and financial intermediation); public enterprises (improving management, pricing, employment practices, and contractual relationships between enterprises and government, sale or transformation of enterprises, and the like); prices and incentive systems (where actions are sought to correct major distortions, particularly in agriculture and energy).

Sector loans, in turn, include reforms of the same type, but narrowed in scope to the issues of the particular sector. For example, the fertilizer loan to Nigeria supported reforms in the fertilizer subsector such as reductions in

---

[12] SALs (and other sector adjustment loans) are generally disbursed in two tranches—the first when conditions of effectiveness of the loan have been met, the second when a number of specified agreed policy actions have been taken to the satisfaction of the Bank.

subsidies, commercialization of fertilizer retail channels, and improvements in procurement and marketing methods.

Discussion of the rationale for the particular measures that, in the Bank's view, form a desirable package of policy reforms would go beyond the scope of this paper. The general objective can be stated as the pursuit of greater efficiency in the use of resources through greater reliance on economic incentives, that is, a set of prices that best reflect real scarcities. Such prescriptions do not rule out the existence of an active public sector or various forms of government intervention, both of which are needed to correct private sector deficiencies and market failures.

A number of lessons from these new forms of lending have been learned already. These, in brief, are as follows.

First, preparation of SALs and similar operations, especially for the first and second time, requires large amounts of policy-focused economic and sector work and, from the earliest stages, continuous exchanges with the government concerned. These procedures will ensure mutual understanding, prevent false starts, and avoid exaggerated expectations.

Second, it is more important and more effective to design a program focused on essential and feasible reforms than to seek overall coverage. While the urge to be comprehensive is perhaps a natural reflection of the extent of the problems faced by many countries, there is clearly a danger in attempting too much relative to a government's political and administrative capabilities.

Third, expectations as to the time needed to effect policy changes, especially institutional reforms, have often been overoptimistic. Such changes must be conceived within a period of several years and supported through a succession of SAL or similar operations. Another lesson is clear regarding timing: while undertaking reforms during a crisis may instill a sense of necessity that may previously have been lacking, it is even better to tackle problems before a crisis.

Fourth, an important dimension—indeed, one which is the essence of the kind of structural adjustment supported by the Bank—is in the durability of the changes sought, in other words their institutionalization. Immediate changes in prices or levels of expenditure may be needed to pursue short-term stabilization. Ensuring that future price changes can be effected more smoothly or preventing abrupt cuts in investment or consumption require closer monitoring, more realistic programing, and more systematic policy analysis—rather than cyclical spurts of planning activity—by the central government and parapublic agencies. Introducing the necessary changes in organization, in personnel, and in habits is what institutional reform is about.

Such changes are also needed to increase management flexibility and therefore improve the response to exogenous factors not foreseeable at the time that structural adjustment programs are prepared.

Sectoral allocations and types of projects

The sectoral composition of the Bank's lending program to Africa (see Tables 1 and 2) has changed in the last quinquennium in ways that reflect both the concerns expressed in the "new agenda" and the lessons from experience noted earlier.

Agriculture's priority is reflected in the continuing share in total lending: about one fourth on average over the last four years. The absolute amounts, however, have not increased steadily, and its share is less than the peaks attained at the end of the 1970s and in 1981. There are two reasons for this. The first is simply that other sectors, where lending has been modest in the past, are naturally becoming more important. Industry is the main case in point. This sector now absorbs about the same volume of lending as agriculture, reflecting the effort of governments, with Bank support, to diversify production and exports. The second reason is that the relatively high rate of failure with agricultural projects (including livestock) has indicated the need for a pause and a reassessment of the present portfolio in this sector and probably for some reorientation of the program (see below).

The growth, in absolute and relative terms, of nonproject lending is a reflection of the SALs and sector loans discussed in the previous section.[13]

As noted earlier, the emphasis on infrastructure (transportation, energy, telecommunications) has naturally diminished over the years even though as an overall strategy it still absorbs the greatest share of Bank lending (about 28 percent in FY1984). Within this category, for obvious reasons, energy has regained some of its past importance (in relative terms) and the number of projects has increased greatly in the last few years with more operations in the oil and gas subsectors.

Finally, the continuing concern for poverty alleviation and the need to meet the costs of rapid urbanization have led to a modest (relative) expansion of lending for urban development and water and sewerage.

In terms of types of projects the trend in recent years has been and will

[13]The figures in Tables 1 and 2 refer to a somewhat more restrictive definition of "nonproject" lending than the one discussed previously as illustrated by the list of operations in Table 6.

continue to be in two directions that directly address problems noted earlier. One is maintenance and rehabilitation. This is accomplished through regular projects, for example, to repair roads and provide equipment and technical assistance to public works departments, and also to a large extent through sector lending of the kind discussed a propos the diversification of lending instruments. For example, the import reconstruction and the export rehabilitation credits to Ghana financed spare parts and equipment renewal for the transport sector, and for the cocoa, timber, and gold-mining subsectors. Groups of public enterprises in need of rehabilitation and revolving capital benefit from SALs (Senegal, Côte d'Ivoire, Malawi, Togo) or from sector loans (Madagascar, Morocco).

The second line of "new style" projects mainly is being developed in agriculture where two major needs have become increasingly manifest: research (especially for food crops) and an appropriate institutional framework (for research, for national extension services, for marketing, for policy analysis). These incipient projects involve a financial dimension and an immediate impact which may be more modest and less visible than more traditional agricultural or area-development projects, but are nonetheless building the foundations for future agricultural progress. Institution building, including strengthening of existing institutions, is also, as noted earlier, an essential component of SALs and sector-adjustment operations.

Resource shifts within the Bank

The priority given to Africa, and sub-Saharan Africa in particular, is also manifest in the reallocation of the Bank's administrative and staff resources. Over the last four years the Bank has been reallocating relatively more resources toward the departments that deal with sub-Saharan Africa (the Eastern and Southern Africa and the Western Africa Regional Offices) both to help develop the pipeline of operations for future years and to increase the scope and enhance the quality and relevance of economic and sector-policy work. For FY1985, within an overall zero-growth budget for the total complex of the Bank's operating departments, increases in staff resources have been authorized for only the two African Regions. In 1982, 20 (later 25) new positions for secondment of staff to governments in IDA-eligible sub-Saharan countries were also authorized and have been filled. The number of Bank resident missions also has been increased, so that out of 33 such offices in developing countries worldwide, 21 are now in sub-Saharan Africa.

Finally, the Bank has, in agreement with the government concerned, reactivated or created aid-coordination arrangements (consultative groups or otherwise) in addition to the eight that were in existence before 1984. For example, two such new groups met at the end of 1984, for Ghana and Senegal, and financing pledges in support of the policy reforms undertaken by these two governments were made which would probably have been difficult to obtain otherwise.

Collaboration with the Fund

Active collaboration between the Bank and the Fund has become much closer on African countries over the years for two interrelated sets of reasons. In the first place, it is a practical necessity, resulting from the much more extensive, and in cases more prolonged, involvement of the International Monetary Fund since the mid- or late-seventies in countries where the Bank has been active for a long time (see Table 7). In the second place, it has become increasingly clear that the issues of stabilization, adjustment, and growth cannot be dissociated from one another. Thus, the primary concerns and areas of competence of one institution relate directly to the activities of the other.

For example, as already noted, the question of the appropriate nominal exchange rate (a primary concern of the Fund) cannot be dissociated from the question of the level of domestic producer prices (which is of direct interest to the Bank); the objective of overall fiscal balance (of concern to the Fund) is closely linked with the generation of public savings (of concern to the Bank); the size of the public investment program, a component of aggregate demand, interests the Fund, while the composition of the program is typically reviewed by the Bank and clearly the two aspects are not entirely separable; similarly, the Fund will be concerned by the level and growth of domestic credit, but the Bank is interested in the sectoral allocation of credit and may be particularly concerned by the financial health of specific recipients of credit, such as public enterprises.

These interconnections and areas of overlapping interest require that diagnostic analyses and policy recommendations be, in some fashion, coordinated and made consistent. This is done through systematic exchange of information (while preserving the confidentiality of information given by a government for use by one of the institutions only), as well as exchange of ideas and comparison of economic projections in respect, for example, of future availability of external financing in support of a particular program.

Where major adjustment issues are at stake, both institutions have to coor-

Table 7. Stand-By and Extended Fund Facility Programs in Africa, FY1980–84

	1980	1981	1982	1983	1984
Central African Republic	S-B	S-B	(S-B)	S-B	(S-B)
Congo	(S-B)				
Côte d'Ivoire		EFF	(EFF)	(EFF)	(EFF)
Egypt	(EFF)	(EFF)	(EFF)		
Equatorial Guinea		S-B	(S-B)		
Ethiopia			S-B	(S-B)	
Gabon	(S-B)	EFF	(EFF)	(EFF)	
Gambia	S-B	(S-B)	S-B	(S-B)	S-B
Ghana	(S-B)				S-B
Guinea				S-B	(S-B)
Kenya	S-B	S-B	S-B	S-B	(S-B)
Liberia	(S-B)	S-B	S-B	S-B	S-B
Madagascar		S-B (x 2)	(S-B)	S-B	S-B
Malawi	S-B	S-B	(S-B)	S-B	EFF
Mali				S-B	S-B
Mauritania		S-B	S-B	(S-B)	
Mauritius	S-B	S-B	S-B	(S-B)	S-B
Morocco		EFF	S-B	(S-B)	S-B
Niger					S-B
Rwanda	S-B	(S-B)			
Senegal	(S-B)	EFF	S-B	S-B	S-B
Sierra Leone	S-B	EFF	(EFF)		S-B
Somalia	S-B	(S-B)	S-B	S-B	(S-B)
Sudan	EFF	(EFF)	S-B	S-B	(S-B)
Tanzania		S-B	(S-B)	(S-B)	
Togo	S-B	S-B	(S-B)	S-B	(S-B)
Uganda	S-B	(S-B)	(S-B)	S-B	S-B
Zaïre	S-B	(S-B)	EFF	(EFF)	S-B
Zambia	(S-B)		EFF	S-B	(S-B)
Zimbabwe		S-B	(S-B)	S-B	(S-B)

Note: Parentheses indicate a continuing program. Where, in a given year, a new program replaces an existing one, only the new program is indicated.

dinate their programs and their financing. For all countries where SALs have been approved by the Bank, Fund-supported programs were already in place or were initiated in close parallel. This has been done because in such cases there was invariably a need for demand-management measures to address a short-term balance of payments deficit, while policy and institutional reforms addressing more directly the supply response over the medium term were covered under general or sectoral structural-adjustment programs supported by the Bank. Also, the financing plan for the balance of payments requires, in most cases, involvement of several sources of funds—the Fund, the Bank, other official bilateral and multilateral agencies, and, as the case may be, commercial banks as well. Coordination of the financing package is done simultaneously or in steps, formally (as in consultative groups chaired by the Bank) or informally through a succession of bilateral contacts, by the Fund or the Bank, or both. In frequent cases debt rescheduling is an important component of the financing plan. As is well known, rescheduling through the Paris Club (official creditors) and the London Club (private creditors) today requires prior agreement on a program between the Fund and the country concerned. As the medium-term character of adjustment programs, especially in Africa, has been increasingly recognized by the parties concerned, the Bank has been asked by the Paris Club to present its views on particular countries' medium- and long-term prospects in anticipation of eventual rescheduling exercises. This should contribute to a better integration of actions to resolve the debt problem within longer-term adjustment and growth programs.

Because programs supported by the Bank and Fund are closely interdependent, collaboration between the two institutions is necessary. This, however, is a complex affair, considerably more complex than coordination between the various professions involved in building a house, to take a popular analogy. Differences between the two institutions therefore do occur occasionally: regarding the evolution of the external "parameters," or the governments' capacity to implement desirable measures, or the likely supply response of the economy, and so on. These are areas where there is no revealed truth, and opinions may naturally diverge. They can best be resolved by continuing dialogue and acceptance of compromise in the best interest of the countries which both institutions seek to assist. At the same time, agreement on the twin objectives of adjustment *and* growth are fundamentally shared by the Bank and the Fund.

Conclusions

The paper has covered the widening range of the World Bank's activities in the many and diverse countries of Africa over a long period of time. Even so, the coverage is not complete. For example, the activities of the International Finance Corporation and this institution's plans for a broader involvement in the development of African private enterprise have not been mentioned. Neither could this review be specific in respect of particular countries or particular Bank operations.

Even within the confines of this presentation, there is no firm conclusion I can offer. As I emphasized earlier, the agenda that has emerged since the beginning of this decade is still very much with us, even though real progress has been achieved both by the African countries and by the aid community. Africa has shown remarkable resilience in the face of adversity, and governments almost everywhere on the continent have begun to implement serious adjustment programs. Some additional concessional resources are being mobilized from a group of industrial countries (quite apart from their response to the drought), and most bilateral aid programs now give high priority to Africa.

The Bank for its part has tried to improve prospects for Africa by adapting and diversifying its lending instruments, by providing better focused and relevant advice to governments undertaking policy reforms, by actively seeking to mobilize additional resources, and by strengthening coordination with other sources of assistance, bilateral and multilateral, notably with the Fund.

Efforts in all these directions will have to continue, but we need continuously to assess the direction and efficiency of the Bank's country assistance. We must interrogate ourselves and try to find answers satisfactory to all on issues such as the following. Regarding the appropriate policy content of structural and sectoral adjustment lending: what is the minimum, feasible reform package that will have a real impact? Regarding issues of balance: to what extent should new forms of lending displace regular projects that more directly promote investment? Regarding directions: how can the objectives of poverty alleviation and rural development be protected or restored? How can efforts within Africa be effectively supported toward economic integration which so predominantly and justifiably feature in the Lagos Plan of Action?

All these questions involve difficult trade-offs—or else they would not be difficult questions. The Bank will continue to seek realistic answers to them in the context of a continuing and strengthened partnership with those primarily interested, that is, the African countries themselves, which ultimately will reap the benefits, if the answers are right, or bear the costs, if they are wrong.

Comments

Philip Ndegwa

I enjoyed reading Mr. de Azcarate's paper for many reasons. His historical analysis is useful in understanding the evolving relations between African countries and the World Bank and some of the factors behind a number of past policy changes in the Bank's approach to Africa. Incidentally, Mr. de Azcarate's analysis also reminds us that the science of modern development economics is very young indeed and is still evolving. Mr. de Azcarate's paper is also refreshingly frank in some parts. For example, he accepts that the World Bank's approach to African problems in the past may have had some shortcomings. I shall say more about this important matter later. Finally, in his reflective moments, Mr. de Azcarate offers a number of excellent observations and ideas for the future.

For these, and other reasons, careful reading of Mr. de Azcarate's paper will show that he has achieved more than what he modestly says, in his introduction, was his intention. Though I regret that my discussion must be highly selective and some of the comments I shall make might sound rather critical, I am sure that it is more a matter of emphasis than major difference in objective or philosophy.

Mr. de Azcarate does not, as he says in the first sentence of his paper, discuss adjustment or stabilization. He has concentrated on what he calls "the evolving role of the Bank" in Africa. It may be that Mr. de Azcarate recognized, and, if so, quite rightly in my view, the difficulty of discussing stabilization or adjustment when these subjects are narrowly defined to mean that the main policy thrust should be on reduced demand. Such a definition, in the context of the overall situation facing African countries, with low and declining incomes, dependence on one or two commodities for export earn-

---

Author's Note: The views expressed in these comments are not necessarily those of the Central Bank of Kenya nor of the Government of the Republic of Kenya.

ings, a lack of integration of national economies in the sense that monetization of the economy has a long way to go, high and rising unemployment, and disintegrating infrastructural facilities partly because of lack of spares, is difficult to understand or accept intellectually. As I have said elsewhere, in the situation in which African countries, especially sub-Saharan African countries, find themselves, so-called stabilization programs should be consistent with, and pursued within, measures aimed at raising the rates of development in general. If that is not done, the programs will not make much sense. In fact, one could think of cases and circumstances in which such programs could make the whole national situation worse.

The paper lacks a sense of immediacy or urgency although the desperate situation facing most African countries calls for urgent and appropriate attention. In fact, it would appear as if the author seems to think that continuation of the present rather gentle and evolutionary response to the crisis facing Africa will be sufficient. In my view, the situation facing Africa is unique and alarming, and unless urgent and adequate measures are undertaken now, the future is going to be a horrible one, with things getting out of hand and resulting in the actual disintegration of some of the countries.

The author does not (perhaps because of modesty) stress the importance of the World Bank (and the Fund) to Africa within the prevailing and foreseeable international environment of development assistance and trade. There can be no doubt whatsoever that the role of the World Bank in Africa is now of critical importance and will continue to be so for the next 15 to 20 years. This is so because of the nature of the development problem in the continent, because of the size of the countries and the fragile structure of their economies, because of the African countries' so-called lack of creditworthiness, because of their present levels of external indebtedness, because of the falling levels of official development assistance, and so on.

A few more words on this point are in order. First, it is true, as Mr. de Azcarate says, that Africa's share in the distribution of IDA resources has increased recently. But that needs to be seen historically because, for many years, most of IDA resources went to Asia, with Africa getting only a little. The main point, however, is that Africa desperately needs a greater flow of concessionary resources, and the Bank should respond to that need with the same commitment it did for Asia when most of IDA resources went to that region. That commitment needs to be, for a number of good reasons, deliberate and publicly declared.

Second, I want to say something about the structural adjustment loan program of the World Bank. Mr. de Azcarate's paper contains an excellent section on the lessons learned so far from this program. In particular, I like the reasons he gives to explain the difficulties encountered in preparation and implementation of SAL in a number of cases. Taking Kenya as an example, there is no doubt whatsoever that the reasons indicated by Mr. de Azcarate are responsible for preventing the World Bank from reaching agreement with Kenya for the third SAL. In particular, the SAL program for Kenya has involved too broad a coverage of areas in which reforms should take place. Moreover, the time scale expected for implementation of policy changes has been completely unrealistic. The fact that this is happening in a country which has performed very well and to the satisfaction of the Fund in virtually all the major policy areas on which the World Bank and the Fund usually focus (exchange rate policy, interest rate policy, wages policy, fiscal policy, import liberalization) indicates clearly that there is something seriously wrong in the design of SALs, at least for Kenya.

I am spending a bit of time on the SAL because it is precisely the kind of program that is needed in dealing with the African crisis. Unfortunately, the difficulties encountered in the administration of SALs appear to be used as an excuse to move away from that kind of program to the so-called project forms of support. While not condemning project-based programs, especially when they are well designed, it is my view that SALs and the extended Fund facility program of the Fund are the appropriate mechanisms needed in dealing with the African crisis. Further, those mechanisms should be used as learning processes and opportunities for promoting meaningful dialogue between the World Bank, the Fund, and donor countries. One feels that there is much too much rigidity on the part of the Bank and the Fund: a reasonable degree of flexibility is absolutely necessary in the African case.

Mr. de Azcarate does not deal explicitly with an important question: why has development performance in Africa been so hopelessly poor? For example, why are people in some countries now poorer on average than they were 20 years ago and after the two U.N. Development Decades? As we continue to see, many explanations have been given, with the emphasis put on those explanations which serve one's intentions better. Some of the explanations offered include too rapid rates of population growth, unfavorable terms of trade, misguided economic management policies, and activities of multinationals. In offering these and other explanations there has been a growing tendency to allocate blame—with the donors stressing the internal weaknesses in the African countries, and with the latter stressing external factors and the injustices of the existing international order.

Fortunately, the World Bank's recent reports on Africa have helped to stimulate a more objective discussion of the matter. It appears to me, however, that these reports, and now also Mr. de Azcarate's paper, minimize the effects of external factors in Africa's development. In fact, in Mr. de Azcarate's paper there is no reference at all to the growing protectionism now being practiced by the industrial countries. While that protectionism is particularly serious for the middle-income countries of Latin America and Asia (because they produce more manufactured goods for export) there is no doubt that both tariff and nontariff barriers in the industrial countries are a major problem for a number of African countries, especially those with recognizable opportunities of performing better economically through exports.

It appears as if the donor countries are now concentrating, in explaining why Africa has not achieved better economic development performance, on internal factors as a way of justifying their reduced levels of support to African countries. The argument appears to run something like this. If only African countries could rely more on the market mechanism and do something about their rates of population increase, their agricultural pricing policies, their exchange rate policies, and corruption, development would be assured. But, in my view, while measures in those areas are needed and should be undertaken immediately where that is not being done, they will never be sufficient for the job. Appropriate international measures are also desperately needed. As we discuss the "new agenda," however, African countries can do no more than take note of the "new politics" of the donors and its consequences: reduction in aid, more protectionism, and the fact that desired and necessary reforms in the international economy will not be introduced in the near future. In any case, it is now clear from the experience of the last few years that at the international level the industrial countries are interested only in those measures of direct and immediate advantage to themselves.

One other thing we have learned over the last few years is that only the poor countries are expected to practice rational economic principles (e.g., to rely on the market, not to adopt protectionist measures, to avoid government budget deficits). In the industrial countries such practices are regarded as sensible. Obviously what we are seeing is exercise of political power with its inevitable consequence of double standards and other selfish measures.

When one looks at the situation in those terms, it becomes clear that the World Bank and the Fund have a most important role to play in educating their rich members and applying more effort and imagination in raising resources for their African members.

An important area in which the World Bank can and should do something to help Africa is in the parastatals sector. A lot has been said in recent years about parastatals in Africa, and I believe that many African countries are now convinced that policy changes and reforms in that regard are necessary. The World Bank and its International Finance Corporation could be extremely useful in mobilizing private external capital required in the reconstruction of the parastatals. The Bank's thinking at one time appeared to be that government departments could not be entrusted with the responsibility of implementing certain projects because of civil service salary structures or because of the need for more direct donor involvement, and therefore parastatals had to be established in order to receive the Bank's support. Many parastatals continue to contribute a great deal to the development of the countries concerned. What is now needed is a kind of second-stage operation in the development of parastatals which involves reorientation of the overall policy, changed working relations with government, consolidation, and privatization or divestiture where feasible. The Bank should be an active participant in this process.

We are happy to hear from Mr. de Azcarate that the Bank will continue to pay attention to the maintenance and rehabilitation of the existing infrastructural facilities. This is to be welcomed because in many parts of the continent existing roads and railways are in a deplorable and deteriorating state, and therefore the first job should be to put them back into working order, just as this is what needs to be done in the industrial sector. In the case of transportation facilities, however, there is need for the Bank to extend its interest. In particular, better road and rail links between African countries are desperately needed to support intra-African trade and economic cooperation in general. It is not always recognized that in addition to a lack of communication links between neighboring countries in some cases, transportation of goods in Africa is at least 50 percent more expensive than in Asia. The World Bank is well placed, because of its experience and influence, to play a leading role in overcoming this major obstacle to African countries' development based on economic cooperation and other forms of self-reliance.

I have dealt with Africa's external indebtedness in some detail in a paper prepared for the Third World Foundation Conference to be held in Zimbabwe later this year. For the present purpose I would like to make several points. First, the small figures involved should not give the impression that the debt problem in Africa is small. The President of the World Bank has himself said that many sub-Saharan African countries face serious debt problems. Second, the debt situation in Africa must be seen as an integral part of the overall development problem facing the continent and not as something that can be dealt with in isolation and on a country-by-country basis. In that sense, I am in disagreement with what Mr. de Azcarate says in his paper. Third, the debt situation, the declining overseas development assistance, and the growing unwillingness by private sources of capital to lend more to Africa all mean that the World Bank and the Fund must give more support, direct and indirect, to African countries.

Mr. de Azcarate has a few paragraphs on what he refers to as the Bank's collaboration with the Fund. I am sure all my colleagues will be happy to hear that there is now active collaboration between the Bank and the Fund in dealing with African countries. The two organizations have the same interest in most of the macroeconomic policies, such as exchange rates, internal prices, and trade policies. But unfortunately the programs through which they deal with African countries are not closely coordinated. For example, it is not easy for a country to deal with a Fund stand-by program while also working on a Bank's structural adjustment loan program that has a different time frame. Even receiving different missions which ask more or less the same questions can be very expensive to African countries. I have suggested to the two organizations that the best way in which to promote collaboration between themselves, on the one hand, and the African countries, on the other, is through simultaneous programs of structural adjustment loans and extended Fund financing.

No one disagrees with the intentions of the "new agenda." What needs to be stressed, however, is that the new agenda calls for a new thinking and philosophy for the World Bank and for other donors and a new thinking and philosophy for the African countries themselves. I want to give one good example of how this new thinking and philosophy would work. That example concerns food supply. I believe all those concerned now accept that food aid will not solve the food problem in Africa. The solution is greater food production, and what the donors should therefore do is give much greater support to agricultural production within the continent itself. Within that program the countries able to produce agricultural surpluses would be encouraged to do so, and those surpluses used as food aid to those countries unable, maybe because of such factors as climatic conditions, to produce adequate food for themselves. Financial resources are needed to support farmers, build roads and storage facilities, and also to finance surpluses. On the part of the African countries, there must be a firm recognition that in addition to more effort and appropriate policies to achieve greater agricultural production (better farmer prices, appropriate land policies, better oriented extension services) economic cooperation in agriculture is as important as in industry.

In other words, a departure from the past is needed in dealing with food supply. It is also needed in other sectors: we should not rely on a gentle evolutionary process to deal with the development crisis facing African countries. In that connection we should also now move to more realistic ways of analyzing the problem by looking at the real situation in physical terms. What needs to be done to reduce unemployment by, say, 50 percent? How are the increasing numbers of people to be fed? What about literacy, water supply, shelter? When one looks at those physical requirements needed in 2000 (and we do know already how many people there will be in Africa then), it becomes clear that the present techniques of looking at the problem are inadequate. In terms of the usual orthodox economic analysis, achievement of those physical targets would need growth rates of incomes never heard of before, and certainly several times the rates normally used in orthodox economic planning. Since that income approach is not useful, what other approaches and strategies do we use? In short, a ''new development economics'' is also needed.

John Williamson

I was pleased that Governor Ndegwa suggested that structural adjustment lending and the extended Fund facility should be done jointly because that is a cause which I have also attempted to explore. It does not appear to have evoked any sympathy among the developing countries. Indeed, the latest communiqué of the Group of Twenty-Four had what appeared to be an explicit repudiation of that idea. I think that what worried them is what they call ''cross conditionality,'' which is the notion that neither the Bank nor the Fund would lend unless the conditions of both were satisfied. Ideally, that type of consideration ought not to be there; but we have seen that among many African governors those misgivings are very real. I want to suggest to the Fund staff that one of the requirements that would need to be met in order to give reassurance to countries that it was a good idea to go ahead with joint Fund-Bank programs would be an assurance that the Fund would be prepared to reinforce success rather than to demand additional policy changes whenever it makes a loan. This issue has arisen in the past in the case of India. The Fund, as I understand it, essentially took the view that the

Indians had brought their macroeconomic policies into order and all its management wanted was assurances that they would remain in order. That was a very proper attitude. Unfortunately, there have been other countries, equally deserving, that have not obtained that type of response from the Fund. I wonder what would happen in the African Department if, for instance, a request for support came from Botswana (which was used by the Fund staff as an example of a country that is managing its policies well). Would the Fund staff be prepared to take the bureaucratic risk—it is a risk—of simply saying, "Your policies look good to us; we are prepared to endorse them as they are?" Or would they demand further changes? The bureaucratic risk is that if they do the latter and the program then breaks down, they end up in that uncomfortable corner since the country performed as it was required in terms of the instruments, but it did not achieve the objectives. In that case somebody in the Fund is going to want to know why the staff agreed to a program like that. This bureaucratic risk is one that the Fund staff ought to be prepared to take in order to give countries the confidence to undertake programs jointly with the Fund and the Bank. I think the Bank also would have to make some adjustments. Mr. de Azcarate said, in effect, that "when we have a structural adjustment lending program we think of all the things that the Bank would like to see done in the country." I think the Bank has to be a little more disciplined in its structural adjustment programs if countries are going to see them as the constructive way forward in the future that, in principle, they ought to be.

Let me also add a word on the international context. When we speak of the burden of adjustment, that plea is clearly directed to the international community, the major industrial countries, and not to the management or the Fund staff as such. Let me suggest that sharing the burden of adjustment is not a good slogan to use in that context. The reactions which you will get if you use that slogan among the industrial countries are complex. Americans may think you are joining with them and calling on the Japanese to relax their trade restrictions; the Japanese may think that you are joining with them and calling on the Americans to reduce their budget deficit; or they may all think that you are calling on them to reinstate inflation; and none of those would win a sympathetic response. Clearly, the policies regarding aggregate demand that are pursued in the developed countries are a matter of vital importance to developing countries, as well as developed countries, and it is surely legitimate for developing countries to express their views on those issues in councils like the Interim Committee and the Fund Executive Board. Indeed, I would very much hope that in those fora, the developing countries would try to strike a blow against the rather primitivist tendency in economic philosophy, incorporated in the Fund's current *World Economic Outlook*, where one finds the view expressed that budget deficits in Germany or Japan are going to do all sorts of terrible things to the world economy. Surely, none of us believes that. So, there are certainly some issues which can legitimately be raised there.

But more crucial for developing countries is the issue of protectionism. That is where developing countries could make some very specific points, in a very telling way, because that is where their interests are on the same side as the rhetoric of the developed countries. The next time President Reagan lectures the International Monetary Fund Annual Meetings about the "magic of the market," it might be useful if somebody from a country like Swaziland were to get up and say, "Well, let us have a free world market in sugar and let us see the magic of the market work in that context. Give us a chance to adjust. We think we can do it perfectly well if you give us a chance." That, I think, would have far more impact than suggestions for sharing the burden of adjustment. Let me also add that the attitude which the developing countries are taking at the moment, in regard to a new GATT trade round, is a great mistake. They have more potentially to gain from this than the industrial countries and they should be in the forefront of pushing a new GATT trade round which would have developing-country interests at its center.

Reply

Luis de Azcarate

Let me try to respond to comments directly relevant to my subject, which has been the role of the Bank in adjustment and growth in Africa. I shall for convenience consider them under six headings: IBRD and IDA allocations, role of structural adjustment loans and other instruments, debt, food, urgency of the "crisis," and Bank-Fund collaboration.

IBRD and IDA Allocations

What limits IBRD lending to Africa in the first place is not resources; it is the state of countries' creditworthiness. What limits IDA lending in the first place is the level of resources. Performance, that is, policy performance, however, is an important factor for both; for IBRD-eligible countries because poor performance will weaken or altogether destroy their creditworthiness, for both IBRD- and IDA-eligible countries because poor performance will mean lower returns on the use of scarce resources.

Of course, we realize that creditworthiness and performance are judgmental matters. We use such quantitative measures as are available and meaningful as well as our staff's best qualitative judgments to determine IBRD and IDA eligibility in principle. At this time only a handful of countries (in sub-Saharan Africa) are IBRD borrowers; you are well aware which. Some also are ''blend'' countries receiving both IBRD and IDA funds, that is, when creditworthiness is still limited and per capita income below the IDA eligibility threshold. Some have in recent years graduated from IDA into full IBRD status (e.g., Cameroon), others have in fact become pure IDA when their margin of creditworthiness has eroded (e.g., Senegal).

While we realize that Africa's needs are enormous and most countries face special difficulties, we cannot at this time consider allocating more than about one third of IDA-7 resources to sub-Saharan Africa, for the reasons I indicate in the paper. With that share the per capita allocation to sub-Saharan Africa is on average much higher than for any other eligible group of countries. Despite the relative financial strength of China and India, these countries have very large masses of poor people. Bangladesh, for example, faces developmental difficulties as intractable, or worse, than many African countries. An allocation from IDA of 50 or 60 percent, as suggested in one of the papers presented to us, is frankly not a reasonable proposition at this time.

Let me add an important note in this connection. Much more than in the past, I suspect the donors to the special facility for Africa, and to IDA as well, will judge the merits of concessional assistance to Africa (however insufficient we may all think its level is) on the basis of results. This means an obligation for the Bank to apply these scarce resources where the conjunction of need and policy actions by governments offers the best chances for success for promoting adjustment and growth.

Role of Structural Adjustment Loans and Other Instruments

Governor Ndegwa says that the structural adjustment loans is precisely the kind of program that is needed in dealing with the African crisis but he notes also that there is something seriously wrong in the design of the structural adjustment loans at least for Kenya. He also sees ''the difficulties encountered in the administration of structural adjustment loans . . . as an excuse to move away from that kind of program to the so-called project forms of support.''

I think I can summarize my views on this by saying that a diversified diet is best. And as a result of the evolution I describe in my paper, I believe the Bank does now offer a wide selection of instruments to all its borrowers. Structural adjustment loans certainly have their place in the menu for some countries under some circumstances. Associated with the quick disbursing aspect of the loan or credit—a most valuable component in times of balance of payments difficulties—they support a coherent and broad package of policy reforms designed to permit or enhance future growth. But they are also complex, time-consuming operations in design and preparation. They are hard for governments to implement at the desired pace in all their components. They are difficult to monitor and therefore to assess as successes or failures. And there is no agreed analytical model underlying them as there is, to some extent, in the case of Fund programs.

In advocating a diversified diet I do not want to dissuade any country from considering structural adjustment loans (in fact, I believe more structural adjustment loans are currently under preparation for Africa than for any other region) but rather suggest that one should not minimize the merits of other forms of lending that also respond to real needs. Regular projects, first, are needed to raise gradually the levels of investment which are now at dangerously low levels in most countries, as I note in the paper. At the same time, projects can be of very different kinds and address maintenance and rehabilitation requirements and not just new fixed investment.

Sector adjustment lending, in turn, which has been growing fast in the last few years, can combine several advantages. These loans focus on fewer, sector-specific objectives and policy actions and thereby establish a simpler, more direct link between lending and performance. They are also less complex to prepare; at the same time more detailed, and still manageable action programs can be designed, provided of course that appropriate sector work has been carried out before. Being more focused and simpler, they are easier to monitor. Finally, the application of funds may be for general balance of payments purposes, or to meet sectoral current input requirements or to finance elements of a sectoral investment program over a period of time or a combination of the above. Also, a sector can be defined functionally, say, to encompass a group of public enterprises across traditional sector boundaries.

Debt

Governor Ndegwa comments that "the debt situation in Africa must be seen as an integral part of the overall development problem facing Africa and not as something which can be dealt with in isolation and on a country-by-country basis." He disagrees with what I say on this.

Since I say very little on this topic in the paper let me try to be a little more explicit. First, I do mention in the paper the two issues of debt and resource transfer as being "closely interrelated" and I think therefore that I am in agreement with Governor Ndegwa on the first proposition of his commentary. I do think, however, that in considering these two issues together, as he suggests, a country-by-country approach is more advisable than one solution that would cover all of Africa or a large number of countries at the same time. One quite empirical reason is that this approach has worked rather effectively so far, at least by avoiding the worst (i.e., country default or bank collapses). Second, as mentioned in my paper, country debt situations differ widely within Africa (some have large commercial bank debts, others little, some mainly trade arrears, others heavy debt with official bilateral donors, others more debt with multilateral "preferred" creditors, others with East European countries and so on). Overall economic prospects are also different from one country to another. Also, blanket solutions across countries would raise problems on equity grounds: creditors, I suspect, are probably more willing to relieve the debt of those countries that are trying to help themselves more vigorously.

But all this, again, is not to say that "the solution" is at hand. Indeed for the most indebted African countries, the years 1985–87 are going to be most difficult (in part because of past reschedulings). It is those countries also that obviously most need measures of debt relief through Paris and London Clubs where appropriate, additional external resources from the Bank, the Fund, and others, and adjustment policy measures. All this said, the search for imaginative approaches should obviously continue.

Food

In calling for "a new thinking and philosophy for World Bank and other donors" in order to meet the "new agenda," Governor Ndegwa focuses on food supply. This is an appropriate example. Let me simply say in this respect that the Bank is quite prepared to assist in accelerating food production in Africa, as it has in the past. All rural development projects include food output components, but I have noted also in my paper that rural development projects had faced technical, institutional, and management problems and that new approaches were needed. It should be noted also that policy reforms in agriculture, as we discuss them with African governments as part of our sector work or in the context of lending operations, are meant to address the problems of food production, food marketing, food exports and imports as much as those of export crops. While, as for any other operation, we are concerned that programs to enhance food production be cost effective, we recognize at the same time that determining the cost and value to be attached to ensuring food security and not just increases in output is a difficult question in concept and in practice. The Bank is currently working on this important issue.

Urgency of the Crisis

I suppose Governor Ndegwa's main criticism of my paper is that it "lacks a sense of immediacy or urgency although the desperate situation facing most African countries calls for urgent and appropriate attention." Governor Ndegwa adds ". . . the author seems to think that continuation of the present rather gentle and evolutionary response to the crisis . . . will be sufficient."

If this is the impression given I certainly have failed to convey at least an important part of the intended message, for which I must apologize. On the other hand, urgency is of course a matter of scale: at least I hope to have shown in the paper that over the long history of Bank involvement in Africa there has been a rather remarkable evolution of the Bank's approaches and instruments and a real effort at adapting to the continent's specific needs.

When one looks back at only the last four or five years—a short period for a large international organization established about 40 years ago—it is hard, I believe, not to consider the following as real achievements: the introduction of structural adjustment loans—a completely new instrument; the special action program; the development of various forms of sector adjustment lending; the replenishment of IDA, albeit at unsatisfactory levels, under extremely difficult circumstances; the establishment of the special facility in less than one year's time. Furthermore, the Bank has during this period shifted considerable administrative and staff resources toward the operational units in the Bank dealing with Africa. Finally, I think the Bank as much as any other institution can also be credited for having publicly called attention to the plight of sub-Saharan Africa, not least through the issuance of three special reports since 1981 (to which Governor Ndegwa refers), and for having reiterated the need for prompt action (including on long-run issues such as population) by the countries themselves and by the international community. Moreover, together with the Fund, we have sought to mobilize other external resources in cases where these were urgently required in support of major policy reform programs. Ghana is a case in point.

Nevertheless, the Bank is not a crisis institution. It is not well equipped to respond to the immediate needs arising from sudden balance of payments difficulties, drought, or other natural disasters. Other national and international organizations are. Nonetheless, the Bank does assist in reconstruction operations with quick-disbursing loans, say, following an earthquake or civil strife. In Africa we have done so for Nigeria and Uganda, for example.

When we talk about the African crisis, however, we all have in mind, I suppose, that set of problems that is precisely not amenable to quick solutions: population growth, the allocation of investment resources, the sluggish growth of agriculture, institutional reform in the public sector, and the like. It is in these areas that the Bank, in my view, has shown considerable flexibility and imagination, although much remains to be done, and we are by no means entirely satisfied by the results so far.

Bank-Fund Collaboration

Governor Ndegwa notes that "Bank and Fund programs . . . are not closely coordinated," that the time frames of stand-by Fund programs and Bank structural adjustment loans are different, and that "separate Bank and Fund missions asking more or less the same questions can be very expensive to African countries." He calls for "simultaneous programs of structural adjustment loans and extended Fund financing."

Because, as Governor Ndegwa rightly indicates, there are areas of overlapping interest between the Bank and the Fund, coordination of actions between the two institutions is essential. While subscribing entirely to this general principle, I also noted in my paper that legitimate differences of views on the relevant issues could occur and that the governments in the end have to make the final choices in a consistent manner.

Nevertheless, beyond these broad principles (and both the Fund's and the Bank's board of directors have again recently reviewed and discussed these principles in depth), practical coordination and resolution of differences is best done on a country-by-country basis.

At the same time, I should be quite frank and admit that (in my own experience) while some governments tend to detect lack of coordination at the slightest appearance of differences between the staff of the two institutions, others also become very suspicious that total coordination might mean "ganging up" against the government or imply a de facto imposition of cross-conditionality between the Fund's and Bank's respective programs. I am sure you all realize that sometimes the staffs of our two institutions have to achieve a delicate balancing act!

I agree with Governor Ndegwa that the alliance of extended Fund financing and structural adjustment loans programs is a natural one. Indeed, such combination was the case for the first programs implemented in Africa: Kenya, Senegal, and Côte d'Ivoire are examples. The programs of action under each type of arrangement, however, do remain distinct as they fulfill complementary but different objectives, follow different processes, and are monitored under different sets of quantitative or qualitative standards. Furthermore each institution retains, as it should, complete independence of judgment as to the degree of achievement of the agreed programs by the government. In short, there are good or at least natural reasons why the respective programs supported by the Bank and the Fund may not move in full harmony.

The question of disbursement provides a good example. In designing a program the Fund will make an assessment of all the projected financing flows to the country over a given period. These naturally include disbursements from Bank loans and IDA credits based, I suppose, on the tentative projections that appear in our loan documentation. But besides the fact that these projections tend to be optimistic, the actual rate of disbursement for each operation will depend on the particular pace of advancement of each operation, be it road construction, crop development, or some policy action under a structural adjustment loan or otherwise. Acceleration of implementation in one case may compensate for deceleration in another, or it may not. In other words, the profile of total disbursements from the Bank to a particular country is a function of a complex set of factors most of which will not be directly related to the financing plan of the balance of payments. Under the best of coordination efforts, therefore, plans and "actuals" may diverge. Realism in projecting the future as well as frequent and prompt exchange of information between Bank and Fund staff will, as in other areas of coordination, help minimize such discrepancies.

PART 3

Adjustment in Africa: What Can Be Done?

Carlos Massad

I believe that my role is to bring the perspective of the Latin American experience into the discussion, and I have a good deal to say about its most relevant aspects; namely, the vital importance of external factors in the crisis, both in the upturn as well as in the downturn; the expansionary fiscal policies that could not be sustained; the absence of sufficient pragmatism to appreciate the adaptations required in traditional policies to make them more effective; the inappropriate timing of certain policies; the unexpected consequences of others; the case (and there is at least one) where the traditional indicators of good economic behavior—fiscal balance, domestic credit, and reserves—were all showing results that gained the praise of many observers while in reality overwhelming imbalances were building up in the economy and finally brought on disaster. The next issue of the *Journal of Development Planning*, which I have been invited to edit, will review some of the experiences in Latin America, and in Africa, as analyzed by distinguished economists from all over the world.

But let me begin by telling you what I have learned here.

First, let me say that the mere fact that this meeting has been organized highlights the preoccupation of central bank authorities with their search for new solutions to a new problem: the superimposition of recessionary adjustment on a trend of slow growth (or even economic deterioration in some cases) and the tragic results of a prolonged drought. Such a coincidence of negative factors can only bring, in the short run, immense human suffering that cannot be ignored.

I have learned that, as in the case of Latin America, present adjustment needs are mainly the result of external factors whose negative behavior was not adequately predicted.

I have learned that, as in Latin America, the African countries found that those factors cannot be influenced by their governments, but are the result of policies that the industrial countries found to their advantage to put into effect: terms of trade that deteriorated dramatically, interest rates that rose to unprecedented levels, protectionist policies that prevent or limit the expansion of exports, and drastic changes in the structure and direction of capital movements in the world economy, capital movements that are now absorbed by the richest members of the international community.

I have learned that, once again as in the Latin American case, international organizations have put their resources at the disposal of the deficit countries, but it is the implacable constraint of the inadequacy of such resources and the need to ration them, rather than purely objective analysis and recognition of present realities, which dictates the nature as well as the speed of adjustment.

Finally, I have learned that there is diversity in Africa, just as there is in Latin America. So, the solutions to problems that are substantially shared by all may legitimately differ from one country to another because of differences in structure, resource endowments, or political preferences.

What can be done to overcome this set of circumstances? Obviously, at the core of the problem lies the foreign exchange constraint, and this must be overcome either by increasing the pool of financial resources available or by making external support less necessary.

The Fund and the World Bank are helping the countries obtain additional resources by prompting commercial banks to maintain or even to increase their commitments.Such efforts must continue, but more is needed, particularly in the form of concessionary loans or grants. Governments provide such resources, and the Fund and Bank could use their influence to secure these resources. Obviously, an increase in the capital of the Bank, the resources of IDA, and in Fund quotas could go a long way to alleviate the present problems. It is the task of the less developed members of both institutions to continue pressing for such an increase, as well as for additional substantial allocations of SDRs. I must say that I am not very optimistic about the probability of success of this particular course of action, however, unless desperate reactions by some country or countries highlight the urgency of providing additional concessionary resources. I do hope that solutions will be found before desperation inspires actions that in the end will damage the whole international community.

There are two ways of reducing the need for external assistance. First, and most important in present circumstances, is to secure the recognition by industrial countries of the global effects of their policies and, in particular, of their negative effects on the developing countries. Such recognition should lead to a modification of these policies or to compensation for their negative effects on others. The Fund and the Bank have only moral suasion to offer in this regard, whereas they are well equipped with strong incentives for action by debtor developing countries.

Expansionary policies in the industrial countries could bring the terms of trade of African countries into more normal ranges, thereby wiping out a substantial proportion of their present need for assistance. Protectionist measures could be rolled back, helping both the price and quantity of African exports. Decreases in interest rates would help to alleviate the foreign exchange constraint. In other words, a monetary system that is more symmetrical in incentives and disincentives is a necessity if we want to minimize the danger of recurrence of present problems. Positive action could be expected in this general area, but most projections emphasize the great uncertainty as regards future growth rates of the world economy. Anyway, here again it is up to the developing countries to continue pressing for a reform of the international monetary system that would bring about a more balanced and stable economic environment for all. Some new thinking is required to find ways to create incentives capable of inducing the industrial countries to assume their due role in the adjustment process of the world economy.

An objective assessment of probabilities indicates quite clearly that the courses of action mentioned above will not yield results in the short run. Again, the main burden of action to overcome the foreign exchange constraint seems to fall upon domestic adjustment policies designed to redress large imbalances, to promote the allocation of resources to the production of tradables, to alleviate food scarcities, and to improve the general efficiency of the economy.

Adjustment is not made in a vacuum and is not painless. It would be a mistake to adjust without keeping in mind the strategic objectives of the economy. Unless this is done, such objectives will never be achieved. What happens is that lack of financing alters the normal relationship between short-term and long-term policies: while short-term policies should normally be conceived as tactical measures necessary to achieve strategic objectives, this concept requires financing in order to overcome short-term deviations without making substantial policy changes. When financing is not available, the relationship between short-term and long-term policies is severed, and the long-term result becomes the consequence of short-term policies aimed at solving emergencies rather than setting a general course for the national economy. Here the Fund and the World Bank could make a decisive contribution by recognizing and accepting the long-term economic strategies of African countries and placing short-term assistance and policy recommendations within that context.

Integration has been mentioned as a strategic objective and as such should be supported and promoted by international organizations. The Bank and the Fund must make a special effort to explore ways of explicitly recognizing, in their conditionality, the long-term strategic economic objectives of developing member countries. Of course, for the institutions to recognize such long-term objectives, the countries themselves must be able to set out such objectives meaningfully, not just as a set of good wishes and particularly without contradicting their declared objectives with their own policies. Such contradictions will eventually destroy the credibility of the countries.

Within the limitations of present resources, I believe that much could be done to enhance the pragmatism and the flexibility of the Fund and the Bank. For example, the question of the distribution of the cost of adjustment domestically could be pointed out, and if results are found undesirable, means could be designed to modify them. Recognition should be made of the common practice of covering payments arrears through unofficial channels or through overpricing or underpricing in external trade, so that what is registered as an ''arrear'' is actually nothing but a prospective capital flight. Growth rates and employment levels could be set, when feasible, as explicit goals of adjustment programs in the medium run, and explicit allowance could be made for changes in external variables or others outside the control of the authorities in order to avoid the need for frequent renegotiations and waivers. The distribution of Fund support could be changed during the program, if necessary, in order to obtain better results in supplies and in confidence generated.

These, as well as many other ideas, have been put forward during these three days, and I am convinced they merit closer attention by the international organizations of which our countries are members. They are not presented in ways that lend themselves to immediate application, but we can certainly reflect upon them. I believe there is no impediment to the establishment by Fund and Bank staff, under the authority of the Managing Director of the Fund and of the President of the Bank, task forces specially assigned to reexamining resource use and policies within the institutions with a view to introducing into them additional pragmatism and flexibility—two words that Mr. Ouattara used to characterize the work of the Fund. Institutions must always be reviewing their policies. This is the occasion, I believe, to initiate a special review—formulated by the Governments of African Central Banks and conveyed to the highest officials of each institution by the African Executive Directors—that will allow the institutions to serve their members better.

M. Narasimham

The serious economic and financial problems affecting African countries are both generic in that they are common to other developing countries and specific in that some are peculiar to sub-Saharan Africa (SSA).

The papers prepared for this symposium more than adequately delineate the global or aggregative factors that have caused the present crisis in sub-Saharan Africa. The first oil price increase worsened the terms of trade of oil-importing SSA countries as it did of other oil-importing developing countries. SSA countries, as the papers bring out clearly, met this problem by greater recourse to external borrowing, in large measure from the commercial markets. This appeared appropriate when world trade was buoyant and money could be borrowed from commercial markets at negative real rates of interest. The much more serious crisis that affected oil-importing developing countries following the second oil price increase affected African countries perhaps even more severely. Once again, terms of trade turned sharply adverse and this circumstance coincided with the global recession which seriously weakened export markets of African countries and was also responsible for a sharp downward turn in the prices of their major export commodities. Protectionist tendencies were also strong and gained further momentum in the industrial countries. The increase in interest rates and the consequent additional burden (in domestic currency) of debt servicing at a time when exchange earnings were themselves under pressure aggravated the debt crisis, especially in the context of the larger proportion of external debt owed by African countries to private financial institutions. Higher interest rates made access to the commercial banks prohibitively costly (even assuming a willingness on the part of the lenders to provide more credit). All this also coincided with the withdrawal of various special facilities introduced by the Fund in the wake of the first oil crisis (Trust Fund, oil facility) or their severe constriction (compensatory financing facility, extended Fund facility). The combination of more severe external payments and a drying up of external financing facilities affected all developing countries, but African countries suffered perhaps more in view of their greater vulnerability to external shocks and greater external dependency in trade and finance. The drought in SSA further added to the pressure on their external payments position by increasing the need for food imports and also widened the domestic gap between supply and demand with its inevitable inflationary consequences. The combined result has been that growth in most SSA countries has slowed down sharply. In combination with continuing high levels of population increase of 3 percent or more, this has meant declining per capita income, fewer employment opportunities, and consequent social and political tensions.

African countries, therefore, are bearing the weight of adverse cyclical and conjunctural factors on underlying structural inadequacies. There is clearly a wide consensus on the need for adjustment in the face of the current crisis, but—and this is not surprising—little agreement on how adjustment is to be financed and on what terms. Structural inadequacies call for structural adjustment in respect of the irreversible element in the deterioration in terms of trade, but the superimposition of conjunctural factors also calls for the more conventional short-term adjustment financing. Unfortunately, this period also witnessed a pressure on the Fund's own resources which was, I believe, a factor in the tightening up of its conditionality. The dominance of countries wedded to orthodox demand management in the decisionmaking levels of the Fund was also a factor in reducing the availability of Fund assistance and hardening the terms on which such assistance was provided.

The adjustment process, it was recognized, needed financial underpinning on the sound principle that finance without adjustment would be pointless and adjustment without finance not feasible. Nevertheless, the terms on which finance was provided, with its heavy demand-management orientation and the tight performance criteria laid down, made the adjustment program itself difficult to implement.

Given the structural basis of the maladjustment, obviously the correction would have to be structural and therefore gradual and over at least a medium time frame. The extended Fund facility was instituted in the 1970s with precisely these objects in view, but by the early 1980s had become an endangered species. There were, to be sure, examples of such arrangements, but by and large these arrangements collapsed for one reason or another, and there were many victims of this collapse in Africa. At present, there is only one extended Fund facility program in operation in Africa and this itself is testimony to the fact that few African countries have been able to avail themselves of this facility because of difficulties in satisfying the rigorous criteria of policy change expected of them under such programs. It is easy to be critical of domestic policy inadequacies as a factor explaining the collapse of such programs. Papers by the Fund staff itself make this point. Domestic financial policy inadequacies often are equated with expansionary credit policies, and it is easy to derive from this the need for curtailment of domestic credit expansion, which is at the core of demand-management prescriptions. If, on the other hand, the problem is of failure of supply, as often is the case, demand management is not likely to help and would only aggravate the problem associated with reduction in incomes and purchasing power caused by supply failures. Though it has been argued on behalf of the Fund that, consistent with the principle of uniformity of treatment, it seeks to tailor its adjustment packages to the specific requirements of different countries, observed experience has shown that most adjustment programs contain a standard mix of policies consisting of curbs on domestic credit expansion, import liberalization, and policy adjustments in interest and exchange rates, producer prices, and the operation of parastatals.

What can be done about adjustment in Africa? As I see it, the main issues that need to be addressed are (a) growing food insecurity in many African countries, (b) the weakening of export markets and export commodity prices, and (c) increasing aid dependency. It would be presumptuous for anyone to suggest answers, but I would strongly endorse the line taken by Mr. Loxley in his paper about the need for alternative approaches to stabilization, both on the practical ground of the failure of the present approaches and the theoretical argument based on the structural character of the problem. There is hence a need to fit the adjustment program in as an element of growth and investment and not as a distinct, let alone contrary, exercise. Growth in its widest sense is no more than a structural transformation of an economy, and structural adjustment in the medium term can be regarded as having ingredients of success only when it is treated as an element of investment and growth. I would entirely agree with Mr. Loxley's structuralist approach and his view that strengthening the food production base should command high priority. Further, in the sub-Saharan context, despite the fact that external trade constitutes a significant proportion of GDP in relation to, say, low-income Asia, it is a matter for discussion whether the external sector should be corrected through more emphasis on exports if this will increase the exposure and vulnerability of African countries to the vicissitudes of international economic conditions. In the light of food insecurity, the adjustment effort should place emphasis, as Mr. Loxley pointed out, on stepping up the production of basic and essential commodities, especially food. To the extent to which this is done, both the vulnerability to external trade variations and domestic inflation would be corrected by adequate food supplies. The Indian experience in this area is not without significance. Import substitution—in this case of a basic wage good—may have greater relevance in the medium term than export expansion. The second relevant area of structural adjustment is intraregional trade, consistent with the Lagos Plan of Action. As regards exports to areas outside Africa, it is debatable whether they should take the form of a further augmentation of supplies of presently exportable and exported commodities or whether there should be selective diversification of exports with greater value added.

While I fully endorse the general thrust of Mr. Loxley's paper, I must express my reservations about one point, his suggestion that the quantum of investment in SSA countries needs another look while greater attention is paid to the quality of investment and increasing the returns on investment. Apart from the higher costs and delayed returns involved in cutting back investment expenditures, resulting in underfunding of ongoing projects, even assuming such cutbacks are feasible politically or otherwise, there is a more serious economic argument. Cutting back on infrastructure can only compound problems for the future. No one can dispute the importance of quality of investment and the need to obtain higher returns. Low productivity of capital is a luxury that poor countries can ill afford. Capital is their scarcest resource, and every effort obviously needs to be made to reduce incremental capital output ratios (ICORs). Some papers refer to the need for "quick-yielding" schemes. In their very nature infrastructural investments are not quick yielding. The returns on them also compare unfavorably with returns on investments directly related to productive activity. But without infrastructural investment, even production-related investments cannot be expected to yield returns adequately or even quickly. Unfortunately, ICORs for infrastructural investment tend to be high for inherent technological reasons but without infrastructural investment we cannot have low ICORs elsewhere. Even enhancement of food production requires considerable low-yielding and slow-yielding infrastructural investment. A price must thus be paid in the early stages of development for providing necessary infrastructure. Here we have a problem with the Fund's demand-management programs that set (in most cases) subceilings on credit extension to the government sector as part of credit ceilings in the list of performance criteria. Infrastructural investment is generally the domain of the public sector (as the private sector in most developing countries is either unable or unwilling to enter the area in any substantial way). The requirements of such investment as part of structural adjustment could run counter to the prescription of severe limits to public-sector borrowing. If ceilings on domestic credit expansion (DCE) have to be set, there is indeed a case for not subdividing it into the public sector and the rest—a subdivision deriving from a suspicion or even conviction about the suboptimal efficiency of the public sector in all cases. In any event, from the point of view of overall monetary expansion and accepting for the moment the logic of the somewhat simplistic monetary model applied by the Fund, it is the overall expansion of DCE and not of its subsectors that should be relevant.

Further, in the operation of the programs, instead of a rigid application of the ceilings (as at present) where even a small degree of noncompliance of subceilings (even if the overall ceiling is complied with) invites suspension of drawings in the absence of waivers (and waivers are becoming infrequent), consideration should perhaps be given to a prorating of the drawing in relation to the extent of performance or, putting it another way, the degree of deviation from the ceiling. This would be clearly better than the present all or nothing approach. One could also refer to the suggestions made earlier to establish a range of ceilings rather than a specific figure. The information and data base in several developing countries do not permit such precise quantification, and one is reminded of the old adage that it is better to be vaguely right than precisely wrong. Precise quantification is also related to specific dates. But markets are fragmented and imperfect, and sometimes seasonal factors, including weather, make fulfillment of performance tests on specified dates difficult. Sometimes there is a temptation to window-dressing and this can give rise to institutional memories that could affect the Fund's perception of the credibility of and its confidence in the country concerned.

If one accepts that structural adjustment in the gradual and medium term, and concentrating on supply augmentation is the alternative, two questions arise. First, what is the role and relevance of the Bank's structural adjustment lending program in Africa? Second, what is the role for the Fund in this situation?

As regards the first, structural adjustment lending that provides quick-disbursing assistance untied to projects is certainly welcome, but the conditionality prescribed by the World Bank on macroeconomic policies comes close to the conditionality prescribed by the Fund that has been the cause of so many problems. Superimposed as it is on the Fund's conditionality, it constitutes, in Mr. Loxley's phrase, a "double dose of external leverage." SALs have been marked by a fairly standard set of policy prescriptions relating to the operation of the pricing system, interest rates, exchange rates, the trade regime, and the like—all very similar to the standard prescriptions enjoined on borrowing countries by the Fund in its supply-oriented aspects. Growing collaboration between the Fund and the Bank would, in normal circumstances, have been a welcome feature, but when one institution makes a precondition for sanctioning loans or permitting tranche drawings that the country must arrive at an agreement with the other, borrowing countries find they have little outside choice, especially with the deterioration in the overall aid climate and the slowdown in commercial bank lending. Structural adjustment lending was designed to provide countries with a line of finance for a long enough period, beyond the normal period of the extended Fund facility to effect necessary structural adjustment, but SALs, though untied to projects, are a far cry from the program lending for which developing countries have been pleading. The stringent conditionality accompanying SALs deprives them of the type of flexibility associated with program lending. If they are to serve the purpose for which they were instituted, clearly conditionality needs to be suitably tailored to the structural characteristics of the borrowing country. SALs are, in a manner of speaking, extended extended Fund facilities. Their similarity of policy mixes makes one wonder whether, in the light of experience with extended Fund facilities, there is any reason to be more hopeful about SALs. Though SALs were introduced with considerable fanfare about four years ago, there is already some evidence of disenchantment with their performance and even their appropriateness. The use of sector adjustment loans is a recognition that SALs perhaps are taking on more in policy reform than they can effectively handle. SALs certainly would help where countries need a program of assistance to induce fuller utilization of existing capacity, and it would perhaps be appropriate to look at them as instruments for more efficient and optimal utilization of capacity rather than as instruments of wide-ranging policy changes. At the same time, SALs are no substitute for the more conventional project financing with its stress on supporting investment.

In other words, conditionality should be broad based and country specific rather than based on a standard mix of market-oriented policies on the supposed ground that these policies are better geared to provoking the appropriate supply responses. The alignment of policies with market forces does not fit well with the diversity of social and economic systems of the members of the two international financial institutions. Even in Africa there is wide diversity in economic organization and there are varying degrees of state intervention in the economic process.

If they are to be successful, adjustment policies have to be framed within a viable and feasible framework. Ignoring social tensions and political compulsions is an invitation to failure of the programs. Fund conditionality guidelines recognize the importance of social and economic conditions, but in practice the standard mix of demand-management policies and market-oriented supply policies has not evidenced an awareness of political and social realities in Africa and elsewhere. There are, of course, a few examples of reasonably successful Fund programs where the appropriate emphasis on supply augmentation has figured (e.g., India), but these are all too few. The more general case is for deflationary adjustment, though the Fund was designed to provide finance to correct maladjustment without undertaking deflationary adjustment. Financial accommodation from the Fund was seen as an alternative to deflationary adjustment and not as its instrument. Unfortunately, contemporary experience points the other way.

In the ultimate analysis the ability of the Fund and the Bank to assist countries undertaking adjustment programs also calls for additional financial resources for these institutions. Mr. Sanusi's paper rightly refers to the inadequacy of Fund resources and calls for an enlargement of quotas with more weight to the developing countries. This is altogether appropriate. SDR allocations also need to be resumed again with more weight for developing countries. The political economy that marks these issues, however, does not suggest that we are likely to have either of these in the near future.

Where then do we go? To suggest that conditionality should be softened will not get us very far. As long as the powers that control the Bank and the Fund take their current position, we cannot seriously expect any softening in their stance with regard to conditionality. It is not so much softening that we have to plead for but conditionality appropriate to the circumstances of the borrowing country, an acceptance of the need for gradualism (and not shock treatment) for the correction of the maladjustment, and the provision of adequate finance on terms that do not add significantly to the debt-servicing bill. One-year stand-by arrangements are relevant to disruptions in economic activity that are amenable to correction in the short term, but are clearly not appropriate where the problem is more fundamental. In the case of the Fund, this calls for a reversion to greater use of the extended Fund facility and full restoration of the enlarged access policy. The recognition of the structural character of the problem fits ill with the current preference for one-year stand-by arrangements, characterized by their short-leash approach. Formulating a program on a three-year frame but using one-year stand-by arrangements seems a contradiction. Three one-year stand-bys do not make one three-year extended Fund facility, as the whole conspectus is different in the two cases. Apart from this, there is need to restore the low conditionality character of compensatory financing facility, not merely making it, in Mr. Sydney Dell's phrase, "the Fifth Credit Tranche," as at present. Equally, there is need to restore the full access rights originally envisaged under the enlarged access policy. The perverse result of an increase in quotas under the Eighth Review has been that the absolute limits of access to Fund's resources have been reduced for most African countries. If the enlarged access policy is not to be a misnomer, the reversion to earlier levels is necessary. The Trust Fund repayments should also be effectively redeployed in the form of new Trust Fund allocations. I would prefer this to the return flow being used for an interest subsidy account. The point has been made about Fund facilities not being cheap and that further recourse to the Fund would add to the burden of debt servicing. African countries already face a serious debt-servicing problem, and for many of them there is a real possibility of a negative transfer of resources. In this context I would suggest that the Fund reinstitute the facility it once had on a general basis, but now allows only in exceptional cases, of permitting countries to pay their Fund charges in local currency. The charges would remain a liability for the country and under normal circumstances would cut into the reserve tranche through increasing the Fund's holding of national currencies above 75 percent. This could be met by treating charges accumulated as a floating facility that does not cut into the reserve tranche. It might be argued that the Fund needs current income in SDRs to be able to pay interest to the creditor countries of the Fund. A symmetrical exercise of adding to the creditor countries' positive balances with the Fund the interest to be paid to them should meet this particular objection. A point has been made by the Fund that it seeks to play a gap-filling role and catalyze resources from other contributors, be they banks or governments. While this is understandable, the failure to obtain the full quantum of the desired minimum of resources should not cause the Fund to withhold its own contribution. This could only aggravate the problem for the deficit country.

The measures outlined above are within the domain of the Fund's Executive Board and perhaps the Interim Committee and do not call for the type of amendment to the Articles or reference to the Board of Governors as would be the case with regard to quota increases, SDR allocations, and the like. These reforms are undoubtedly important and necessary, but in all realism one has to accept their improbability in the near future.

Given the circumstances of low-income countries, particularly in SSA, these modifications in policies and procedures would be first steps. Even they may not be enough. A reference may also be made to the need for more equitable sharing of the burden of adjustment. The present system makes the entire burden of adjustment devolve on borrowing deficit countries. In the discussions we have heard about the Fund's role in surveillance and its efforts to bring about a measure of reciprocal adjustment by the surplus industrial countries through its regular consultations with them. Notwithstanding statements to this effect, the results of such surveillance on domestic monetary policy more compatible with international monetary and exchange rate stability and on reducing the rigors of protectionism and expanding capital flows to the developing countries do not indicate any such positive influence. If surveillance indeed has had such effects it must be regarded as a very well kept secret. The answer, therefore, lies perhaps in adjustment through collective self-reliance in Africa through greater food security, through greater effort in reducing the dependence of domestic economies to external vicissitudes in trade and development assistance and in conserving investible resources, both domestic and external, for the betterment of social conditions at home. This is a strategy, as Mr. Loxley points out, quite different from the thrust now followed by the international institutions of integrating countries more into the world economy. But it is also a strategy consistent with the adjustment and growth needs of Africa and one endorsed in the Lagos Plan of Action.

One final point. No one questions the seriousness of the African crisis nor the inadequacy of existing financial flows in relation to that critical situation. By all means the point should be made that Africa should get more, but I hope not to be misunderstood in saying that the case for assistance to Africa stands on its own and not in terms of comparing it with assistance to other regions of the world. A reference was made in one of the papers that three countries in South Asia, namely India, Bangladesh, and Pakistan, get 50 percent of IDA money. Apart from the fact that the present level of IDA assistance to these countries is below this figure, it needs to be pointed out, as Mr. de Azcarate has done in his paper, that in per capita terms African countries got more concessional funds than their South Asian counterparts. The net aid to India, for instance, is about $2 per head per year, which can by no means be regarded as large, given the poverty in the country. There are perhaps more absolute poor in the South Asian subcontinent than the entire population of Africa. Poverty is grim and degrading wherever it occurs and should not be viewed in regional or continental terms. I would, in all humility, submit that such comparisons only strengthen those seeking to divide developing countries from presenting a common front for additional resource transfers to the developing countries. Africa's needs are clearly great and have an independent justification, and that itself should be a sufficient argument for increased assistance.

John Williamson

In recent years I have been much preoccupied with problems in Latin America, and that is the fault of the Fund because, when I was employed by the Fund for two years, I got married to a Brazilian, and that somehow diverted my attention. It has been a great pleasure to come back to Africa and have this opportunity of taking a long, hard look at the problems here. I want to offer some reflections on both the areas of agreement and the areas of disagreement I have noted.

I have been impressed by the breadth of agreement on the diagnosis of the problems faced by Africa. Clearly, it is unnecessary to emphasize the hostile external environment yet again. Another area of agreement concerns the importance of underlying resource problems. The fact is that desertification is not just an ecological disaster, but has become a macroeconomic disaster for a whole range of countries. Third, I find it refreshing to find a willingness on the part of African Governors to recognize the policy errors of the past. So there seems substantial agreement on diagnosis of the problems.

I think that I have to say to my friends in the Fund that they would do themselves a service if they were equally willing to recognize there have been errors on the part of their organization. I cannot understand why they are so unwilling to admit this in public because in private I find them much more frank. When, for example, yesterday, I criticized the Fund at one point for its unwillingness to give a more or less unconditional endorsement of the present macroeconomic policies of Colombia, I was told afterwards that, in fact, since the last time I had discussed that subject, the Fund has done essentially that. While they are willing to make this type of adjustment in their policies, which shows they are capable of having second thoughts, why are they not capable of manifesting it a little bit more in public? In a group like this I think it would be refreshing to have a little more of that type of open-mindedness.

I also find more agreement on the nature of the solutions, in general terms, than I had expected to encounter ex ante. No one has challenged the need for adjustment. No one has denied that that includes the provision of appropriate incentives. Again, there has been a recognition of the importance of efficiency in the parastatals. There is a recognition, which I think is fairly new in Africa, that population growth is a major problem that has to be tackled as a matter of urgency. There has been a great deal of agreement, even among Fund staff—and I think perhaps this represents a change in their position—that import substitution in terms of food production should at this stage become a priority. I have also found it encouraging to discover that the preferential trade arrangements in East and Central Africa are being pressed far more vigorously than I had realized. Finally, I think there is a general recognition that these problems are difficult and that there are no panaceas, that what is needed is a consistent package which, to be successful, has to be believed in by both the country and the Fund and Bank.

Under certain circumstances, where the initial situation is sufficiently disastrous (the example of Ghana was one that we heard about), a remarkably quick turnaround can be produced by the application of a consistent package. Unfortunately, however, there is clearly not a meeting of minds yet on what the elements of such a package should be. I want to offer some thoughts to supplement those of colleagues who have spoken before on what constitutes a sensible package.

I am in agreement with Mr. Lawrence on this matter, except in one respect, which concerns his interpretation of what Professor Loxley said yesterday. I agree with almost all the individual points in John Loxley's paper. I agree with the desirability of structural adjustment, in the sense of adjustment that emphasizes expanding supply rather than compressing demand. I agree with the stress on the need for more finance, and for that finance to be available earlier in the adjustment process to finance import increases. I think this is a valuable point, to which the Fund has responded in certain instances. The emphasis on import substitution in food I have already mentioned, as well as the reorientation of investment toward "debottlenecking" on rehabilitation and the emphasis on income distribution. I agree with all of those individual points, but at the end of the day I do not feel that those add up to a coherent *alternative* to a Fund program, so much as a set of detailed improvements which, however important, have to be taken in conjunction with policies regarding exchange rates, interest rates, demand management, and import liberalization. Hence I will comment on those four elements of the package, and the attitude which I would like to see the Fund adopt toward them.

First, the question of exchange rates. I believe it is absolutely fundamental to any viable adjustment program that the exchange rate be brought to and maintained at a realistic level. I think that is essential because it gives the right incentives for rational long-run diversification. I agree that this can, in African conditions, only be expected to take effect in the long run in many cases. There will be exceptions where the economy has broken down in a way that the Ghanaian economy had done, but by and large the beneficial effects will be long run.

The short-run effects of exchange rate action may be negligible, or, if many countries are doing the same thing at the same time, the short-run effects may even be perverse, because of the terms of trade effect. Nevertheless, to get the incentives right for long-run adjustment, a competitive exchange rate is imperative. At times that might have the disadvantage of creating rents going to sectors which one does not particularly want to collect rents, but I am always assured that the Fund is flexible in allowing a government to tax rents under those circumstances.

It seems to me that in recent years the Fund record in trying to calculate appropriate exchange-rate changes has been quite good. If I have a criticism of the Fund in this direction, it is that it did not ask enough of some African countries in the period of easy conditionality from 1979 to 1981. It was no service to give countries money in difficult circumstances which were going to get worse without asking for measures to give a reasonable prospect of recovery in the medium term.

I would also like to comment on the question of immediate versus gradual exchange-rate adjustment. When an exchange rate is vastly overvalued, the effects of correcting it immediately may be very harsh. On the other hand, the reason for an immediate adjustment is the need to preempt capital flight. It depends on the particular country: if exchange controls are so tight that one does not have to worry about capital flight, it will be feasible to devalue in a series of steps. But with a vastly overvalued exchange rate, to say that one is doing half of what is needed today and will do the other half next year is in most countries asking for disaster. Hence I would expect that it will usually be necessary to make a quick adjustment even though the effects may indeed be very difficult—because the alternative would be even worse.

Once the initial adjustment has been made and the rate is appropriate, gradual adjustment should be the order of the day. That is something which I have been preaching for 20 years, since I first wrote a piece about the crawling peg. I am delighted to find that in Kenya exchange-rate policy has now come around to pegging to a relevant basket and changing the value of the peg so as to maintain the exchange rate realistically in the light of differential inflation. I hope that this sensible example will be copied by many other countries.

Second, let me say a few words about interest rates. The Fund keeps telling us that higher interest rates are necessary because of the effect on savings. That is very doubtful. From our textbooks we all remember that income and substitution effects go in opposite directions. Empirical evidence is equally ambiguous—there is no strong evidence of much effect of interest rates on savings, at least once real rates get up into the positive range. Interest rates probably have some effect on investment levels and allocation, but one can have interest rates that are too high as well as too low—indeed, in most of Latin America interest rates are now too high, and the Fund should be urging countries to reduce them. I don't think that is the case in Africa, but we should be clear that the aim needs to be interest rates at an *appropriate* level, not necessarily a higher level.

The critical margin where interest rates have an important impact on the economy of most countries is the external one. An interest rate which is high enough, in conjunction with the expected change in the exchange rate, to avoid creating incentives for capital flight is a necessity.

Third, let me talk about what has been referred to by Mr. Narasimham as demand management. I must, however, register a semantic caveat. I come from Britain, where demand management is used by Margaret Thatcher as a term of abuse to belabor those of her opponents who want to increase demand in order to reduce unemployment. So I think that "demand management" is a good thing. What I don't think is a good thing is cutting absorption irrespective of the state of the economy.

There are three circumstances in which a cut in absorption should be part of a Fund program. The first Mr. Jimenez referred to yesterday, when he mentioned Mexico in 1981, a case of general excess demand in the economy. I think it is revealing that he quoted the case of Mexico, because I cannot think of another country in the whole world (except perhaps Israel) where there has been any general excess demand in the 1980s. There has been excess demand in certain markets because there were no intermediate imports in order to fuel productive industry, but the answer to that is to make available some intermediate goods and not to cut demand further.

The second circumstance obtains where there *may* be a political case for early action to cut demand as much as is ultimately going to be necessary, rather than telling the population that its standard of living is going to fall 2 percent this year, 2 percent next year, and another 2 percent the year after. If living standards have to fall a lot, maybe it is better to do the whole thing immediately and be able to say that from here on things are going to get better, even though this does involve some economic waste. The case has been made recently that this adds to the political viability of a program, and perhaps we should ask ourselves whether this may not be a valid case.

In the third circumstance there is no alternative to cutting demand because of a shortage of external liquidity. If there is no money to finance an interim deficit, then the deficit perforce has to be eliminated immediately. And there is no other way of achieving rapid adjustment except to cut aggregate demand. Of course, a better solution might be to increase liquidity, but that is a plea that has to be addressed to the international community and not to the Fund staff.

Let me turn to import liberalization. This is where I want to draw on European experience. In the 1940s and early 1950s, when Europe also faced extremely difficult problems of balance of payments adjustment, with a great deal of suffering involved in the early years, we did not start by import liberalization. We started by declaring that import liberalization was the aim at the end of the day after recovery had been achieved, and in that way we made sure that there were no incentives for the creation of inefficient import-substituting industries. So it is important to make clear where you are going. But if you have a foreign exchange shortage, I don't think that the first thing to do is to liberalize imports, and I have my doubts about the advice the Fund and the Bank have been giving to that effect in recent years in Africa.

We must recognize that many of the things I have suggested are desirable would require more cash. Supply-oriented adjustment and the avoidance of cuts in demand, except when there is generalized excess demand, will be feasible only if there is more liquidity available to Africa than currently seems in prospect. My view is that the real return on that extra finance would be high enough to cover the cost, although that will not necessarily make the lending attractive to lenders who, because of the problem of creditworthiness in low-income countries, are thinking primarily about getting their money back.

It is important to ask whether and how one might be able to attract greater finance than currently seems in prospect. In this connection I propose to examine what has become a dogma about the revolving character of the Fund's resources. Unlike Roger Lawrence, I accept that the Fund is a monetary institution and should remain a monetary institution, and therefore that its resources should revolve. There is value in having a division of labor. What we must surely do is to reinterpret this concept of the "revolving character" of the Fund's resources before it causes an avoidable tragedy. There are, after all, several possible concepts of the Fund's resources revolving. One would be to say it is Kenya's turn this year, Tanzania's next year, Saudi Arabia's the year after, irrespective of whether they need money or not. That would make the Fund's resources revolve. Another concept is what we actually have: Kenya's turn this year because Kenya needs it this year, but it has to repay in three years irrespective of circumstances. Another concept would be: Kenya's turn this year, provided Kenya needs it and adopts a program that is expected to enable it to repay in three years if external circumstances are reasonably favorable. If external circumstances are not reasonably favorable, an automatic extension should be granted. That would still involve the Fund's resources revolving. This is an interpretation that would make it possible for the Fund to live with what it is going to have to live with in Africa, without abandoning its monetary character and without further intensifying Africa's difficulties.

Larger drawing rights, reversing the move to reduced access in recent years, are clearly desirable. But of course this involves high politics; it is not something that the Fund staff have in their power to give or withhold. I agree completely with what has been said endorsing the extended facility; that was the right model. It should be reactivated, preferably in parallel with structural adjustment lending broader (less niggling) conditionality than in the past. But all of that depends upon our ability to persuade the West to reappraise its attitude and to make available larger but still rather modest sums in order to improve the prospects of civilized adjustment in Africa. The prospects of achieving that are not bright, but we still have to try.

The express willingness to adjust, of the sort we have heard from Governors during this conference, will surely be helpful in persuading those who hold the purse strings to take the case seriously. The position in the West is perhaps slightly more favorable than it has been: those terrible television pictures of the drought have created a new sensitivity to the African predicament. It should be possible to exploit this change in order to impress on the developed countries the importance of making available rather modest sums of money in return for a continuing commitment to adjustment on the part of the African countries, for that is surely a bargain which would be in the general global interest.

Roger Lawrence

I would like to organize my comments around the question of the larger economic environment and its relation to adjustment prospects and programs and give some thoughts on the institutional setting that might foster an adjustment process more suited to the current needs of African countries.

The international environment is characterized by extraordinarily low commodity prices, high interest rates, low levels of import demand in a large part of the developed world, particularly Europe, and reluctance by private financial institutions to lend. All these phenomena are the result of governmental policy and the overall operation of economies in the industrial world. These policies and the way recovery is developing in the industrial countries will have an important bearing on the prospects for an effective adjustment process in the developing countries and particularly in Africa. A few obvious points. The policy of the United States as regards the mix of fiscal and monetary policy and its impact on interest rates have a direct bearing on financial operations of African countries. Levels of interest rates have also, I believe, played a role in the behavior of commodity prices recently, and they have had less direct effects, for example, through their impact on African markets in Latin America.

Moreover, of particular interest to Africa is the speed with which growth takes hold and is transmitted to Europe. This is important, because Europe uses more imported raw materials than does North America and because ties between Africa and Europe are closer than between Africa and other parts of the developed world. So, the whole question of government policy in Europe and European prospects for growth is of great importance. Then, of course, the general financial climate, the adequacy of aid programs, the operations of the multilateral institutions, and the prospects for SDR creation are of particular importance. The new trade negotiations will also affect the external environment of developing countries. A key question for African countries is the extent to which agricultural and related processed products find their way onto the agenda of these negotiations.

I have reviewed these well-known points because of their importance to the adjustment process. Suitable adjustment programs can be formulated only when the external environment is not subject to large, sudden, and unpredictable shifts. What is required is an environment which, if not stable, is at least predictable so that countries can identify the external circumstances to which they are expected to adjust. Now, however, these circumstances encompass a large and growing U.S. budget deficit, a large and growing U.S. trade deficit, a dollar that has risen sharply and is viewed by most observers as seriously overvalued, and rising unemployment in Europe. Few observers believe that these trends can continue. When they change, these trends will alter the external environment. This means that the external situation to which developing countries are being asked to adjust will change further, requiring still further adaptation by these countries. This is an unsatisfactory situation, and certainly developing countries have a strong interest in promoting external stability by encouraging policy coordination in the industrial countries.

If domestic adjustment is influenced by external factors, it is equally true that such adjustment also shapes the external environment. For example, the sharp improvement in trade accounts required in many Latin American countries was accomplished by massive import cuts. This destroyed major export markets for the economies of the North, contributed to the poor economic performance of the North, and has had unfortunate consequences on the demand for African exports and commodity prices. The sudden improvement required in Latin American trade accounts has also led to an unprecedented export push by these countries and is intensifying protectionist pressures.

Devaluation plays a rule in expanding the output of commodities and in depressing their prices. The interrelationship between adjustment and commodity prices is not limited to exchange rate policies, however. In a number of African economies there are plans to expand commodity output that are independent of devaluation. These plans often call for the expansion of a minor export crop. Expansion is viewed at the country level as prudent since it involves the diversification of both production and exports. But again the overall implications for commodity prices of a simultaneous push by a number of individual commodity producers to increase production can be questioned. The policies followed in response to the need to adjust will thus have an important bearing on the operation of the commodity economy. This impact needs to be faced squarely and to be understood fully.

In summary, adjustment programs could be greatly facilitated by a better external environment. That environment, however, will itself be influenced by the character of the adjustment process. As regards African countries, the relationship between domestic policies, the supply of primary commodities, and their prices requires close attention.

Let me turn to the design of Fund programs. Professor Loxley has presented us with a detailed and interesting paper on the adjustment process and adjustment programs and has put forward an alternative program inspired by the structuralist critique of Fund programs. This critique holds that when differences between aggregate demand and supply cannot be bridged by prospective external financing, the resulting gap should be closed as much as possible through increasing supply, directed as needed toward exports and import-competing activities. This is an important concept, because such a process would allow adjustment to be accompanied to the greatest possible extent by growth. Adjustment through supply expansion usually requires restructuring production so as to maximize export revenues and produce more import-competing goods when this can be done efficiently. This in turn requires appropriate incentives to these activities and a reorientation (usually an increase) in investment. Such a process necessarily takes longer to bear fruit than do simple demand contraction and cutbacks in imports. Consequently, adjustment through supply expansion requires more external financial support than do other types of adjustment programs—a point which has been made explicit by Professor Loxley and also by Mr. Mohammed.

If then one is to turn to the Fund and ask it to operate more in this kind of framework, there are two implications which need to be faced squarely. First, the Fund would need more resources and, second, the Fund membership would need to modify somewhat its interpretation of the Fund as a strictly monetary institution. I think it is perfectly feasible and proper for developing countries to request changes on both fronts. But it needs to be said that the prospects for gaining acceptance for these changes are not bright at the moment.

What, then, are the alternatives? The various institutions and governments concerned with the external support of development in a particular country experiencing external payments problems could examine, with the country concerned, its own proposals for medium-term adjustment. This examination would start with the external accounts, with the increase in output necessary and feasible to increase exports or substitute for imports, and with the associated investment program (not only its magnitude but also its composition). Consequences could then be drawn for macroeconomic management. In such an analysis, the macroeconomic demand variables would be the last part of the puzzle to be put in place. This framework certainly has many disadvantages; it is clumsy, and raises and perhaps magnifies all the questions about collaboration between the Fund and the Bank, but it does at least provide a means to examine the size of the required adjustment. If the size of the adjustment implies excessive increases in unemployment, the components would be re-examined to develop a more balanced program. Would not bilateral donors perhaps see advantages in increasing the overall level of resources or in changing the composition of the projects to be financed, if that would mean a less severe retrenchment? In such a framework, Fund programs, although of limited duration, could be seen as part of a medium-term adjustment program.

A. Tadesse Gebre-Kidan

At the outset, let me make a brief comment on two issues. First, when we talk to the Fund, whom exactly are we addressing? As I see it, the Fund comprises its staff, the Management, the Executive Board, the Board of Governors, and through it the international community at large. From that perspective, I think the relevance of this discussion is not intended per se for the consumption of the Fund staff. I thought this should be clarified. Second, with respect to the terms of reference of this symposium, it has been unclear whether we have to confine ourselves to operational matters and some policy matters, or whether we could extend our remarks into fundamental relationships between the Fund and African countries. In my view, the latter cannot be excluded.

It has been amply demonstrated here that a serious and fundamentally critical situation prevails in the African continent. I would like to refer to the ecological developments alluded to in passing by Mr. Williamson. I think we are in for a much more troubled period. A symposium was held on this topic in Brazzaville recently, and one of the speakers, who is among the most eminent scientists in this field, said we may be on the threshold of an era of ecological devastation. Unless the situation is reversed, the physical basis on which everything is built will be destroyed. The need for addressing this problem is urgent.

In addition, the infrastructural base and the level of skill and technology are extremely low in Africa. Because of this, our economies are fragile, our capacity to negotiate with the rest of the world is limited, and we are paying a heavy price, heavier than the rest of the developing world. The realities that we face and the balance of payments problems that we find in Africa are reflections of these problems, nothing less and nothing more. Whatever we prescribe for the continent must emanate from these circumstances. In the current situation and its prospects, many paradoxes are emerging, probably more than ten. In the face of these difficulties, structural adjustment facilities in the Bretton Woods institutions are either being scaled down or withdrawn. There is actually going to be a net outflow of resources from Africa. Direct investment is on the decrease because Africa is regarded as a high-risk area. Domestic saving is extremely low; therefore investment is extremely low, and there is no growth. In the face of the degradation of land, there is paradoxically a population explosion. What does all this mean? There have to be fundamental solutions to such serious problems that are deep seated and accentuated by such paradoxes; otherwise there is going to be a fundamental crisis.

Now, what is to be done? We have been talking about realities over and over again. In my view, there are various types of realities: realities that must be accepted, and others that must be changed. The sort of paradoxes I mentioned, superimposed on the incredibly increased difficulties that we face, can create an outcome that is easy to imagine. The realities that must be changed must be changed through an active effort to address some of the fundamental problems.

We just cannot take a passive attitude to a good number of these problems and cannot count on developments elsewhere to help us out. In fact, when it comes to adjustment measures, sometimes what is good for the rest of the world may be bad for Africa. For instance, there is now an accent on reducing inflation. One way to reduce inflation is, of course, to depress prices for our produce. That has been done and is actually further aggravating our problems. From this perspective I think certain realities must be arrested and reversed so that we can make progress. Otherwise, we are simply presiding over chaos.

At the same time, I know current international and political realities and know we cannot escape from the conclusion that these realities are not conducive to international assistance at this time. Unless we make a serious and massive effort to avert the crisis, the whole situation may be doomed.

Against this background, what can the Fund do? There are two areas for action. One is operational and has been adequately dealt with by earlier speakers; the other is more fundamental. I think there is some hope since the industrial countries accept that the international monetary system leaves much to be desired and that it will have to be reviewed. This is a good beginning.

In this context, what can the Fund do in an expanded and reformed system? I see several roles. First, the Fund should get into action. It should not ignore the smallest countries. It cannot guarantee world prosperity and peace by leaving these countries out. We have the experience in my own country. As you all know, when the League of Nations was approached by Ethiopia for assistance during the Italian invasion, the international community said Italy is more important than Ethiopia. So the League chose to forget Ethiopia's claim and, of course, what that triggered is known to all of you. If we all belong to the same community, organically linked, then we cannot say this is more important or that can be ignored. Yet this is, unfortunately, the attitude that I now detect. There is a tendency to say the African countries should be left to their own devices; and maybe this is founded on a concept that only the fittest should survive. Basically we are not unfit; we are fit, but we need assistance. So in that respect, the Fund should be in the forefront in helping the cause of the smallest members.

Second, with respect to the role it should play vis-à-vis the poorest countries, I agree with the panelist who pointed out that we are not referring to the African countries only, but in this respect we are talking of all the least advantaged countries in the world community. As far as these small and weak countries are concerned, I think the Fund can have four roles. It can remain a monetary institution, as lender of last resort for countries that face temporary liquidity problems. Second, it can reconstitute itself to address their development financing needs in conjunction with other institutions. To this end, various schemes can be devised. For instance, from the total quota, a certain amount could be segregated for this purpose. The basic concept behind that would be that the Fund is an institution devised to ensure prosperity and better living for the whole international community. Third, the Fund can be regarded as an agency for the transfer of real resources from the rest of the world to the least advantaged members of the world community. In simple language, we can regard it as a taxman for the benefit of the smallest countries. This is a concept that transcends national boundaries, and if we all belong to the same international community, I think it is high time that we should start addressing ourselves to this kind of approach. Fourth, I think the Fund can evolve into a protector of its smallest members. It can shield them from external shocks by instituting various equalization measures and other mechanisms.

These approaches involve alternative perceptions and attitudes. If the Fund were framed on this foundation, we would have better prospects for the future. These are challenges that can be put before the international community and the Fund. I hope they will be given due consideration.

Abdoulaye Fadiga

Well-informed observers have dwelled on explanations of why the economic recovery has been much more rapid in the United States and the Pacific Rim countries than in the rest of the world. They state, moreover, that it was not until a particular region was faced with serious financial difficulties that the international community began to express concern and that impassioned discussions of the foreign debt problem took place. If I am making a point of reminding you of these facts today, it is to bring home to you that we, as Africans, are aware of the realities of the world today. For this reason, when we are invited to participate in international conferences, we use the opportunity to inform the world that we are fully aware of the interests that condition international relations and the reality of the situation in the world today. For Africa, however, the situation is today quite simply a matter of survival. We have indicated our desire to exchange viewpoints with officials of the Fund in order to make them aware of our real problems; but we also, and perhaps above all, wished through the Fund staff to draw the attention of the entire international community to our situation.

So as to avoid repeating the ideas developed by previous speakers and watering down our thoughts into mere generalities, I would like to discuss a number of specific problems in the hope that Fund officials will concentrate on them and assist our countries more effectively to pinpoint the challenges.

I would like to begin by identifying measures that could, in my opinion, constitute practical and suitable solutions to Africa's problems and that, if applied effectively, could help our continent to overcome the current crisis. The major concern of the African countries in their relations with the Fund is their access to Fund resources. At the Central Bank of West African States we feel it is essential that the cost of using these resources be studied carefully. At present the cost is in fact high, which means that any major use of Fund resources involves the risk of further damaging the debt profile of our countries. Consequently, we feel that the cost of the assistance provided by the Fund to the African countries should be reduced so as not to jeopardize efforts being made to bring the foreign debt down to more tolerable levels and to create conditions for sustained economic growth. We invite the Fund to examine this proposal, which in our view is quite feasible and could help us specifically to find a solution to some of Africa's problems. The Fund should take appropriate measures to give the African countries greater access to its resources while establishing arrangements for subsidized interest rates through the Trust Fund or some other facility.

Second, the required pace of the adjustment programs, and related conditions imposed by the Fund on countries receiving its assistance, are, in our view, too rigorous. In establishing performance criteria, the Fund missions should from the outset pay more attention to the various implications of the adjustment programs. In this context, the rate of adjustment should be scaled down, enabling the African countries to reconcile adjustment with economic growth more satisfactorily.

Third, Africa's difficulties result essentially from depressed world prices for its raw material exports. This means that the African countries cannot secure from these exports the resources needed to improve production. We feel it important to make World Bank and Fund staff aware of this crucial problem, which urgently requires a solution. At the same time, we would like to help the industrial countries of Europe in particular to understand better the serious consequences of this situation and the need to increase official development assistance. The industrial countries often do not recognize this need for better prices for raw material exports, not least because the African countries themselves, showing an amount of pride unwarranted in the circumstances, do not state their case for higher prices effectively. This attitude on the part of the African countries is even more difficult to justify when you consider that they have every right to demand a fair price for their output, fruit of the labor of millions of their citizens. As governors of the central banks, we face many and varied problems every day, and the staff of the World Bank and the Fund can help us find the appropriate solutions. Agriculture in Africa, whether it be based on single or diversified crops, is hampered by numerous restrictions that prevent it from effectively playing its role as the driving force in the improvement of production and economic growth. All organizations involved in marketing have become well aware of this situation and the Fund can no longer, in our view, ignore it.

Fourth, Fund officials should, in their studies, emphasize not only the need to ensure that the responsibilities and consequences of the debt problem are shared as much as possible between creditors and debtors, but also define the ways and means of achieving this objective. In this regard, we would like to see the Fund adopt a more flexible approach to the question of foreign payments arrears by making this kind of suggestion in negotiations with the creditor countries and private banks. Having become the natural intermediary between the debtors and creditors, the Fund enjoys unquestionable moral influence, and any decision that it would make to provide assistance to its poorest member countries, most of which are African, would have an undeniable positive effect.

As for the World Bank, it must increase its assistance to the countries of Africa. The special fund for Africa does, it is true, constitute a laudable initiative, but the resources currently available through this fund are still quite insufficient. Moreover, it is important to ensure that lenders do not use the creation of this facility as a pretext for rejecting the replenishment of IDA resources. The creation of this fund should not result in the elimination of other special windows, insofar as the special fund is specifically intended to assist the African countries. For this reason, we ask the President and Executive Board of the World Bank Group to refuse to consider any study submitted to them tending to credit the thesis that it is no longer necessary to develop other types of assistance from the World Group because the African countries will be benefiting amply from the resources of the special fund. Moreover, the staff of the World Bank should propose to its governing bodies that the Bank's capital be increased. As directors of the central banks, we all know how much weight we accord to suggestions from our staffs. We base our decisions on the studies that they submit to us. We do not generally amend these studies significantly because they are usually quite relevant. Staff of the World Bank can therefore directly influence the highest decision-making levels there, and we invite them to speak for us before these governing bodies.

The discussions which have taken place over the past three days have also given us an opportunity to express our serious concerns regarding current relations between the World Bank and the Fund. More than ever in the past, it is important that cooperation between these two institutions be enhanced so as to make both organizations more effective. This cooperation, while mutually complementary, should not mean more conditionality. The Bank should not systematically tie structural adjustment lending to the approval of stand-by arrangements with the Fund, as these involve policy measures that are often difficult to implement. Action by these two institutions should rather be simultaneous, with one dealing with short-term problems while the other provides assistance intended to create conditions for long-term economic growth in the recipient countries. Africa will be able to overcome its current difficulties only if adjustment measures are accompanied by action to promote sustained economic growth.

Fifth, the procedures with respect to structural adjustment loans and other forms of assistance must be simplified and made more flexible and the disbursement of funds must take place more rapidly. For their part, the African countries must acknowledge the need to provide the Bank as quickly as possible with the necessary supporting documents justifying their requests for assistance. It would be unrealistic for these countries to ask for loans and at the same time to refuse to provide material proof of their need. Experience has taught me that in economics, in contrast to politics, the longer the implementation of a measure is postponed, the greater the cost and the more serious the problem that remains unsolved.

Alassane Ouattara

We on the staff of the Fund have listened carefully to the views of the governors, and we have tried to explain the policies of our institution, the environment in which we operate, and also the guidelines which we follow for our operations. You have raised important issues. Looking at the different papers, particularly the paper of Professor Loxley on alternative approaches to stabilization, I think the most important issue is the problem of resource flows. I agree that if we had no constraint on the amount of the resources, adjustment would be easier. As you all know, the resources of the Fund are limited. They are limited in duration and they are limited relative to quota. I have indicated that I feel that these resources are expensive for many of the African countries that have fairly difficult debt-servicing problems. It is important, when looking at the problem of access, as Governor Fadiga indicated, that account be taken of this aspect of the problem.

It is important for any adjustment program that the financing be carefully thought through. Without adequate financing, a program cannot work, and Fund support cannot guarantee the success of any program that is underfunded. And in this respect, I noted the concern of most governors regarding Bank-Fund collaboration. We are doing a lot in this area and we will continue to strengthen our cooperation. Over the past few months, we have felt, both at management and staff levels, that for the countries in Africa, given the structural nature of the problems that they face, it would be better to seek greater Bank support. We do want programs negotiated with the Fund to be supported quickly by the World Bank. The Bank and the Fund are working very closely on these matters. The Fund looks at broad macroeconomic policies, but for policies regarding investment programs, rehabilitation of parastatals, and the like, we go to the World Bank to seek their views. We do have the same concern. Adjustment has to go along with growth, and growth requires, as Mr. Lawrence has said, a large amount of investment. Given the low level of savings in Africa, capital flows are clearly necessary to sustain such growth.

Let me turn to the problem of devaluation, exchange rate adjustments, and capital flows. I have noted the concern of many governors that when a country decides to make a substantial change in the exchange rate, adequate resources should be available to the sectors that can profit best from the devaluation. I believe that this is an important aspect of any program.

Apart from the general issue of resources and capital flows, I also feel that institution building is important. Governor Addo has eloquently given us the case of Ghana and has summarized his intervention by saying "the most important aspect of any program is the management of the program." I agree fully with that, and I think that management has to start with the design of the program. The Fund, as you know, has been placing greater emphasis in recent years on supply-side policies, but we still believe that demand management is essential. If you want to have the proper allocation of resources, you do need demand management policies. If you want to obtain higher rates of growth, you do need both demand-management and supply-side policies, and in that respect, the design of a program is a continuing process and has to take into account the most recent developments in the countries.

In the management of any program, the Fund stands ready to help countries through direct or indirect technical assistance, as we have done in many cases. But management is also the responsibility of the African governments. I have been, myself, an official in an African institution. If a team of people are determined to follow the program, to remind the political authorities that there are targets, to remind them that they have made commitments, to remind them that their credibility depends on the outcome of such programs, and, in the end, that the welfare of their people depends on their credibility and determination in trying to achieve their growth objectives, I am sure that implementation will be easier. I indicated that in many countries implementation is a great problem, which we will have to face and try to resolve together.

We certainly have taken the points made about the design of programs. The Fund staff is open-minded on these issues, and I am sure will try, with the experience that we have had, not only in Africa but elsewhere, to continue trying to design better programs. The design of programs obviously calls for a hard look at the problem of conditionality. The Fund is a monetary institution. We have said this: its resources must revolve. These resources can be used by members with balance of payments difficulties, but they have to be repaid and have to be repaid in conformity with a schedule of repayment that has been agreed in advance. Policies have to be designed to take account of this objective. In effect, conditionality is something which is normal.

I think we all agree that it is necessary that adjustment should take into account the particular circumstances of each country; there is a Board decision that stipulates this. And the Fund staff tries to do its best in this regard. Of course, many countries feel that this effort is not sufficient. Here more progress will certainly have to be made. But I will say clearly that I do not believe that a "soft" program is a solution for Africa. We cannot continue to have current account deficits representing 15–20 percent of GDP and think that their financing is sustainable in the medium term. At some stage, with the Fund or without the Fund, one would have to adjust. The imperative of adjustments must be met. As long as policies are well thought through, the support of the Fund is not only direct but also indirect, as Mr. Brau has pointed out, in relation to other creditors through the Paris/London Clubs or bilateral donors.

I have also noted the concern of Governors regarding the timing of measures and giving consideration to political realities. As I said earlier, it is difficult for the Fund to react to these questions because we cannot cite individual cases, but I can tell you that over the past six months since I have been Director of the African Department, I have been involved directly with this matter at the request of the management. The management has asked me to see heads of state to ensure that some of the political decisions are feasible. We do not want unrealistic programs. We want programs that can be financed, that are properly funded, but that have the political support of the authorities. Credibility has to lie first with the country. The country knows best what is the proper time to implement some of the measures, but the political authorities cannot delay indefinitely such an important measure as appropriate pricing policy or exchange rate policy. There may be several ways of improving policy and it is the role of the Fund to advise governments, given our experience elsewhere, what we think may be the best way to approach a problem. But the decision has to lie with the government.

Many speakers have said that we should put more emphasis on supply-side policies. We have been putting greater emphasis on supply-side policies for some time; perhaps the international economic environment has not allowed the benefits of this shift to be seen. I am sure that with the improvement we are experiencing now, this should be more visible. But supply-side policies necessitate the underlying support of demand-management policies. I do not think that in economic policy you can have a one-sided approach. An appropriate mix of policies is required to allow the authorities to achieve the objective they have set out for themselves. And in this area, clearly the Fund continues to attach great importance to supply-side policies.

Several Governors have raised the problem of communication with the Fund, the procedures of the Fund, even the inflexibility of the Fund. We will attach greater importance to the preparation of missions. I have explained to three or four Governors who have requested negotiation missions that I do not believe that a mission should go to a country unless the country is ready to receive it. Some Governors have pressed me to send missions to negotiate a program when we have not been in the country for a year or so. I know the deficiency in statistics in Africa. I do not believe that, after a year of absence, and a lack of communication of statistical data, a Fund mission should go right ahead and negotiate a program with a country. We have to prepare the ground, even if it takes time. So we will try our best to prepare missions, but you have to help in this respect, not only to make sure that the timing is right, but also to ensure the right type of coordination in the country.

I want to assure the Governors that management is ready to continue discussions on these issues, and that we often do this in Washington. Almost every week the Managing Director and the Deputy Managing Director receive governors and ministers from the African countries to listen to their problems and to try to see what the policy constraints are, what the problems of timing are in some of the decisions, and so forth. This we will continue to do. We will continue to do it in Washington, but we also plan to continue to do this in your own countries.

Governors should feel that the door is open in the Fund. We feel that the dialogue must be continuing, that we should try to understand better the constraints of African governments, and that we should try to listen more about some of the types of policies that they feel are not right. But it has to be a dialogue, a two-way exchange. The Governors should also try to listen to the Fund's experience. I told one of my former colleagues that Africa has been independent, on average, for only 20 years. The Fund has been dealing with member countries for 40 years. So we should all address these programs with humility and accept that errors can be made on both sides; but the most important aspect is to work in the interest of the countries, and that is what the institution is for.

Appendix

List of Participants, Authors, and Panelists

Participants

Central Bank of West African States	
ABDOULAYE FADIGA	Governor
CHARLES KONAN BANNY	Director of Research
Bank of Central African States	
CASIMIR OYE MBA	Governor
MAURICE MOUTSINGA	Director of Operations and External Financial Relations
MAURICE DINAMONA	Editor, Central Services Research and Documentation
Botswana	
CHARLES N. KIKONYOGO	Governor, Bank of Botswana
TSIDI M. TSIKATA	Principal Research Officer, Bank of Botswana
Burundi	
A. NTAHONKIRIYE	Governor, Bank of the Republic of Burundi
G. MURANIRA	Fonde de pouvoir principal, Bank of the Republic of Burundi
E. NIBASUMBA	Fonde de pouvoir-adjoint, Bank of the Republic of Burundi
Egypt	
ALY NEGM	Governor, Central Bank of Egypt
A.M. ABOUL SAAD	Deputy Governor, Central Bank of Egypt
ABU BAKR ABDEL ATI	Central Bank of Egypt
MAMDOUH HABSA	Central Bank of Egypt
Ethiopia	
ATO TADESSE GEBRE-KIDAN	Governor, National Bank of Ethiopia

The Gambia	
ALHAJI ABOULIE A. FAAL	General Manager, Central Bank of The Gambia
Ghana	
J.S. Addo	Governor, Bank of Ghana
KODWO BERVELL	Assistant Director of Research, Bank of Ghana
Guinea-Bissau	
PEDRO A.G. GOMEZ	Governor, National Bank of Guinea-Bissau
ALFREDO RODRIGUES SILVA	Director, National Bank of Guinea-Bissau
Kenya	
PHILIP NDEGWA	Governor, Central Bank of Kenya
E.C. KOTUT	Deputy Governor, Central Bank of Kenya
Lesotho	
STEFAN SCHOENBERG	Governor, Central Bank of Lesotho
Liberia	
THOMAS V. HANSON	Governor, National Bank of Liberia
MOSES G. TARBO	Special Assistant, National Bank of Liberia
LAWRENCE M. YATES	Economist, Bank of Liberia
Madagascar	
R. RANDRIAMAHOLY	Governor, Central Bank of Madagascar
PANOEL RAKOTOVAO	Director of Inspection, Central Bank of Madagascar
EMMA RANDREZA	Assistant Manager, Research Department, Central Bank of Madagascar
Malawi	
F.L. MAMBIYA	General Manager, Reserve Bank of Malawi
C.T. MWALWANDA	Director of Research and Statistics, Reserve Bank of Malawi

E.R. GONEKA	Research Assistant, Reserve Bank of Malawi
Morocco	
MOHAMED TAZI	Director General, Foreign Department, Bank of Morocco
Nigeria	
J.O. SANUSI	Executive Director, Bank of Nigeria
N.E. OGBE	Director of Research, Bank of Nigeria
A. OLOYEDE	Principal Economist, Bank of Nigeria
Rwanda	
AUGUSTIN RUZINDANA	Acting Governor, National Bank of Rwanda
Seychelles	
B. RASSOOL	Assistant Director of Research, Central Bank of Seychelles
Sierra leone	
J.T.S. WRIGHT	Deputy Governor, Bank of Sierra Leone
BRIMAH CONTEH	Secretary, Bank of Sierra Leone
Somalia	
OMAR AHMED OMAR	Governor, Central Bank of Somalia
Sudan	
MAHDI AL-FAKI	Acting Governor, Bank of Sudan
Swaziland	
H.B.B. OLIVER	Governor, Central Bank of Swaziland
M.B. SAMKETI	Assistant General Manager, Central Bank of Swaziland
Tanzania	
C.M. NYIRABU	Governor, Bank of Tanzania
D.J. KAMORI	Director, Exchange Control, Bank of Tanzania

I.M. RASHIDI	Director, Economic Research, Bank of Tanzania
A.J. MARWA	Multilateral Division, Bank of Tanzania
A. MSENGA	Personal Assistant to the Governor, Bank of Tanzania
G. MGONJA	Research Manager, Bank of Tanzania
A. SHARIFF	Branch Manager, Bank of Tanzania
J.P. KIPOLOLA	Chief Economist, Treasury
Tunisia	
MONCEF BELKHODJA	Governor, Central Bank of Tunisia
Uganda	
LEO KIBIRANGO	Governor, Bank of Uganda
S.A. OBURA	Deputy Director for Research, Bank of Uganda
Zaïre	
N'SELE EKOFO ANYENGA	Deputy Governor, Bank of Zaire
SAMBA MAWAKANI	Director of Research, Bank of Zaire
Zambia	
DAVID PHIRI	Governor, Bank of Zambia
M. GONDWE	Board Secretary, Bank of Zambia
M. SAKALA	Deputy General Manager, Economic Research, Bank of Zambia
G. MBULO	Economic Advisor, Bank of Zambia
MRS. V. CHONA	Director, Foreign Operations and Budgeting, Bank of Zambia
E. MWILA	Deputy Director, Economic Research, Bank of Zambia
Zimbabwe	
KOMBO MOYANA	Governor, Reserve Bank of Zimbabwe

African Development Bank	
DELPHIN RWEGASIRA	Economic Advisor
E. SANVEE	Resident Representative, Nairobi
African Center for Monetary Studies	
A.B. TAYLOR	Director General
M.I. MAHMOUD	Director of Training
J. TEDAJO	Director of Research
J.H. FRIMPON-ANSAH	Monetary Consultant
Y. EL NIL	Economist
S.M. MALLECK AMODE	Economist
IMF Executive Directors	
ABDERRAHMANE ALFIDJA	Executive Director
E.I.M. MTEI	Executive Director
GHASSEM SALEHKHOU	Executive Director

Moderator

GERALD K. HELLEINER	Professor of Economics, University of Toronto

Authors

LUIS DE AZCARATE	Director, Country Policy Department, World Bank
EDUARD BRAU	Senior Advisor, Exchange and Trade Relations Department, IMF
JOHN LOXLEY	Head of Department of Economics, University of Manitoba
SAMBA MAWAKANI	Director of Research, Bank of Zaire (on behalf of AACB)
PHILIP NDEGWA	Governor, Central Bank of Kenya
ALASSANE OUATTARA	Director, African Department, IMF

J.O. SANUSI	Executive Director, Central Bank of Nigeria (on behalf of AACB)

Panelists

ABDOULAYE FADIGA	Governor, Central Bank of West African States (BCEAO)
ATO TADESSE GEBRE-KIDAN	Governor, National Bank of Ethiopia
ROGER LAWRENCE	Director, Money and Finance, UNCTAD
CARLOS MASSAD	Professor of Economics, University of Santiago
AZIZALI F. MOHAMMED	Director, External Relations Department, IMF
M. NARASIMHAM	Director, Administrative Staff College of India
JOHN WILLIAMSON	Senior Fellow, Institute for International Economics

Discussants

JULIO M. JIMENEZ	Chief, East African Division, IMF
AZIZALI F. MOHAMMED	Director, External Relations Department, IMF
PHILIP NDEGWA	Governor, Central Bank of Kenya
CHARLES M. NYIRABU	Governor, Bank of Tanzania
DAVID PHIRI	Governor, Bank of Zambia
KOMBO MOYANA	Governor, Reserve Bank of Zimbabwe

Observers

E.C. KOTUT	Deputy Governor, Central Bank of Kenya
A.K. MULLEI	Director of Research, Central Bank of Kenya
J.W. MUMELO	Foreign Department, Central Bank of Kenya

C.L. CHANTHUNYA	Senior Financial Expert, Trade, Monetary and Customs Division, Zambia
Z. DEMISSIE	Director of Customs, Trade and Monetary Division, Preferential Treatment Area, Zambia
A.C. FENWICK	Advisor, Research Department, Central Bank of Kenya
M.J.P. KANGA	Assistant Director of Research, Central Bank of Kenya
H. KARANI	Senior Assistant Director of Research, Central Bank of Kenya
W.K. KINYUA	Senior Research Officer, Central Bank of Kenya
JOHN J. STREMLAU	Director, International Division Rockefeller Foundation